Ethnogra
a data-satur

MANCHESTER
1824

Manchester University Press

Materialising the Digital

Materialising the Digital seeks to interrogate the infrastructures, relationships and imaginaries of digital technologies through situated, empirical analyses of the production, circulation and use of digital devices.

SERIES EDITORS:
HANNAH KNOX AND ADAM FISH

Positioned at the intersection of media studies, STS, anthropology and sociology, the series will provide original, critical and theoretically innovative understandings of the implications of digital technologies for contemporary social life. Our intention is that this series will provide a solid ground from which to engage and critique the persistence of utopian, functionalist and dystopic visions of technological futures.

Ethnography for a data-saturated world

Edited by Hannah Knox and Dawn Nafus

Manchester University Press

Published by Manchester University Press
Altrincham Street, Manchester M1 7JA

www.manchesteruniversitypress.co.uk

British Library Cataloguing-in-Publication Data

A catalogue record for this book is available from the British Library

ISBN   978 15261 2759 4   hardback
ISBN   978 15261 3497 4   paperback

First published 2018

The publisher has no responsibility for the persistence or accuracy of URLs for any external or third-party internet websites referred to in this book, and does not guarantee that any content on such websites is, or will remain, accurate or appropriate.

Typeset
by Toppan Best-set Premedia Limited
Printed in Great Britain
by TJ International Ltd, Padstow, Cornwall

For Mary and Dan

Contents

List of figures

Notes on contributors

Anders Blok is Associate Professor in Sociology at the University of Copenhagen and member of the University's Center for Social Data Science (SODAS).

Baki Cakici is Assistant Professor within the Technologies in Practice group at the IT University of Copenhagen.

Joseph Dumit is Chair of Performance Studies and Professor of Science & Technology Studies and Anthropology at the University of California Davis.

Francisca Grommé is a postdoctoral researcher in the Department of Sociology at Goldsmiths, University of London. She is working on the research project Peopling Europe: How data make a people (ARITHMUS).

Hannah Knox is Lecturer in Digital Anthropology and Material Culture at University College London.

Ian Lowrie is an instructor in Sociology and Anthropology at Lewis and Clark College.

Adrian Mackenzie is Professor in Technological Cultures in the Department of Sociology at Lancaster University and researches cultural intersections in science, media and technology.

Mette My Madsen is PhD fellow in the Department of Anthropology at the University of Copenhagen.

Dawn Nafus is Senior Research Scientist at Intel and Adjunct Professor at Pacific Northwest College of Art.

Morten Axel Pedersen is Professor of Social Anthropology at the University of Copenhagen.

Alison Powell is Assistant Professor in the Department of Media and Communications at London School of Economics.

Evelyn Ruppert is Professor of Sociology at Goldsmiths, University of London.

Antonia Walford is a Teaching Fellow at the Centre for Digital Anthropology, University College London, and a Post-Doctoral Researcher at the Centre for Social Data Science, University of Copenhagen.

Kaiton Williams recently received his doctorate from the Information Science programme at Cornell University. He is currently pursuing embedded research with a technology startup in Silicon Valley.

Preface and acknowledgements

This book emerged as the result of a workshop entitled Big Data from the Bottom Up that was held at University College London in October 2015. The workshop was jointly funded by the UCL Big Data Institute and the ESRC Centre for Research on Socio-Cultural Change and was also supported by the UCL Centre for Digital Anthropology which hosted the event. We want to thank all those who attended and participated in the workshop and provided reflections and comments on the contributions. In addition to many of the authors of the chapters presented here, we would also like to thank other workshop participants Allen Abramson, Ben Anderson, David Berry, Anne Burns, Kimberly Chong, Sara Randall, Irina Shklovski and Farida Vis for their contributions. At the Big Data Institute we wish to thank Patrick Wolfe who opened the event for us and also to thank the institute for making available funds for Dawn Nafus to visit UCL as a visiting scholar in the autumn of 2015. At CRESC thanks go to Mike Savage and John Law for their thoughts on the Social Life of Method, and Penny Harvey who has been very involved in CRESC-related research on digital data and whose involvement in a parallel CRESC project run by Evelyn Ruppert on Socializing Big Data contributed to the conceptualisation of this event. Thanks also go to Claire Dyer and Yang Man who provided invaluable administrative support. Jennifer Collier Jennings has provided important community building work at EPIC that has informed much of the thinking here.

Thanks must also go to Manchester University Press who have supported this project from the inception, attending the original event and supporting us throughout the process of putting together this volume.

Other people who have been instrumental to the inception of this volume and the ideas herein include Haidy Geismar, Shireen Walton, Ludovic Coupaye, Damian O'Doherty, Rajiv Mehta, Gwen Ottinger, Randy Sargent, Tye Rattenbury, ken anderson, Suzanne Thomas, Richard Beckwith, the Data Sense team at Intel and many of the students enrolled on the MSc in Digital Anthropology at UCL. Thank you for all of your thoughtful comments and reflections on data, technology and anthropological methods over the past three years.

Finally thanks to our families. Hannah thanks Imogen, Francesca, Beatrice and Damian for being there and holding things together, whilst Dawn thanks Dan, Penni, both Jims and Pattie for their continued support of her adventures.

1

Introduction: ethnography for a data-saturated world

Hannah Knox and Dawn Nafus

It is increasingly difficult to attend to social and political relations in the contemporary world without recognising that they are in some way constituted by digitally generated data. From censuses that describe national populations to polls that predict and chart election outcomes, from audience surveys and click-counters that are used to price advertising to credit ratings and market analyses that determine financial relations, social worlds are entangled with data that is produced, circulated and analysed using computational devices. To paraphrase Walter Benjamin's famous aphorism about the effects of the then new technologies of film and photography on human engagement with the world, 'every day it seems the urge grows stronger to get hold of a subject at very close range by way of its [data]' (Benjamin 2008 [1939]).

During the 2000s, with the continued increase in computational information processing capacity and the huge spread of smartphones and sensors there has been an increasing public concern about the challenge of data's 'bigness' (Anderson 2008; Bowker 2014). Practices of data collection and collation seem to have exploded in recent years with the proliferation of electronically connected devices that are capable of sensing and producing data about the world and circulating that data to a range of users including governments, corporations and individuals. Using analogies from older industries, the economic and social potential of data has led to its characterisation as the 'new oil', offering potentially new revenue streams, new ways of imagining and

governing populations and new methods of verification and accountability. Those who are more concerned about the political structures
and effects of this new resource also talk of data as 'exhaust' – the
byproduct of human interaction that needs to be both 'captured' by
the analytic converter of data science and properly managed and
governed to mitigate the dangers associated with ambiguous attribu-
tion, security, corporate monopoly and nefarious techniques of surveillance and control.

Most recently, other social, political and ethical questions have
arisen about the implications of automation and machine learning.[1]
Newer computational techniques for parsing large datasets focus
mainly on what machines can and cannot recognise, asking whether
some data has enough of the same features as some other data such
that a machine can determine that they are both indeed a picture of
a dog, or a stressed tone of voice. These automation practices intensify
a sense of opaqueness. Many worry that machine learning systems can
grow so complex that it can be difficult even for the very people who
designed the system in the first place to say how machines make the
determinations that they do. Consideration of the social implications
of automation has provided a new realm of debate about data and its
ethical implications. No longer are questions about data merely a
matter of how objects and subjects become known through different
quantities and qualities of data collection, nor are they about who has
and should have access to that knowledge. They have been extended
to incorporate more fundamental questions about what happens to
our sense of what knowledge is when the agents of knowledge production are no longer necessarily even human.

New data relations thus not only raise questions about how to
better know and act upon the world, but also shed light on the
very foundations of what we consider knowledge to be. This book
starts from the conceit that attention to digital data opens up the
possibility of interrogating more broadly the presuppositions, techniques, methods and practices out of which claims about the value
and purpose of knowledge gain power. To talk of digital data is
to talk of one facet of a broader terrain of knowledge production,
of which numerical or digital data is only one part. Seeing data
practices and concerns as a matter of how to more broadly understand and make the world demands then that we locate digitally collected data as one of many ways of knowing, which include critical

reflection, affective experience and, most importantly for this collection, ethnography.

In spite of the level of enthusiasm and debate about the possibilities and challenges of big data, grounded empirical studies of the knowledge practices entailed in contemporary data analytics are surprisingly few and far between. The journal *Big Data & Society* has done much to generate a social response to big data issues but this is one of very few places where ethnographic accounts of big data as a field of practice exist at all. In part this is no doubt due to the time that it takes for ethnographies to work their way through the publishing system. There are some important studies in the pipeline such as Nick Seaver's (2015) doctoral study on music recommendation analysts and Asta Vonderau's current research project on cloud computing, but at the date of writing these are yet to be published. Meanwhile other data-related phenomena such as practices of modelling and visualisation in scientific settings (Dumit 2004; Myers 2015) the appearance of bitcoin (Maurer 2012) and the building of databases for the collation and navigation of hybrid and indigenous knowledge forms (Shrinivasan et al. 2009; Verran and Christie 2014) provide an important starting point from which to approach big data practices ethnographically. Such studies are much needed as a way of cutting through the media hype in business press around big data and its promises (see Boellstorff and Maurer (2015) for early work in this area). But ethnographic studies also offer more than just empirical detail that can provide a reality-check on otherwise hyped phenomena. Ethnography done well also holds the promise of generating a new way of theorising and understanding digital data by building novel analytical concepts that are appropriate to the kinds of relations of knowledge production that digital data itself entails.[2]

This book therefore aims to fill this gap of ethnographic approaches to contemporary digital data by providing a window on to the cultures, practices and infrastructures and epistemologies of digital data production, analysis and use. Understanding the production and use of digital data and its implications for knowledge is an issue that cuts across a huge array of different areas of practice (science, commerce, government, development, engineering etc.) and covering this terrain in its entirety is far beyond the ability of any one volume. In order to provide a path through this complexity we therefore take as our core focus the way in which digital data is troubling and reconstituting expertise. This focus on expertise allows us to do something that is relatively unusual in an edited collection: both to provide a comparative description of a number of empirical fieldsites where communities of experts are self-consciously forming around the new possibilities put on the table by digital data; and to consider how our understanding of the ways experts make and remake digital data might reframe our own expertise as ethnographers. This is not a methods book, but it *is* a book about what digital data is doing to empirical methods that sustain claims to expertise, with a particular focus on its implications for ethnography.

We approach digital data then, as a comment on the relationship between knowledge, expertise and the methods through which knowledge is produced. We do this in order to interrogate whether data practices might be part of a broader unsettling of how to know the social. We focus specifically on the interplay between digital data and ethnography as two ways of understanding contemporary possibilities available for knowing, formatting and intervening in the world. This is not just a book about how ethnographic knowledge can fill in the gaps of data science (e.g. boyd and Crawford 2012) nor is it just a demonstration of how ethnography can shed light on what data science actually is and the effects it produces (although both of these are touched upon in this volume). Rather, the book sets out a more ambitious aim of exploring what might be happening to social knowledge production at the interface of data and ethnography, with a view to outlining new directions in social research and simultaneously attending to the epistemological foundations of that research.

Past experiments in digital data and ethnography

The conversations that this book charts between digital data[3] and ethnography offer, we suggest, a fresh terrain in which to ask questions about the social production of knowledge. However, the question of how to combine data-oriented and qualitative approaches in ethnographic research is not new.[4] Anthropologists have, since at least the 1960s, periodically turned to the possibilities that computation might hold for assisting with anthropological analysis. Gregory Bateson and Margaret Mead's forays into cybernetics as a method for analysing social systems offer an early example of how information-theoretical thinking was incorporated into anthropology and used to reshape a distinctive approach to the discipline (Bateson 1972; Mead 1968). Ecological anthropologist Roy Rappaport's groundbreaking study of the relationship between ritual and ecology offered a similarly systems-theoretical method of socio-natural analysis to chart the relationship between the abundance or scarcity of ecological resources and ritual process, an approach which has more recently been taken up in computer simulation work in Bali by Stephen Lansing and colleagues (Rappaport 1977). Lévi-Strauss meanwhile explored the conceptual potential of computers in the development of structural anthropology and was conversant with the logic of information theory and its influence on structural linguistics (see Seaver 2014b; Geoghegan 2011). Whilst these first theoretical explorations into systems theory and structural analysis took place in the 1950s and 1960s, their influence has gained traction again in recent years and is now felt in much contemporary anthropology, particularly amongst those who study ecological relations and technology (Boyer 2013; Kohn 2013).

As computers developed and became more affordable, a number of anthropologists were quick to explore the broader methodological potential of these new computational devices for assisting with the collection and analysis of field materials. This is outlined in books like Dell Hymes's 1965 volume on the use of computers in anthropology (Hymes 1965). Studies such as Marie Corbin and Paul Stirling's database-supported analysis of kinship and family in Spain in the 1970s established a precedent for the use of computers in anthropological analysis. The Centre for Social Anthropology and Computing (CSAC) was established at the University of Kent in 1986. This remains a key location for discussions and collaborations around the use of computers in anthropological analysis (Ellen 2014).

A parallel field in which anthropologists have played an important part is the study of human–computer interaction. Human–computer interaction (HCI) scholars have a well- established history of entangling digitally produced data with ethnography. During the 1980s for example, anthropologists working at the Palo Alto Research Centre at Xerox Park were noted for bringing ethnomethodological approaches to HCI, which drew on numerical and video data alongside ethnographic fieldnotes to understand the social dynamics of situated computer use (Trigg et al. 1991; Suchman et al. 1999).

Each of these forays into the possibilities that computers might hold for anthropology came at a particular historical moment that brought together specific configurations of people, devices, work practices, questions, theories and intentions. The approach we take in this book is not teleological or historiographic, but rather takes its lead from the contemporary moment, and in particular scholarship that has focused on what has been termed 'the social life of method' (Ruppert et al. 2013; Lury and Wakeford 2012; Marres and Weltevrede 2013). This scholarship argues that social science methods are more than just incremental techniques for understanding the world. Methods are also social phenomena in and of themselves, both because they emerge from particular social worlds that organise ontologies and epistemologies in their own particular ways, and because methods actively participate in the social worlds they were designed to comprehend. Surveys were developed as professional instruments for knowing about the concerns of a population, and became the preferred technique of knowledge production for a technocratic middle class who used them to reshape social relations into practices that could be surveyed and audited (Strathern 2000). Ethnography's origins in colonial encounters provide another notorious example. Empire-building set the context in which 'holistic' understandings of subjugated peoples became necessary. State actors mobilised holism in order to shore up notions of 'tribes' as so many distinct units that could be managed and controlled conveniently as single entities, in contradistinction to white settlers. Turn-of-the-century ethnography is not the same as postcolonial or contemporary ethnography, yet the question of how ethnography relates to, and participates in, wider social conditions remains important. In this sense, contemporary ethnography's encounter with digital data is but a recent unfolding of the longstanding relationship between methods and the social relations they simultaneously examine and create.

These histories are far more complicated than we can address here, but one lesson we take from them is that the development of methods require a critical awareness of, and engagement with, other participants likely to use them. We believe not that scholars should avoid coming up with new methods, lest they participate in a social world one would not have wanted, but that developing new methods requires broader engagement. Indeed, anthropology has been coming to terms with the social life of its methods for quite a long time, whether in terms of the representational politics it participates in (Clifford and Marcus 1986) or in terms of its response to the use of ethnography in other disciplines (Ingold 2014; Madsbjerg 2014).

Whilst it is possible then to construct a history of both ethnography and of the use of computing in anthropology, these brief reflections demonstrate that choices over research method are specific and contingent to the circumstances in which they take place. Even the most exhaustive history of these prior practices would therefore be insufficient to explain the current interest in digital data analysis both outside and within anthropology. To do this we must turn to the current configuration which the chapters of this book elaborate on that combines both the production and the use of new digital data sources, and the form that ethnographic practice takes within anthropology today.

Digital anthropology

For the past two decades, the main debates about computers within anthropology have come under the umbrella of what is now known now as 'digital anthropology'. The aim of digital anthropology has been to study the significance of digital phenomena, which serve both as object of ethnographic enquiry – what happens in online communities, or in data-mediated interactions – and as a methodological puzzle about how come to understand those social worlds. A rich literature on digital methods for qualitative researchers in turn has ensued (Hine 2015; Pink et al. 2016).

A key issue at the heart of digital anthropology has been the way in which 'the digital' raises theoretical questions about how reality is constituted. Notions of 'the digital' perpetuate (unfairly, Boellstorff argues) tropes of 'virtuality' and 'unreality' at the very moment that anthropologists are asking questions about how to move beyond the virtualising concept of culture. That is, in order to understand the variety of existing lifeworlds in their own terms, this persistent trope of digital cultural formations as somehow less real than other cultural forms must be rethought (Boellstorff 2016). The question of how reality is constituted has drawn digital anthropology into the heart of contemporary anthropological debates about ontology and the constitution of sameness and difference (Boellstorff 2016; Knox and Walford 2016). 'The digital' is more than just a new terrain to

interrogate, or a new set of methodological problems and opportunities, but takes us to the heart of the issue of what it looks like to take
seriously other people's ontologies, and the grounds on which we can
say others' worlds are 'the same' as or 'different' from our own.

One of the key anthropological critiques that has been made of data
is that it is an abstraction (Carrier and Miller 1998). As a partial sto-
ryteller that strips away much of the richness of social interaction in
order to render things amenable to mathematics, numbers are thus
seen to form their own virtual reality (Miller 2002). Boellstorff (2012)
argues in contrast that, whether an online game, a cultural construct
or a physical artefact, we need not decide in advance whether something is a virtuality or a reality. We could instead see these entities as
both 'real' and 'virtual' at the same time. This is helpful for rethinking
how we might approach digital data ethnographically. Instead of starting from an assumption that says data's primary status is representational, the chapters in this book examine different data types as things
that have both representational strategies and ontological properties.
Sensor data, for example, attempts to point towards a bodily phenomenon like heart rate at some distance from the sensor technology itself,
while click data is about as close as one can get to the click itself.
Representations and ontologies work differently in both cases. While
both can be overinterpreted, or elude the real object of study, to figure
them both as primarily abstractions – socially performative abstractions perhaps but abstractions none the less – deflects attention from
their reality-producing effects.

This then means we have a particularly thorny 'social life of
methods' issue: ethnographers are required to take seriously the ontological status of numbers and their relationship with an underlying
reality, while also taking seriously the contradictory emic injunction
to always take numbers with a grain of salt, and treat them as virtual
simulacra of the lifeworlds to which they refer. We must do both
of these while acknowledging data's palpable materialities that also
somehow shape-shift into various material forms (graphs, sounds,
sensations etc.) (Berson 2015). These contradictory injunctions make
for a tall order. Digital data, whether a computation of click patterns
or readings from an instrumented environment, involves material
and semiotic forms that are different from previous objects of ethnographic study like online forums or virtual worlds. This requires
that we extend digital methods, while building on the conceptual

frameworks raised by Boellstorff's theorisation of the digital. As the chapters to follow show, computational forms have their own particular ways of creating and erasing both difference and sameness, and scales 'large' and 'small'.

Whose methods?

Recognising the role of methods in constituting social worlds also suggests a further possibility, namely that methods for knowing the world are problems that go beyond professional scholarship. The 'social life of methods' approach suggests that scholarly knowledge production is connected to the world 'out there', and that other people who are not scholars are also capable of creating and using methods. Indeed, when it comes to digitally collected data, techniques for knowing the social through 'transactional' data – that is, data that occurs as the result of everyday exchanges like clicking or using social media, as opposed to data collected for social research – have been elaborated far more rapidly and extensively outside of scholarship (Savage and Burrows 2007). For Savage and Burrows, these developments constitute a challenge to sociological authority, putting sociologists in the uncomfortable role of methods adopter, rather than methods creator. As described by Grommé, Ruppert and Cakici (Chapter 2 below), the introduction of data science methods into European statistical institutes created some consternation, but also the need to develop new professional practices and forms of social capital for constituting proper data science for this purpose. For many new media and communication scholars wishing to understand the cultural and social worlds of social media, this question of who gets to produce knowledge with data has become quite acute. Social media companies' convoluted methods of data handling, often hidden behind claims of intellectual property, pose real challenges to those trying to understand the mechanisms by which social media feeds or online content are organised. Indeed, one methodological intervention in this field has taken the form of an American Civil Liberties Union (ACLU) lawsuit, launched on behalf of media scholars Karrie Karahalios and Christian Sandvig, to persuade the United States government to decriminalise digital methods such as website scraping, which, under an arcane Reagan-era law, remains illegal. These entanglements suggest that, while scholarship remains a distinct place from which to develop methods, we do not live in a social world where we can safely presume that methods necessarily originate in scholarship.

The use of data by computer scientists, social media and consumer health companies to produce knowledge about the social raises well established issues of legitimacy, expertise, dominance and access. Expanding what we mean by method to include research done in the course of everyday living, as opposed to an exclusively professional practice, introduces a much richer set of social dynamics. Consider, for example, Noortje Marres's (2015) work on experiments in green living. Marres is interested in notions of scientific experimentation as a frame with which people come to understand what ecological homes are about. Putting in compostable toilets or solar panels have become, in certain circles, tests of what is possible. These tests shape how some people with green homes relate to one another – an ethos centred more on what was learned about energy consumption or material feasibility than the cultural identities also on display. Similarly, people in the Quantified Self movement who use data to experiment with their health, either out of curiosity or out of necessity, have developed a repertoire of 'paraclinical practices' (Greenfield 2016), procedures that appropriate clinical practices of data collection, experimentation and intervention, repurposing them for radically new ends that include narrative making as well as identifying new interventions.

These examples point towards the *everydayness* of methods as empirical devices (Marres 2017), and a richer social life of methods than the one dominated by the territory-making of high social capital professionals. The everyday use of methods for the production and communication of knowledge also extend well beyond scientific empiricism. For example, numbers regularly feature in the literary and visual arts (Connor 2016; Chilver 2014) not for the purpose of constituting scientific exactness but as a method of bringing into the world experiences of cadences, visual proportions and more evocative imaginations of bigness and smallness (Tufte 1983). When Melanesians display so many shells or towers of yams for exchange, or West African traders use intricate, deliberately crafted methods of reckoning (Guyer 2004), we see readily how methods of counting and reckoning become a nuanced part of everyday lifeworlds.

Following the social life of methods, then, means locating method both in the processes by which the author assembles his or her account and in the social worlds of the protagonists. This book seeks to broaden commonplace understandings of where method might occur, whether that method is ethnographic or computational, or both at the same time, in order to understand more deeply how digital data is becoming implicated in the social worlds that people make. It also acknowledges how various actors are differently positioned with respect to methods of digital data collection and analysis. What presents itself as a methodological question to one actor might be mere substrate for another. For example, 'everyday' experimenters often do not have many choices about how numerical data comes into their worlds, but might be able to resituate it as part of an experimentation process. Data scientists, on the other hand, have fewer opportunities for bringing data closer to situated contexts in which it lives, but often have more complex computational repertoires at their disposal. There is a mutual interdependence at stake, even though these actors might not in the end produce a shared same social world.

Numbers and narratives

The longstanding distinction between qualitative and quantitative knowledge production lies in the background to this rejoinder of digital data and ethnography. If methods have a social life, this distinction becomes not an obstacle to be overcome but a particular social arrangement that needs to be better understood. Numbers and qualities are not inherently opposite ways of seeing the world. Numbers have semiotic qualities (Guyer 2014; Verran 2012) and do more than just measure. Anthropologists have never just ignored numbers as they encounter them in fieldwork, and, while they rarely measure or calculate numerically in creating an account, they are hardly uninterested in quantities or questions of prevalence and scale. Quantitative and qualitative knowledge are not inherently separate, but the distinction between the two has been a longstanding Western cultural cleavage that has had the effect of separating them out. Data practices and ethnographic practices have thus found themselves in different spaces but now, for both material and conceptual reasons (as the chapters of this book attest) they are being brought back together in newly conceived configurations.

To understand the opening up of new connections between these methods it is useful to remember just how much of a cultural project it was to create the association between numbers and notions of objectivity or truthfulness. Ian Hacking (1990) reports that, in the Renaissance period, people who played with dice and coin flips began noticing the intriguing regularities that would later become Gaussian probability theory. Yet their forays were largely considered suspect. Chance was considered dicey; proper, rational thinkers believed in universal natural laws that controlled all things including whether a coin would flip heads or tails at a particular moment. It took a few hundred years for cultural assumptions to form that true and false could be not binary but probabilistic, and that there were reliable mathematical regularities that meant chance could be tamed.

Numbers as a form of attestation, and a way of producing evidence more convincing than personal testimony, began to feature in scientific practice during the Enlightenment period, when merchants also began using them in trading practices in order to improve their social standing. Numbers appear to systematise because they introduce their own, internally consistent formal grammars that are difficult to break (though, as the saying goes, statistics can be considerably much worse than damn lies). That very systematicity became a form of attestation. Numbers served as the perfect language in which mercantile trade could be formalised, through techniques like double-entry bookkeeping and weights and measures standardisation, which served as a kind of testimony that was beyond the merchant himself. The history of the modern fact, as Mary Poovey (1998) puts it, is one that created the separability of measurement from measurer in order to create a form of knowledge production that could rival the moral authority of the church. This notion of separability of measurer and measurement, and the notion of probabilities as a form of objective regularities, took years to intertwine into default twentieth-century notions of 'quantification'.

This longstanding trope of quantification as a kind of machinic objectivity, or direct line into once-and-for-all universal truths, is now under strain. As digitally produced data proliferates, the means that people have for evaluating the relationship between data and what it is supposed to represent are transforming. The unmooring of signifiers from signifieds for example, is at the heart of debates about internet security, identity theft and online fraud. Moreover, as data traces produced by transactional activities are used to steer the relationship between consumers and retailers, the classic problem of the breakdown of a separation between the thing being measured and the effects of measurement itself has become particularly prevalent, with all manner of creative and playful subversions of algorithmic suggestions now proliferating (Merry and Conley 2011).

For data analysts both in academia and in non-academic settings, huge repositories of unstructured data poses other problems. Rob Kitchin (2014) charts the adoption and sometimes rejection of big data methods across the sciences, social sciences and humanities. Kitchin points out that one problem that scholars in the natural sciences have with big data is that it creates 'bigger haystacks' in which to conduct 'fishing expeditions' that end in spurious correlations. In general, the more parameters one has, the greater the chance of spurious correlation. Some data scientists informally say that after ten parameters spurious correlations become highly likely. This scope would all too easily be achieved if one were to try to correlate all the parameters measured by an activity tracker with data retrieved from a weather data service. Kitchin observes that these conditions make it crucial to have deeper discussions across disciplines, including the natural sciences, about the importance of critical reflexivity and acknowledging the situatedness of one's own methods in sorting out which correlation is spurious and which is not. He argues that in the broader course of scientific research that largely goes unpublished – problem selection, hypothesis selection, and early trial and error – critical reflexivity indeed is as epistemologically significant as deduction, but under-acknowledged. If early exploration becomes datafied, and if exploring a problem now involves exploring a dataset, perhaps experiments can be designed on the basis of that exploration rather than assuming that data is there for the purpose of proof. In these circumstances, Kitchin argues, unspoken practices of research might be talked about more openly. Computational methods for exploring, rather than 'proving', might in fact be what is being developed in big data. It is certainly central to the suggestion of many of the chapters of this collection.

What scientists might only ever recognise as the 'exploration phase' could be one way in which ethnographers might create an opening into big data as both method and fieldsite. Indeed, that is precisely where ethnography's epistemological strengths lie. Following the threads of connection in an open-ended way, and thinking critically about how those threads cohere whilst knowing all along that they will only ever be partial and contingent, is perhaps core to the

ethnographic enterprise. As Knox, Mackenzie and My et al. demonstrate in their chapters, ethnographers are less daunted by the large
haystacks that other researchers find so troubling. To do fieldwork is
to live with sensorial excess. Our haystacks are always 'too large'
regardless of whether the social order we are examining is as vast as
global capital flows or as seemingly 'small' as village kinship practices
(Strathern 2004). They are consistently large because

> social anthropology has one trick up its sleeve: the deliberate attempt
> to generate more data than the investigator is aware of at the time of
> collection. Anthropologists deploy open-ended, non-linear methods of
> data collection which they call ethnography ... Rather than devising
> protocols that will purify the data in advance of analysis, the anthro-
> pologist embarks on a participatory exercise which yields materials for
> which analytic protocols are often devised after the fact. (Strathern
> 2004: 5)

Ethnography is not, however, the infinite tracing of all threads. We
cut the network at a certain point (Strathern 1996), usually the point
at which we believe our gathered partialities have a plausible coherence. This is the exact opposite of the epistemological premises taken
by Gaussian probability theory, the theory on which the bulk of
twentieth-century quantitative methods are based. In introductions
to probability theory, the examples of coin flips or dice rolls are commonly used to show how to calculate odds. Instructors use the examples because they make it easy to concretely imagine a field of infinite
exact flips of the same coin. The notion of a probability distribution
relies on a notion of infinite 'tries' – that if I were to consistently roll
the dice, and the dice were not loaded and the table was flat and there
were no other conditions to affect the outcome, we could conclusively
say that the odds of rolling a six are one in six. As students learning
about probabilities, we might then learn that if we were to ask African
Americans the same survey questions as White Americans, a conclu-
sive result would be the result that showed the same distribution time
and time again among the two groups, as if one were rolling dice.
This possibility of the repeat of the roll of the dice is crucial to the
production of modern facts (here, the difference between two groups).
It yields the truth effect of a once and for all claim, universal across
the proclaimed boundaries of the problem. Here, a true claim would

hold across all African Americans and White Americans (unless, of course, circumstances fundamentally change).

In ethnography, however, there is no roll of the dice time and time again. Our focus is often on the contingent nature of social relations, making clean and clear repeatability difficult to imagine, and shaky grounds on which to attempt an analysis. Many of us in turn hold a suspicion of universalising intellectual manoeuvres on both epistemological and ethical grounds.

The style of statistics we have just described is radically changing in the context of big data. The centuries-old dilemmas in Hacking's work about natural laws versus probabilistic knowledge is being revisited in the current debates about 'frequentist' versus 'Bayesian' approaches. The 'frequentist' side of this debate draws on the Gaussian notions of predictability and probabilities that we have just described. The Bayesians draw inspiration from Thomas Bayes, an obscure early eighteenth-century statistician largely ignored until the advent of computer science and now celebrated as a kind of founding father of big data parsing techniques. To continue with the coin toss example, a Bayesian, like an ethnographer, would be inclined to reject the premise that there might be an infinite field of coin flips, each exactly the same as the next on the grounds that that convenient abstraction does not reflect the world as it exists. Instead, Bayesians are much more inclined to think about the situation in terms of what we can say descriptively about the conditions, and how probable it is that that situation will occur. In the coin toss example, that might translate into an attempt to calculate the probability of the angle of the coin's launch, or the force used.

This manoeuvre in some ways echoes Hacking's 'determinism' of natural laws (Hacking 1990), in as much as there are substantive claims being made about the factors in play. While Bayesians resemble Hacking's 'determinism', Bayesian calculations are far less deterministic in the contemporary usage of the word than a frequentist approach. In the frequentist approach, numbers focus on regularity of outcome. They are used to purify the experiment away from prior knowledge. Frequentists start out with a hypothesis that they show to be true or not, while in Bayesian work the hypotheses themselves can be probabilistic as well as the outputs. Bayesian approaches do not attempt to say what is true or not true in an overall manner, but make explicit, and mobilise, prior knowledge. When that prior knowledge turns out to be wrong, a Bayesian analysis would go back and run the calculation in an adjusted manner. This builds into the mathematical procedures a stronger notion that situations are *likely* to change. This is one reason computer scientists talk about 'machine learning' as a form of big data analysis – machines create these iterative loops and refinements relatively easily. The notion of learning here is less an anthropomorphism than an admission of the idea that the results depend upon prior assumptions. To claim, as early pundits did, that big data was free of *a priori* theoretical knowledge is to misunderstand entirely the situated nature not just of data collection, but of how big data statistical techniques actually work (see also Bowker 2014).[5]

In this way, Bayesian approaches to assembling data always start with a notion of partiality and contingency that we more readily take to be ethnography's bread and butter. It is a view of probability as 'orderly opinion, and that inference from data is nothing other than the revision of such opinion in the light of relevant new information' (Kotz and Johnson 2012). Bayesians then do not attempt to 'devise protocols that will purify the data in advance of analysis', as Strathern put it (2004: 5–6), but fold in 'impure' propositions on an ongoing basis. They do exactly what Strathern says ethnographers do: revisit the analytical device used after the fact, once new information is known. (Though, as John Cheney-Lippold (2011) argues, the bounds of 'learning' in Bayesian computation are necessarily much narrower than in ethnography. Changes to how social categories are encoded in the computation are much harder to make than changing the elements associated with that category.) These incremental buildups of beliefs do not require reference to infinite sampling as the standard of evidence. Nor do they point towards a goal of universal truth. Bayesians do not tame chance, they proliferate it.

It would be false to say that the current preference for Bayesian techniques in contemporary computer science has created a flood of ethnographers using them to trace webs of cultural significance. There are very few who would even be in a position to do so. It would also be false to say that Baysesians never use frequentist techniques, or fully subscribe to the epistemological implications we have just drawn. There are likely more positivists than post-positivists currently using those techniques. Bayesian approaches to computation nevertheless do something epistemologically significant for ethnographers. They leave open the possibility of situated knowledge production, entangled with narrative, in ways that frequentist approaches foreclose or render invisible.[6]

Digital data and the sociology of knowledge

With the development of new computational techniques for approaching numerical or digital data, a number of social scientists working primarily in the field of science and technology studies and the sociology of knowledge have begun to interrogate the potentially profound epistemological implications of big data analytics. Muniesa (2014), for example, has focused on financial markets to show how the semiotic aspects of a calculation – how a number is meant to mean – matters profoundly to the relationships it performs. Thrift (2004), on the other hand, has noted that the sheer quantity of calculations required in big data analytics also becomes a change in quality:

> In recent years the activity of calculation has become so ubiquitous that it has entered a new phase, which I call 'qualculation' … where many millions of calculations are continually made in the background of any encounter. It is no longer possible to think of calculation as necessarily precise. (Thrift 2004: 584)

In other work, Thrift argues that specific numerical compositions become 'calculative infrastructures' that bring a set of actors and actions into relation to one another. They create the conditions of possibility for a particular set of connections and disconnections. Often for indicators in the commonsense understanding of the term – a Consumer Price Index, or Gross National Happiness measure – their capacities to configure social relations become apparent when we ask what exactly these things indicate, and how. Who is implicated and who is excluded? Blok and Pedersen (2014) echo Thrift's 'qualculation' in their description of their own field research as a 'qualiquant experiment', a concept that is extended in their chapter in this collection on transversal collaborations. They note that new polyphonies can emerge in intersections between different modalities of 'data' both ethnographic and numerical. Additionally, a recent ethnographic experiment called 'ethnomining' collected digital data deliberately for research purposes and then discussed it with the participants themselves (Anderson et al. 2009).

Latour (2002) and Latour et al. (2012) push this thinking even further, by linking the epistemological promise of big data analytics to a much longer-standing, if only recently resurrected, debate between Gabriel Tarde and Emile Durkheim. Latour et al. (2012) argue that the prospect of being able to capture, mine and newly represent digital traces represents a way of comprehending social patterns that profoundly breaks from the Durkheimian traditions that dominated twentieth-century ways of knowing the social. Durkheim saw social structuring as something that takes place outside the individual, and thus surveys were used precisely to de-individualise matters, and to decouple the hypothesis from any particular instance. In this way, surveys evoked the infinite flipping of a coin, and were largely processed in frequentist ways. Tarde, however, was sceptical of Durkheimian structure, and saw instead a perpetually emergent flow of discrete interactions between individual persons. Individual persons are not discrete, autonomous, rationally calculating individuals in the Tardean view; they are *a priori* social, configured by transactions experienced previously. The conditions of possibility created in one transaction potentiate what is conceivable in another, not unlike a Bourdieuan notion of disposition (1977). In this way, Tarde does not rely on unseen overall structure to account for coherence and patterning. Venturini and Latour see his work as questioning sociology's 'fictive distinction between micro-interactions and macro-structures' (Venturini and Latour 2010: 4) and providing a theoretical basis for the kind of rejoinder between the qualitative and the quantitative that we discussed earlier.

Venturini and Latour point out that digitisation further exposes the fictive nature of this distinction. It has also meant that a Tardean sociology is more conceivable now than it would have been in his own time, when those transactions barely left a trace. Now many of them do, if partially and inconsistently. Tarde imagined that social transactions would be countable, and even speculated about a future 'gloriometer' that would measure reputation and would invite people to make use of those metrics in ways not unlike contemporary social media. One implication, then, is that digital data created in the course of social interactions are not just 'bigger' than surveys. They are ontologically quite different, much more like the objects of material culture research or archival work. They also have the potential to elaborate forms of knowledge that conceptualise social regularities quite differently from Durkheimian traditions.

All of these works meld 'data as thing in the world' and 'data as method' (Nafus 2016) into slightly different configurations, and tighten the connection between the two in different ways. Collectively, they make a solid case for an ontological and epistemological entanglement in a data-saturated world. This in turn raises two questions for ethnography. On the first hand, there is the question of what the appearance of big data is doing to the established opposition between quantitative and qualitative methods. Our exploration of Bayesian techniques and Strathern's partial connections has hinted at some of the reasons why ethnography and data analytics might have more in common that it seems at first sight, though the chapters to come have much more to say on the matter. On the second hand, if new forms of data are redistributing expertise, then the usual object of ethnographic critique (the reductionist quantitative researcher) and the usual response to this critique (the need to fill in the gaps with ethnography) both need revisiting. The book tries to address both. It asks how ethnography figures as a specific knowledge-producing practice in a data-saturated world, and it asks where more productive objects of critique might lie if method cannot be located *a priori* in particular researcherly figures or practices. It does so by approaching data and ethnography not as things to be compared but in terms of the shared concepts and practices that appear to be at stake in current attempts at knowing the world. If knowledge production can be thought of as a kind of interdisciplinary trading zone (Galison 1996), the chapters collected here suggest that with the advent of digital data there are renewed potential grounds for tradability. At the same time, just as Hacking noted that early dice rollers had no idea they were experimenting with long-term epistemological transformations, so too does our present condition make it impossible to fully say what kind of epistemological transformation we might actually be in.

Whilst we cannot provide an ultimate answer to the relationship between digital data and its epistemological implications, this collection none the less aims to provide an orientation device that might aid our capacity to see where things are changing, where conventions are being disrupted and where forms of knowledge and social organisation look likely to endure. The way we do this is to return to our central interest in what digital data is doing to different forms of expertise – both quantitative and qualitative.

The book is structured so as to help the reader navigate through this sometimes disorienting terrain of border crossings, combinations and experimental collaborations. It starts with a consideration of data science, understood from the perspective of ethnography. Data scientists are frequently heralded as the powerful experts of a new digital social order. The first question we pose is who are these experts and where did they come from? Part I addresses this question through three comparative ethnographies of emerging data science. In Chapter 2 Francisca Grommé, Evelyn Ruppert and Baki Cakici take us into the world of national statisticians in Europe to explore how statistical knowledge is being reworked in response to the appearance of new kinds of data. Focusing on the procedures by which data scientists are recruited by national statistical agencies, we learn about the core qualities and competencies that are attributed to an ideal data scientist. Here Grommé et al. trace the fault lines between established and new forms of expertise, and highlight how what is required of data scientists is not just data analysis skills but also an aptitude for collaboration, a potential for learning and a capacity to imbibe the habitus of what it means to be an official statistician.

In Chapter 3 Ian Lowrie takes us to Russia and to the university courses where data science is taught. Lowrie provides us with insights into the relationship between that expertise which is necessary to being a data scientist and that which differentiates data science from other disciplines. Here, we find a similar tension being played out between mathematics and data science that we saw in the previous chapter, cast here as a tension between pure and applied knowledge. In the Russian setting, to be a data scientist is to be able to turn the science of mathematics and statistics to productive and useful ends. Although hard skills constitute the heart of data science in the classroom, purely classroom-based or textbook-based instructional learning misses a huge part of what it means to be a data analyst – an observation picked up later by Joseph Dumit in the interview that concludes this book. In Russia, the urge to 'keep learning' is treated by Lowrie less as a process of cultivating unique skills and more a process of developing a new kind of practical craft.

In Chapter 4, Kaiton Williams takes us to Jamaica where there have been ongoing attempts since the early 2000s to generate a successful digital economy on the island. Williams's focus on a developing economy opens up attention to the often invisible geopolitics of data analysis, charting how those who service the data analysis needs of call centres, offshore banking services and low-wage data processing have to grapple with the racialised imaginaries of what data science is and what it should be. Far from data science being a utopian or flat space of knowledge production, the chapter reminds us how fields of expertise work to reconstitute geographies of inclusion and exclusion. Here, we also get our first glimpse into the way in which ethnographic experiments with data traces might be deployed reflexively to shed light on where boundaries can and cannot be traversed. Williams introduces our first experiment in the form of an attempt to critically deploy data as a way of pushing back at the inevitable social positioning of the researcher that take place in all ethnographic research.

Part II of the book moves us from ethnographies of data science to three chapters which pay close attention to different social lives of data and the ways of knowing that they entail. Turning from the culture of data science to the ontologies of data and their entanglements with other forms of expertise including ethnography, these chapters unpack what kind of relational assumptions are at play in different data practices – both qualitative and quantitative.

In Chapter 5, Antonia Walford explores the role that databases and practices of collection play in the creation and stabilisation of environmental data. Moving beyond the idea of the database as a technology of storage, Walford draws our attention to the centrality of sharing, circulation and reuse of data within archival practice and thus expands our understanding of the relational promise that data practices enable and extend. Describing the work of those who have been trying to develop audacious new methods of global environmental data collection, Walford unravels the relational commitments of people, environments and technologies that the practice of collection and the ordering of scientific knowledge entail, highlighting how data does not do away with but rather profoundly changes the structured relationship assumed between data parts and archival wholes.

Staying with climate scientists, in Chapter 6 Hannah Knox takes up a question posed in Walford's conclusion about the implications of the relational understanding of data for the practice of ethnography. Knox responds to this by asking whether numerical data might provide a hinge point around which climate modellers and ethnographers could enter into a more productive dialogue. Launching from the social/natural boundary-crossing posed by the anthropocene, and focusing comparatively on how climate modelling and ethnography produce knowledge via data, Knox asks whether there might be a way of reformulating ethnography's relationship to data in a way that allows ethnographers to hold on to the reality that climate data narrates, whilst still acknowledging the relational and emergent character of anthropogenic climate change. In her conclusion Knox makes a tentative proposition as to what this might look like by engaging with practices emerging from the fields of architecture, art and design.

In Chapter 7, Adrian Mackenzie asks a similar question of a very different context by posing the question: how can we do an ethnography of a very large number? In the context of big data, and of claims that are made as to the power of large numbers, an attention to the question of how we and others actually engage big numbers is crucial. Attempting to engage ethnographically with the number of code repositories stored on the GitHub platform (29 million), Mackenzie explores what a big number like this actually is, asking: How is it composed? Calculatively ordered? Used to figure specificity and difference? Large numbers are crucially shown to be both integral to the functioning of data infrastructures *and* central to the imaginaries that such infrastructures produce and proliferate. Numbers are thus shown to be not only tools that can be used by researchers to illuminate relations but also lively subjects with whom ethnographers should learn to engage in all their ontological complexity.

With a better grasp of how both data scientists and ethnographers can and do produce knowledge through data, Part III presents specific examples of how this reformulated understanding of both data analysis and ethnography is producing collaborative experiments in 'data ethnography'. In Chapter 8, Mette My Madsen, Anders Blok and Morten Axel Pedersen describe a collaborative experiment with data scientists at the University of Copenhagen which has attempted to create a picture of the 'social fabric' of a cohort of students by combining qualitative and quantitative data on their movements and practices. Madsen et al. use the term 'transversal collaboration' to denote the messy, emergent and uneven nature of the collaborative work required to produce provisionally stabilised knowledge about a shifting social field. In this description, the subject and object of research are constantly under a process of reconfiguration, with Madsen et al. deploying ethnography simultaneously as a means of reflecting on data collection and a way of doing data collection itself.

In Chapter 9 Alison Powell reports on another experiment in which she devised a method for engaging data that she calls 'data walkshops'. This method works to draw out the phenomenological dimensions of data by eliciting embodied and emotive responses to the city as a datafied landscape. By attending to how 'data walkshop' participants came to engage with data as part of the fabric of urban life, Powell develops an approach to quantification that draws on ethnography, critical mapping and art practice to deepen our appreciation of what numbers in situ do to social relations. This method is used in this chapter to develop a critique of a functionalist vision of smart cities and their social effects, but it also presents a method which might be deployed in a much more diverse range of settings.

In Chapter 10 Dawn Nafus also describes her own experience of engaging publics with data, in this case focusing on people's relationship to increasingly ubiquitous streams of sensory data. Nafus outlines several of the lessons she has learned over the past ten years through her involvement in projects that have used qualitative, quantitative, textual and visual methods to help people think about different forms of sensory data that their devices are producing. As in Madsen et al.'s chapter, what emerges is a description both of how data science changes ethnography and of how ethnographic sensibilities affect the design of data analysis platforms. For example, when one approaches data in an ethnographic mode, flaws, gaps and ambiguities in data become not problems to be solved but sites of productive engagement through which people begin to engage, think and interrogate the relations that might lie behind data traces. That ethnography might demonstrate the qualitative potential of data itself is indeed one of the key insights of this volume and one that is taken up in our final section of the book.

The final contribution is an interview that Dawn Nafus conducted with Joseph Dumit at the University of California Davis about a new data-science curriculum that Dumit has been developing with colleagues in computer science. Drawing on his experience of speaking to Silicon Valley companies in putting together the course, Dumit characterises the kind of approach to understanding data that the course advocates as what he calls a 'third thing', that requires not just quantitative or qualitative expertise but something that lies at the interface of these two disciplinary traditions. This third thing is indeed the thing that our collection of chapters attempts to interrogate, something which we label variously as 'data studies', 'critical social data science' or what we have called in this introduction 'data-ethnography'. Whatever we term it, our aim has been to gather together ethnographer-practitioners who are attempting to dwell in this third thing in order to offer both a theoretical and a practical orientation as to how a fresh relationship might be forged between ethnographers inspired by the world-making possibilities of digital data, and data scientists committed to using data to interrogate and understand a world of unfolding social complexity.

Notes

1 For example the Royal Society published a report into Machine Learning in April 2017 that outlined the challenges and potential of machine learning for contemporary society (Royal Society 2017).

2 This claim builds on discussions in anthropology about anthropological theory as discussed for example in the journal *Hau: Journal of Ethnographic Theory*, and in publications such as Lebner (2017).

3 In this book, when we say 'data' we are generally referring to digitally collected numbers, words, images etc. We recognise of course that data can also refer to ethnographic evidence of various kinds. Different anthropologists have different views on the matter of whether the written reflections, notes, materials and photographs that mark traditional fieldwork can be called 'data'.

4 This is also pointed out by Nick Seaver (2014a) in a blog post on the Savage Minds website: https://savageminds.org/2014/05/19/computers-and-sociocultural-anthropology/.

5 Debates about how much substantive prior knowledge one needs in fact do rage within communities of machine learning specialists. Computer vision developers, for example, debate about whether it is better to make assumptions about the physics of light in getting a machine to discern that a picture of a dog is indeed a dog, or whether to do it on a 'purely statistical' basis. 'Purely statistical', however, does rely on some prior input – it is more that the developer has less of a notion of what that input means semantically, if anything (Suzanne Thomas, pers. comm.).

6 Of course, here we acknowledge that there is no shortage of frequentists who, with great care and self-reflexive sensitivity, take pains to situate what they learn through frequencies and avoid God trickery. Our point

is merely that the philosophical premises, grounded in a certain history, start with a notion of 'infinite' coin flips or dice rolls or chances to count a population in a particular way, that invites the sorts of universalising claims that ethnographers are so quick to object to.

References

Anderson, Chris. 2008. 'The End of Theory: The Data Deluge Makes the Scientific Method Obsolete'. *Wired*, 23 June. http://archive.wired.com/science/discoveries/magazine/16–07/pb_theory [accessed 4 March 2018].

anderson, Ken, Nafus, Dawn, Rattenbury, Tye and Aipperspach, Ryan. 2009. 'Numbers Have Qualities Too: Experiences with Ethno-Mining'. *Ethnographic Praxis in Industry Conference Proceedings* 1: 123–40.

Bateson, Gregory. 1972. *Steps to an Ecology of Mind: Collected Essays in Anthropology, Psychiatry, Evolution, and Epistemology*. St Albans, Australia: Paladin.

Berson, J. 2015. *Computable Bodies: Instrumented Life and the Human Somatic Niche*. London: Bloomsbury.

Benjamin, Walter. 2008. *The Work of Art in the Age of Mechanical Reproduction*. London: Penguin (original German edition 1939).

Blok, Anders and Pedersen, Morten Axel. 2014. 'Complementary Social Science? Quali-Quantitative Experiments in a Big Data World'. *Big Data & Society* 1(2): 1–6.

Boellstorff, Tom. 2012. '"Rethinking "Digital" Anthropology'. In *Digital Anthropology*. Edited by Heather Horst and Daniel Miller. London: Bloomsbury Publishing, 39–60.

Boellstorff, Tom. 2016. 'For Whom the Ontology Turns: Theorizing the Digital Real'. *Current Anthropology* 57(4): 387–407.

Boellstorff, Tom and Maurer, Bill. 2015. *Data: Now Bigger and Better!* Chicago: Prickly Paradigm Press.

Bourdieu, P. 1977. *Outline of a Theory of Practice*. Cambridge: Cambridge University Press.

Bowker, Geoff. 2014. 'The Data/Theory Thing'. *International Journal of Communication* 8(2043): 1795–9.

Boyd, Danah and Crawford, Kate. 2012. 'Critical Questions for Big Data'. *Information, Communication & Society* 15(5): 662–79.

Boyer, Dominic. 2013. *The Life Informatic: Newsmaking in the Digital Era*. Ithaca, NY: Cornell University Press.

Carrier, James G. and Miller, Daniel. 1998. *Virtualism: A New Political Economy*. Oxford and New York: Berg.

Cheney-Lippold, John. 2011.'New Algorithmic Identity: Soft Biopolitics and the Modulation of Control'. *Theory, Culture and Society* 28(6): 164–81.

Chilver, John. 2014. 'Number Intersecting with Art: Three Studies'. *Distinktion: Scandinavian Journal of Social Theory* 15(2): 239–49.

Clifford, James and Marcus, George E. 1986. *Writing Culture: The Poetics and Politics of Ethnography.* Berkeley, CA: University of California Press.

Connor, Steven. 2016. *Living by Numbers: In Defence of Quantity.* London: Reaktion Books Limited.

Dumit, Joseph. 2004. *Picturing Personhood: Brain Scans and Biomedical Identity.* Princeton, NJ: Princeton University Press.

Ellen, Roy. 2014. 'A Short History of Anthropology at the University of Kent, 1965–2014'. Available at: www.kent.ac.uk/sac/files/history.pdf [accessed 4 March 2018].

Galison, Peter. 1996. 'Computer .Ssimulations and the Trading Zone.4'. In *The Disunity of Science: Boundaries, Contexts, and Power.* Edited by Peter Louis Galison and David J. Stump. Stanford: Stanford University Press, 118–57.

Geoghegan, Bernard Dionysius. 2011. 'From Information Theory to French Theory: Jacobson, Lévi-Strauss and the Cybernetic Apparatus'. *Critical Inquiry* (autumn): 96–126.

Greenfield, Dana. 2016. 'Deep Data: Notes on the N of 1'''. In *Quantified.* Edited by Dawn Nafus. Cambridge, MA: MIT Press, 123–46.

Guyer, Jane I. 2004. *Marginal Gains: Monetary Transactions in Atlantic Africa.* Chicago: University of Chicago Press.

Guyer, Jane. 2014. 'Percentages and Perchance: Archaic Forms in the Twenty-First Century'. *Distinktion* 15(2): 155–73.

Hacking, Ian. 1990. *The Taming of Chance.* Cambridge: Cambridge University Press.

Hine, Christine. 2015. *Ethnography for the Internet: Embedded, Embodied and Everyday.* London: Bloomsbury Academic.

Hymes, Dell. 1965. *The Use of Computers in Anthropology.* London: Mouton and Co.

Ingold, Tim. 2014. 'That's Enough about Ethnography!' *Hau: Journal of Ethnographic Theory* 4(1). http://dx.doi.org/10.14318/hau4.1.021 [accessed 4 March 2018].

Kitchin, R. 2014. 'Big Data, New Epistemologies and Paradigm Shifts'. *Big Data & Society* 1(1): 1–12.

Knox, Hannah and Walford, Antonia. 2016. 'Is There an Ontology to the Digital'. Cultural Anthropology Website, Theorising the Contemporary, 24 March. https://culanth.org/fieldsights/820-digital-ontology.

Kohn, Eduardo. 2013. *How Forests Think: Toward an Anthropology beyond the Human.* Berkeley: University of California Press.

Kotz, S. and Johnson, N.L. (eds). (2012). *Breakthroughs in Statistics: Foundations and Basic Theory.* New York: Springer Science & Business Media.

Latour, B., Jensen, Pablo, Venturini, Tommaso, Grauwin, Sébastian and Boullier, Dominique. 2012. 'The Whole Is Always Smaller than Its Parts: A Digital Test of Gabriel Tardes' Monads'. *British Journal of Sociology* 63(4): 590–615.

Latour, Bruno. 2002. 'Gabriel Tarde and the End of the Social'. In *The Social in Question. New Bearings in History and the Social Sciences*. Edited by Patrick Joyce. London: Routledge, 117–32.

Lebner, Ashley. 2017. *Redescribing Relations*. London: Berghahn Books.

Lury, Celia and Wakeford, Nina. 2012. *Inventive Methods: The Happening of the Social*. London: Routledge.

Madsbjerg, Christian. 2014. 'Happy Birthday, Now Grow Up'. www.epicpeople.org/happy-birthday-now-grow-up [accessed 7 January 2017].

Marres, Noortje. 2015. *Material Participation: Technology, the Environment and Everyday Publics*. Basingstoke: Palgrave Macmillan.

Marres, Noortje. 2017. *Digital Sociology: The Reinvention of Social Research*. Cambridge: Polity Press.

Marres, Noortje and Weltevrede, Esther. 2013. 'Scraping the Social? Issues in Real-Time Social Research'. *Journal of Cultural Economy* 6(3): 315–35.

Maurer, Bill. 2012. 'Late to the Party: Debt and Data'. *Social Anthropology* 20: 474–81.

Mead, Margaret. 1968. 'Cybernetics of Cybernetics'. In *Purposive Systems*. Edited by H. von Foerster, J.D. White, L.J. Peterson and J.K. Russell. New York: Spartan Books, 1–11. http://cepa.info/2634 [accessed 4 March 2018].

Merry, S.E. and Conley, J.M.. 2011. 'Measuring the World: Indicators, Human Rights, and Global Governance'. *Current Anthropology* 52(3): S83–S95.

Miller, Daniel. 2002. 'Turning Callon the Right Way Up'. *Economy and Society* 31(2): 218–33.

Muniesa, Fabian. 2014. *The Provoked Economy: Economic Reality and the Performative Turn*. London and New York: Routledge.

Myers, Natasha. 2015. *Rendering Life Molecular: Models, Modelers, and Excitable Matter*. Durham, NC: Duke University Press.

Nafus, Dawn. 2016. 'The Domestication of Data: Why Embracing Digital Data Means Embracing Bigger Questions'. *Ethnographic Praxis in Industry Conference Proceedings* 1: 384–99.

Pink, Sarah, Horst, Heather, Postill, John, Hjorth, Larissa, Lewis, Tania, and Taachi, Jo. 2016. *Digital Ethnography: Principles and Practice*. Los Angeles: Sage.

Poovey, Mary. 1998. *A History of the Modern Fact: Problems of Knowledge in the Sciences of Wealth and Society*. Chicago and London: University of Chicago Press.

Rappaport, Roy A. 1977. *Pigs for the Ancestors: Ritual in the Ecology of a New Guinea People*. New Haven: Yale University Press.

The Royal Society. 2017. *Machine Learning: The Power and Promise of Computers that Learn by Example*. London: The Royal Society.

Ruppert, Evelyn, Law, John and Savage, Mike. 2013. 'Reassembling Social Science Methods. The Challenge of Digital Devices'. *Theory Culture & Society* 30(4): 22–46.

Savage, M. and Burrows, R. 2007. 'The Coming Crisis of Empirical Sociology'. *Sociology* 41(5): 885–99.

Seaver, Nick. 2014a. 'Computers and Socio-Cultural Anthropology'. Blog post on https://savageminds.org/2014/05/19/computers-and-sociocultural-anthropology [accessed 31 May 2017].

Seaver, Nick. 2014b. 'Structuralism: Thinking with Computers'. Blog post on https://savageminds.org/2014/05/21/structuralism-thinking-with-computers [accessed 1 June 2017].

Seaver, Nick. 2015. '*Computing Taste: The Making of Algorithmic Music Recommendation*'. Doctoral Thesis, *University of California at Irvine*.

Shrinivasan, Ramesh, Boast, Robin, Furner, Jonathan and Becvar, Katherine M. 2009. 'Digital Museums and Diverse Cultural Knowledges: Moving Past the Traditional Catalog'. *The Information Society* 25 (4): 265–78.

Strathern, Marilyn. 1996. 'Cutting the Network'. *Journal of the Royal Anthropological Institute* 2: 517–35.

Strathern, Marilyn. 2000. *Audit Cultures: Anthropological Studies in Accountability, Ethics and the Academy*. London: Routledge.

Strathern, Marlilyn. 2004. *Commons and Borderlands: Working Papers on Interdisciplinarity, Accountability and the Flow of Knowledge*. Oxford: Sean Kingston Publishing.

Suchman, Lucy, Bloomberg, Jeanette, Orr, Julian E. and Trigg, Randall. 1999. 'Reconstructing Technologies as Social Practice'. *American Behavioural Scientist* 43(3): 392–408.

Thrift, Nigel. 2004. 'Movement-Space: The Changing Domain of Thinking Resulting from the Development of New Kinds of Spatial Awareness'. *Economy & Society* 33(4): 582–604.

Trigg, R.H., Bødker, S. and Grønbæk, K. 1991. 'Open-Ended Interaction in Cooperative Prototyping: A Video-Based Analysis'. *Scandinavian Journal of Information Systems* 3: 63–86.

Tufte, Edward. 1983. *The Visual Display of Quantitiative Information*. Cheshire, CT: Graphics Press.

Venturini, Tommaso and Latour, Bruno. 2010. 'The Social Fabric: Digital Traces and Quali-Quantitative Methods'. *Proceedings of Future En Seine*

2009: Cap Digital. www.medialab.sciences-po.fr/publications/Venturini_Latour-The_Social_Fabric.pdf [last accessed 21 February 2018].

Verran, Helen. 2012. 'Number'. In *Inventive Methods: The Happening of the Social*. Edited by Celia Lury and Nina Wakeford. London: Routledge, 110–24.

Verran, Helen and Christie, Michael. 2014. 'Postcolonial Databasing? Subverting Old Appropriations, Developing New Associations'. In *Subversion, Conversion, Development: Cross Cultural Knowledge Exchange and the Poltics of Design*. Edited by James Leach and Lee Wilson. Cambridge, MA: MIT Press, 57–77.

Part I

Ethnographies of data science

2

Data scientists: a new faction of the transnational field of statistics

Francisca Grommé, Evelyn Ruppert and Baki Cakici

National statistical institutes (NSIs) have historically sought to be a single point of truth about states. Their publications, as recent press releases point out, communicate objective statistics, such as 'In October 2016, the French business climate is stable' (INSEE 2016) and 'Finland's population in September for the first time closer to six than five million' (Saari 2016). Such statements may come across as 'dry' and 'factual'. Yet, they are the result of the painstaking work of translating questionnaires, surveys and registers into statistics that seek trust and legitimacy from governments, corporations and publics. Such trust is in part generated by the application of international quality standards for accuracy, reliability and timeliness that national statisticians appeal to in carrying out their role.

The availability of new data sources – or big data – such as that from mobile phone locations and sensors is introducing new possibilities for the generation of official statistics. For instance, rather than the population register, counting Finland's population could be based on the number of residents who own a mobile phone. However, existing methods for official statistics are not suited to the analysis and interpretation of this data. Data science and data scientists are increasingly identified as the discipline and profession necessary for realising the potential of these new data sources, which require skills and knowledge of analytic techniques not typically used in official statistics such as machine learning, algorithms and predictive modelling. In this regard, big data is introducing to the repertoire of official statistics not only new forms of data but also new valuations of professional skills and expertise, or, as we conceptualise in this chapter, of cultural and symbolic capital (Bourdieu 1984).

In the making of official statistics, what exactly comes to count as data science and the profession of data scientist is not self-evident. While there is much talk about a new science and profession,[1] a science of data dates back to Peter Naur's *Concise Survey of Computer Methods* (Naur 1974), which is often cited as the source of the term 'data science'. Naur defines data science as 'the science of dealing with data once they have been established, while the relation of data to what they represent is delegated to other fields and sciences' (Naur 1974: 30). Various genealogies from computer science, statistics, economics and corporate sources point to other well-known names in statistics alongside Naur, including Gottfried Wilhelm Leibniz, Thomas Bayes, Florence Nightingale and John Tukey, among others (Cukier 2010; Loukides 2010; Patil and Davenport 2012; Donoho 2015). Contemporary definitions of data science and data scientists are much more closely associated with big data, another recent term, and the definition of data scientists as experts who work with big data is cited in recent literature examining data science practices (Kitchin 2014; Ruppert, Law, and Savage 2013; Burrows and Savage 2014; Gehl 2015; Halavais 2015; Pasquale 2015).[2]

Our concern in this chapter is how data scientists are being defined in relation to national statisticians and how both professions are objects of struggle with ambiguous outcomes. While the concentration of the generation, accumulation and ownership of big data in the hands of private-sector corporations has been well documented and argued, our interest is in professional struggles over the legitimate authority to generate official knowledge of the state. We refer to this struggle as the politics of method in which the objects of study and the professions that study them are being defined at the same time (Savage 2010). This entwinement of objects and professions means that this struggle is consequential for how national statistical institutes define and bring into being official statistics as matters of government (Desrosières 1998; Ruppert 2012). However, how national statisticians position themselves in relation to data scientists is the outcome not only of discussion and debate but also of specific material-semiotic practices such as experiments, demonstrations and job descriptions. Furthermore, this struggle is not delineated by national interests and practices (or to any other level or scale), but part of transnational negotiations, contestations and tensions that cut across numerous NSIs and international statistical organisations.

These are the main arguments of our analysis of fieldwork that we draw on in this chapter, which involved a collaborative ethnography of several NSIs and international statistical organisations in Europe.[3] By observing meetings, conducting interviews, shadowing statisticians, observing experiments and performing participatory exercises, we attended to how practices traverse, travel between and connect sites and scales.[4] This is what we refer to as a 'transversal' ethnographic method (see Scheel et al. 2016), which involves working across national and disciplinary boundaries, spatial scales, individual(ised) projects and standardised or predefined research techniques. In practice, it required the work of several researchers to follow, engage and establish relations with different fieldsites (and each other) and connect or contrast observed practices across sites. The method allowed us to analyse the implementation and use of new data sources and analytics in official statistics as the outcome of innumerable distributed practices, negotiations, struggles, tensions and constraints that traverse NSIs and international statistical organisations. By following the details of these rather mundane and situated bureaucratic practices we identified how data science and the profession of data scientist are being constituted in relation to national statisticians. As we note later in the chapter, this did not mean the practices we observed were the same or equally distributed or that there was consensus and settlement on definitions across actors and sites. Rather, following situated practices enabled us to trace repetitions of the activities, stakes, rationalities, claims and arguments shaping the formation of these professions as well as their objects.

We first establish a conceptual understanding of how valuations of professional skills and expertise in relation to big data constitute cultural and symbolic capital and are changing the relations between factions of professions within the transnational field of statistics. We then take this up to discuss an NSI recruitment practice where job interviews enact a version of data science and the profession of data scientist anchored around declarations of accumulated skill and potential. Next, we show how being a data scientist in relation to official statistics is a matter not only of possessing specific skills but also of acquiring certain sensibilities. We discuss how a habitus for data science is shaped through the material-semiotic practice of the data camp. Finally, we outline how the object of data science, big data, is consolidated through repetitions of definitions and appeals to 'learning by doing' at international conferences and meetings to distinguish the data scientist from the iStatistician and defend the role of NSIs in the legitimate production of official statistics.

Data scientists: field, capital, habitus

Pierre Bourdieu's (1984) conceptualisation of fields, capital and power provides us with a way to understand the formation of the figure of the data scientist in relation to the making of a professional field.[5] Bourdieu understands a field as a dynamic configuration of relational positions occupied by actors who compete with one another over recognition of the forms of capital that shape their relative positions and in turn power and authority. Within any given or emerging field actors seek to maintain or improve their positions in relation to each other through the valuation of different forms of capital, including cultural, economic, social and symbolic capital. It is then through the accumulation of these various forms of capital that their relative positions are established within the field (Bourdieu and Wacquant 2006: 127–8). While Bourdieu's studies were mostly confined to the nation and in particular to France, others have taken up this conceptualisation to understand inter- and transnational fields. Most notable are studies in the fields of international law (Madsen 2014, 2011; Dezalay and Garth 1996) and international political sociology (Bigo 2011). In Didier Bigo's understanding of a transnational field, the 'national' is not simply replaced by the 'transnational' or the 'global'. Rather, he advances that the transnational exists in the form of transnational networks and practices of professionals who 'play simultaneously in domestic and transnational fields' (Bigo 2011: 251). In this view, a transnational field is constituted by networks and practices between and amongst professionals who act at various non-hierarchically ordered scales of the transnational, national and local. It is through struggle and change that new kinds of practices and forms of expertise emerge and become recognised as legitimate in the production of knowledge within a field (Bigo 2011: 240–1).

It is through such simultaneously national and transnational networks and practices that statisticians have operated and worked since the late nineteenth century but especially during the period following the Second World War to make up a transnational field of statistics. Through working with and in relation to professional organisations such as the International Statistical Institute (ISI) and the International Association for Official Statistics (IAOS),[6] and international governing organisations such as the United Nations Statistical Division (UNSD) and the European Statistical Service (ESS), they have come to constitute one faction of actors who have forged a transnational field of statistical practice. Like other fields, they form one faction of a broader field that includes statisticians who work in different capacities within government but also in the academy and commercial and nongovernmental sectors. And like other fields it is dynamic and has undergone specific transformations as a result of changing methods, technologies and governing strategies, problematisations and rationalities but also as a result of struggles within and between factions.

Rather than mapping the dynamics of this transnational field and the dynamics of who constitute its stakeholders, factions and their relative positions, we focus on changing valuations of methods, technologies, expertise, skills, education and experience in the making of data scientists, especially in relation to national statisticians and in turn the recognition of different forms of cultural capital within the field. It is through structured social practices and structuring fields that various agents and their interests generate forms of expertise, interpretations, concepts and methods that collectively function as fields of power and knowledge. This is one of the lessons of Bourdieu's (1984) studies on the ways in which fields of knowledge constitute fields of power. As Mike Savage (2010) has documented, these struggles constitute a *politics of method* through which statisticians and other stakeholders (demographers, data scientists, domain specialists etc.) both within and outside NSIs struggle over the technologies, truth claims, budgets and methods involved in the production of official statistics in order to improve their relative position. Rather than possessing and having fixed advantages, resources and skills are 'mobilized to achieve advantage and classify social distinctions' within this particular context and field (Halford and Savage 2010: 944). It is through such mobilisations that new skills and expertise and the rise of new professions and positions such as data scientists, data wranglers and data infomediaries get valued and recognised. Another site of these struggles is that of university curricula and professional training programmes in data science, for example.

However, struggles also occur through myriad material–semiotic practices that demonstrate and challenge competing methods and truth claims. The stakes are thus not only relative power and capital but also what Bourdieu refers to as the exercise of symbolic violence over the production, consecration and institutionalisation of forms of knowledge:

> Symbolic power is the power to make things with words. It is only if it is true, that is, adequate to things, that description makes things. In this sense, symbolic power is a power of consecration or revelation, the power to consecrate or to reveal things that are already there. (Bourdieu 1988: 28)

While Bourdieu does not express this as performative, he asserts that a description 'makes things'; from populations to the economy and the making of professions, the outcome of struggles thus also involves the constitution of the object itself.

While many objects of struggle constitute the field, a prominent and current one in relation to official statistics is the framing of the threat (or not) of a new faction (and its definition) called the 'data scientist'. The faction emerged in relation to the technological expertise required to analyse big data, a term that became pervasive around 2011. Its proponents promised a new science of societies that challenged existing forms of data and knowledge such as that generated by traditional methods and practices of national statisticians. While many commentators called it a hype, the prevalence of and claims about data science and data scientists became an object of struggle within the field:

> On the other hand, the Big Data industry is rising: the huge volume of digital information derived from all types of human activities is being increasingly exploited to produce statistical figures. These figures often make use of data from private institutions or companies. Leaving aside the current public debate on whether companies which collect the data should own the data and could use them for another purpose without consent, these new statistical figures may be seen as competitors of traditional official statistics.[7]

Reflecting on this struggle some two years later, the then Director General of Eurostat argued that 'we are at the edge of a new era for statistics' as 'data is raining down on us' and, as he further put it, others are claiming that the data revolution could make national statisticians obsolete.[8] With a chief data scientist now located in the White House, what then is their relation to the chief statistician, he asked?

> Ignoring these new developments, official statistics would lose relevance in future and risks to be marginalised similarly to what happened to the geographical offices with Google or TomTom heavily investing into satellite images, aerial photographs and topographic maps.[9]

It is in response to this question that national statisticians over the past several years have struggled to define the profession of data scientist as well as their position in relation to it. But in doing so they have been reconstituting their profession as well as their object, official statistics. At the same time, as Bourdieu also advances, it is because of their similar socialisation, career trajectories, interests and practices that they have a shared habitus and in turn can develop a common sense of the stakes. There is a correspondence or homology between social positions of agents and their dispositions, and their ways of perceiving and evaluating. Dispositions are an embodied state of capital, which Bourdieu names habitus, a system of lasting dispositions that integrate past experiences. Acquired dispositions are part of one's habitus, are internalized, embodied social structures, and a 'primary form of classification that functions below the level of consciousness and language and beyond the scrutiny or control of the will' (Bourdieu 1984: 466). Rather than there being a mechanical or direct relation (e.g. reflection) between social positions and preferences, the concept of habitus captures how the dispositions of similarly positioned agents are defined relationally and in distinction from all others. The dispositions of others therefore serve as negative reference points. When social differences as embodied dispositions get translated into choices, then they serve to strengthen social distinctions (Bourdieu 1984).

In various contexts from small meetings in national offices and analyses in official documents to those of international task forces and conferences, national statisticians discuss, debate and struggle over the practices of data scientists, their valuation and what they mean for the authority of their data, expertise and the knowledge that they generate. While often non-coherent and involving contradictory claims, at the same time, there are recitations, repetitions and reiterations of truth claims about what is the problem, what are the solutions and so on. There are also patterns and momentary settlements about the constitution of both the profession of the data scientist and its relation to that of the national statistician. This struggle is the focus of our analysis below. In doing so we follow Judith Butler (1990), who argues that it is through such citations, repetitions and resignifications of claims that truth is not just described but performed. In brief, this is what Butler draws attention to in her take-up of J.L. Austin's (1962) theorising of speech acts.[10] While some speech acts are descriptive of a state of affairs (what Austin named constative), others are performative (what Austin named illocutionary and perlocutionary). The latter have a force that creates a potential effect in a state of affairs that they seek to describe. What determines whether this force will have an effect is whether there is an uptake, that is, changes in a state of affairs such as the adoption of new conventions and practices.

For us, the force of recitations, repetitions and reiterations of claims about the data scientist and national statistician is to be found in their uptake in specific material-semiotic practices such as experiments, demonstrations, and job descriptions. That is, while discursively performed, definitions of what is at stake, problematisations and solutions are also constituted through doing things. Struggles are performed not just through words but through what national statisticians do. Drawing on Engin Isin and Evelyn Ruppert's (2015) conception of digital acts, we examine how statisticians define and differentiate the data scientist from their craft through not only what they say but what they do in practices such as data boot camps, hackathons, innovation labs, method experiments, job descriptions and sandboxes. Furthermore, it is through such doings that the habitus of the data scientist is constituted and experienced.

We thus attend to struggles within the field as involving how national statisticians talk about, define, problematise and become data scientists but also what they do, their practices and how through these they also define, distinguish and dispositionally come to occupy their position within the transnational field. To capture the recognition of different types of capital we do not only draw on literal references to data science and data scientists in our analysis. When referring to 'the data scientist' or for that matter 'national statistician' moreover, we are adopting the terminology of the field. Our intention is not to suggest that there is one universal characterisation of professions but that there are specific formulations within different practices.

Recruiting data scientists

Our first practice concerns the recruitment of data scientists, where the same process is used to interview and assess several candidates. The recruitment process materially frames data science through job interviews, where applicants appear in front of a committee and convince the committee that their previous experience and knowledge are sufficient for the role of the data scientist, while the committee itself judges whether the applicants' responses fulfil the requirements. The process is discursively framed through application documents, including the job description, guidance for candidates, sample multiple choice tests and other supporting texts. The recruitment process constructs a kind of data scientist, clearly defined and framed prior to the encounter. However, the definition does not end with the documents supplied by the employer. It is further refined through the submitted CVs, the performance of the candidates and the discussions of the committee. It is not merely an exercise of fitting people into checkboxes, but rather the definition of the task and job are changed and refined throughout the process.

In this section, we draw on material gathered while shadowing a statistician in 2015 as she interviewed applicants for data scientist posts distributed across several departments within the government. The interview committee included two other civil servants, one from the human resources department of the NSI, and one from another government agency. Each interview lasted from 45 minutes to one hour. The candidates were also required to take a multiple-choice test in an adjacent room following their interview, which included questions on basic statistics knowledge such as term definitions, probability calculations etc. Their eventual placement would be in various institutes within government, but their assignments were to be decided after the interview process.

The job description document presented an ideal type for the data scientist: a collection of skills in programming/computing, data and statistics. The interviewers were asked to formulate questions that assessed the candidate's competency in different skills. They were provided with a 'marking matrix', a document listing the categories and the grades they should use to assess the performance of the interviewees. The marking matrix referred back to the ideal type, distributed over two categories of questions, 'job-specific' and 'competency', each with four subcategories. Job-specific categories referred to the technical skills of data scientists, including computing (mostly related to programming languages), scripting (related to statistical tools such as R, SAS, SPSS), software (referring to 'Big Data technology' such as NoSQL, Hadoop, Spark, etc.) and statistical skills (referring to traditional statistics knowledge, which test should be used for which problem, how to determine if a sample is representative, etc.). The competency category referred to broader skills, applicable for all civil service positions, defining a common core of skills and attitudes that civil servants are expected to possess. These included collaboration, personal improvement, meeting deadlines, leadership and communication (including the ability to explain technical issues to non-technical audiences).

To be accepted as data scientists, the candidates needed to demonstrate statistical expertise. Several questions at the interview were designed toward this end, such as 'How do you know if your result is statistically significant?', or 'How did you know if your sample represented the population?' When one of the candidates provided inadequate answers to these questions, the interviewers added a note to his application during the assessment round, asking him to 'Please look at the statistical techniques required [for the position]'. When asked about tools, most candidates brought up Matlab, SAS, SPSS and R as familiar software. In particular, R was discussed as an open-source tool, being 'less clunky than SPSS' in the words of one candidate.

The interviewers queried the applicants' familiarity with big data through questions such as: 'What did you learn from your experiences working with big data projects?' One candidate replied with 'use fewer programming languages', displaying a familiarity with data science practice by referring to the shared perception of the proliferation of tools and languages. Through his answer, the candidate implied that some technologies were used for the sake of having used a new technology in the project, and that these types of activities did not belong in proper data science.

Following each interview the interviewers were required to individually assign different scores to the eight subcategories using a scale from one to seven. The evaluation also involved a multiple-choice assessment for some categories, where the interviewers were expected to tick under 'positive', 'needs development', or to leave it blank. After the interviewers filled in their forms individually, they were also required to reach consensus on the final assessment of the candidate, although this did not prove very difficult for them as their final scores in most categories were either the same or differed by only one point. During one such discussion, one of the interviewers stated that, given sufficient background in other related tasks (for example a quantitative PhD, or prior experience in statistical programming), the candidates would be able to pick up some of the skills even if they did not seem to possess them at the time of interview.

Data scientist as accumulated skill and potential

Who are the data scientists as enacted by the job interview? They are able to program, acquire new technical skills quickly, have basic statistical knowledge, be familiar with the discourse of big data, be reflexive about not only the division between the highly techni-cal and the traditional statistical but also their own position within various government departments. They are not merely programmers or developers as they possess statistical expertise, but they are also more than just methodologists as they do not rely on other develop-ers to conduct their study or produce their results. The data scientists combine statistical knowledge with new forms of data analysis. At the same time, the data scientists of the job interview are not hackers. They do not solve problems through small, localised fixes. Instead, they follow specific methodologies informed by traditional statistical practice. In short, the job interview enacts the data scientist as a set of skills and attitudes. Candidates are expected to possess capital in the form of particular accumulated technical skills such as statistical analysis and programming that can be converted to advantage in the ongoing struggle to define the field of data science (Halford and Savage 2010).

The data scientists sought in these interviews are not bound to a specific government task or practice. They can be placed in different government departments, but still contribute their own set of skills independent of domain. In other words, the capital of the data scientist is highly convertible, it allows them to work in different domains with the same set of skills. However, these posts are all part of gov-ernment, and the recruited data scientists are thus expected to perform as civil servants, in ways listed under the competencies category of the marking matrix.

The candidates need to possess certain cultural capital such as statistical expertise and related technical skills to succeed in the recruitment process, but, as the interviewers also acknowledge, they are evaluated in relation to their potential to become data scientists. That is, being a data scientist involves a process that builds on capital that a candidate already possesses but through which they must demonstrate the capacity to learn and acquire yet unknown skills. To become a data scientist, in other words, is an ongoing process of accumulating capital by engaging with different fields and acquiring additional skills such as new programming languages, or familiarity with new data analysis tools as technologies change and evolve. Rather than settled, the data scientist is understood as a profession constantly in-the-making.

The recruitment of new data scientists valorises new skills in the statistical practices of government. However, skill alone is not sufficient but must be bundled with other forms of capital such as statistical knowledge, as well as a particular habitus as we discuss in the following section. However, in this specific job bundle, technical skills count for more when granting legitimacy to the performance of the data scientist candidate. Candidates argue for why different skills should be considered part of the bundle, attempt to configure what cultural capital advantages data scientists and thereby define who should count as one. Some skills, for example familiarity with database management, once relegated to IT specialists, now play a much more prominent role defining the skills of government statisticians.

The question and answer format of the job interview enacts a kind of data scientist, anchored around verbal declarations of accumulated skill coupled with the evaluation of their potential. However, as we have already suggested, being a data scientist also involves cultural capital understood as the acquisition of particular sensibilities. In the next section, we discuss the shaping of a data science habitus through our investigations of data camps.

Data camp: from skills to sensibilities

Big data sensibilities

As NSIs start experimenting with big data statistics, they need employees not only with data science skills but also with 'big data sensibilities', as stated by a senior national statistician. In this section, we discuss the shaping of what we call a data science habitus, embodied cultural capital that includes skills, tastes, habits, normative inclinations and other knowledges that are not normally made explicit. Indeed, in the absence of a singular definition of data science, the shaping of a habitus functions to form who are data scientists and how they differ from or resemble national statisticians. We discuss one practice through which a habitus is shaped to suggest that it is not only acquired through discursive practices, but also through practical exercises such as experiments, sandboxes and boot camps that test, develop and demonstrate the possibilities of new data sources and analytic techniques.

The specific material-semiotic practice we discuss is a data camp in which national statisticians, students, and PhDs in computer science and related disciplines participated. The aims of the camp were to develop uses of big data for official statistics; to increase statisticians' knowledge and familiarity with techniques; to profile the NSI as a future employer for data scientists; and to strengthen the ties between the NSI and the university. The camp was modelled after a hackathon, and included skills training, lectures, presentations and, of course, collaborative work. We suggest that these practices 'make explicit' (Muniesa and Linhardt 2011) what big data sensibilities might entail.

Data camp

During the data camp, twenty participants and seven mentors from the NSI and the university stayed on a university campus for a week. The mixed NSI-university teams worked until late at night on topics such as profiling Twitter populations and using road sensor data as an indicator of economic growth, not even stopping work during the 'data dinners'. The participants engaged in three main activities. The first and central part of the data camp was collaborative work. To get statisticians up to speed with the programming languages and software necessary for processing and analysing large datasets (in this case mainly Spark and Hadoop), skill training sessions were provided during the first days. At the end of each day, members of the group evaluated their findings and identified problems they were struggling with. The second main activity was attending lectures by academic or professional experts, for instance on 'Big Data processing principles' or 'Setting up research questions'. The third main activity was participation in the final presentation day. The teams presented their results for the NSI and university higher management. The event took place in the VIP room of the university, and included a ceremonial signing of a memorandum of understanding about future collaboration between the two institutions.

A closer look at these activities indicates that, for statisticians to work with Big Data, they need to acquire more than skill. Regarding collaborative work, participants stated the relevance of algorithms by referring to the commands and codes that help them execute a wide variety of automated work: converting datasets, classifying data for more insight and analysis, codes that extract and select relevant data, mining text, calculating values, and finally implementing analytic models. 'Algorithms' therefore covered a wide variety of automated work. In their evaluations and reports; however, participants emphasised the relevance of algorithms to process data and to get insight into datasets. As one participant stated in his project report: 'The initial work focused on accessing and getting to know the data. We tried Spark-R and Pig-Latin for this. Since using Pig-Latin was successful, we did not try any other language. Pig-Latin was used to study the data set in more detail.'

Such statements of relevance, we suggest, amount to more than acquiring necessary skills. The participants articulated that it required an 'appreciation' of algorithms. For instance, one of the outcomes of an evening evaluation session was that 'algorithms love statistics' (see Figure 2.1). Yet the participants also experienced that algorithms did not necessarily make data processing a quick and simple task. Data from sources such as Twitter differed from administrative sources, and required extra attention due to the variations in their formats and their changeability over time. One NSI participant commented on the relevance of the location of commas, and the elaborate work required to prepare datasets for analysis. This work, the group commented, required patience. As automated correction and processing work also happens at NSIs, using algorithms and cultivating patience were not entirely new for statisticians. What was new, however, was a conception of a relationship between algorithms and statistics. Statisticians expressed an imagined closeness between algorithms and statistics (and therefore themselves) that helped them not only understand but also capitalise on data.

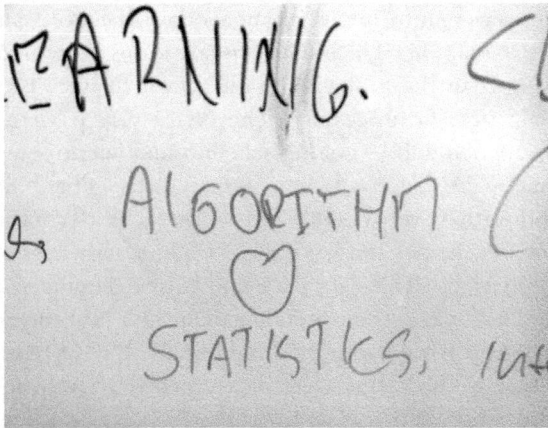

Figure 2.1 The love of algorithms: the data camp's whiteboard after group evaluation

Two lectures on visualisation were especially instructive about data science sensibilities. The first lecture covered the practices of a NGO working according to the principle of 'objects of concern'.[11] They stated that this might mean increasing the visibility of a local phenomenon (like deforestation) on a map, in order to draw attention to it. 'You have to take a position', the organisation's CEO stated, 'not exaggerating is making a choice as well'. Similar practices were adopted by the teams for different purposes. For instance, one team created a threshold for visualising a phenomenon because they thought it would help their analysis.

The second lecture by an NSI statistician contrasted with this practice. When the presenter was asked whether his visualisations had an explicit political viewpoint, he responded that he left the politics to the audience, 'so you [analysts and statisticians] don't have to make choices'. The sensibilities negotiated here concerned relations between what they considered to be realities and their representations. As summed up by one of the mentors: 'You lie a bit with statistics … you have to torture them until they confess.' The lecture shows that national statisticians are not unfamiliar with such practices, even though they usually argue for the objectivity of statistics in public settings (as argued in Desrosières 2001).

The lectures were informative about another aspect of a data science habitus in-the-making. The NGO visualisations were aesthetically more pleasing than the NSI visualisations, which were presented as mostly an aid to data processing. The NGO visuals were detailed, interactive, applied subtle colour schemes and were easy to grasp because they were based on geographic maps. The NSI visuals, although innovative, were clunky, less concerned with continuous and cohesive colour schemes and less easy to read for audiences other than national statisticians. The data camp mentors encouraged attractive visualisations by stating their preferences; as one NSI mentor stated: 'It would be great if we had something like the [NGO] visualisations on our website.' The teams were also coached actively to produce such visuals.

Appreciating the aesthetics of visualisation is relevant for two reasons. First, attractive visualisations draw in audiences. Second, and what we highlight here, they also serve as analytic tools. Visualisation is not only an end-product but a method for the analyst to understand large volumes of data that are not easily analysed using traditional techniques such as graphs. Aesthetics contribute to this aim, in the form of contrasts, colours and animations that facilitate analysis. So, while maps, graphs and diagrams have always been part of statistical analysis, the difference here is the appreciation of, and the acquisition of a taste for, the possibilities of advanced aesthetics.

A final sensibility was introduced by the NSI mentors in the context of preparing for the closing presentations: doing result-oriented pro-jects for a specified group of users. This included requirements typical for NSIs whose role is to supply statistics to clearly defined user groups such as departments and government agencies. Working within gov-ernment, they are accustomed to contributing to public discussions and policy-making as a professional responsibility. As the mentors also reminded, making a convincing case requires indicating, or at least hinting at, the value (or 'business case') of projects. Alongside these sensibilities, being inquisitive and taking risks were appreciated and encouraged by the participants, the mentors and higher management. As the Director General of the NSI stated on the final presentation day: 'Especially experimentation I liked very much.' In sum, the data camp showed how the statisticians' norms of contributing to government policy and debate co-existed, and sometimes clashed, with an appreciation of experimentation and a sensibility for doing trial-and-error work. Statements such as 'there is a lot in the data' often helped resolve such frictions because they indicated that a trial-and-error process might lead to results at a later stage.

A data science habitus for official statistics

Various elements of a new type of cultural capital were recognised through the data camp: tweaking representations of reality; a feel for the business case and users; the aesthetics of visualisations; experimentation; patience; and an affinity for and appreciation of algorithms. In addition, the data camp allowed statisticians to build personal networks of support and generate demonstrations of their capabilities that might allow them to operate according to these sensibilities in their statistical institutes.

The foregoing is not exhaustive or comprehensive nor an account of the formation of a universal data science habitus. Rather, it is an account of practices involved in the shaping of a set of 'data science sensibilities' specifically in relation to a faction of the transnational field of statistics. Which sensibilities are valued and become part of a habitus that individuals start to embody happens through training, and, in this case, by doing things (cf. Dobbin 2008; Franssen 2015). These sensibilities are not separate from but a consequence of changing relations between statisticians, forms of data and their methods of analysis. Working with algorithms and visualisations, as we have noted, requires sensibilities for aesthetics, patience and a closeness to data that are otherwise not easily interpretable. These are dispositions of 'how to be with data' that form a shared habitus.[12]

In sum, the shaping of this habitus required practical exercises that put something to the test in order to be actualised. This is what Fabian Muniesa and Dominique Linhardt refer to as 'making explicit' (2011). Such actualisation does not unfold without problems, hesitations or tensions, as exemplified by the tension between trial-and-error work and producing short-term results. Making things explicit is exactly that: making sensibilities visible and putting them up for consideration, debate or negotiation. The significance of practical exercises is also recognised in appeals at international conferences and meetings where repetitions of definitions of big data lead to appeals to 'learn by doing' and in this way differentiate the data scientist from the 'iStatistician'.

Towards the iStatistician: define, demonstrate, differentiate and defend

We need more investment, more infrastructure, more innovation, being 'smart', raw data into intelligence, skills needed, competitiveness, and so on. The repetition was rather numbing.[13]

This quotation comes from a fieldwork memo that noted the mundane repetition of arguments of statisticians across various international meetings. Rather than deepening over time, such arguments usually remain undeveloped along with the uncritical adoption of the oft-repeated claim that big data is 'raw'.[14] These repetitions highlight that what is understood as data science and in turn a data scientist happens through not only 'doing things' but also discursive practices of imagining and defining the object of concern. Like other professional fields, this takes place in complex networks of interactions and exchanges from small meetings and official documents to those of international task forces and conferences where national statisticians discuss, debate and struggle over definitions.

In this section, we draw on practices that involve presentations and discussions at international meetings we observed. These include, for example, task forces of Eurostat and various meetings of population and housing experts at the UNECE and Conference of European Statisticians. Presentations invariably included a series of repetitions that were not defended as much as put forward as something that everybody knows. We identify four repetitions: *defining* what big data is, how it is better than traditional sources, and what skills it demands; *demonstrating* how big data can or cannot deliver official statistics; *differentiating* the data scientist from the figure of the iStatistician; and *defending* the authority of NSIs to establish, and evaluate adherence to, the legitimate criteria for the production of official statistics.

Define

'Big Data is characterized as data sets of increasing volume, velocity and variety; the 3 V's.'[15]

The emergence of new professions involves identifying and defining an object of concern that calls upon new skills and expertise not currently being met. For this reason, defining an object and profession are very much entwined. When national statisticians defined big data they usually adopted the '3 Vs', one of the most prominent repetitions in this and other fields. It is a definition born of industry, though taken up and in some cases expanded within the academy.[16] One definition offered at an international meeting built on this formulation to highlight how it gives rise to new IT issues compared to more traditional data sources:

> Big data is data that is difficult to collect, store or process within the conventional systems of statistical organizations. Either their volume, velocity, structure or variety requires the adoption of new statistical software processing techniques and/or IT infrastructure to enable cost-effective insights to be made.[17]

Over time, the definition was further expanded:

> Every day, 2.5 quintillion bytes of data are created. These data come from digital pictures, videos, post to social media sites, intelligent sensors, purchase transaction records, and cell phones' GPS signals, to name a few, and comply with the following attributes: volume, velocity, variety, veracity, variability and value, in other words: Big Data.[18]

Such definitions led to repetitions of how big data is 'better' than data from traditional sources such as censuses and surveys. Most commonly, these potential improvements were identified in relation to the European Statistics Code of Practice, which defines five aspects of statistical output quality: relevance; accuracy and reliability; timeliness and punctuality; coherence and comparability; accessibility and clarity.[19] That big data could possibly meet these principles better than existing forms of data was key to its evaluation and the identification of what is at stake.

Definitions and valuations of big data were then often translated into the skills required and in turn what constitutes a data scientist. At one international meeting, a national statistician described 'hard-core data scientists' as having broad knowledge plus specialist skills and being people who can work with big data systems and process knowledge.[20] At another meeting a statistician stated that what he observes is that workers in other disciplines such as computer scientists have been quicker to adopt these skills and they are taking up the 'high' positions that economists once did; that they sell themselves better; and that it is harder for statisticians because their interests are substantively different.[21] In these ways, how national statisticians defined, problematised and valued big data was very much entangled with how they then came to identify the forms of cultural capital that make up the profession of a data scientist.

Demonstrate

The role of repetitions secured a relative settlement on a definition, problematisation and valuation of big data, and in turn the skills that it demands. But, while necessary, such definitional settlement remained insufficient as it lacked specificity in relation to how Big Data would practically compare to longstanding and trusted official statistics. If the profession of data science and in turn the scientist are to be relevant to the field of statistics, then experiencing, testing and demonstrating – or as commonly recited 'learning by doing' – was required. Laboratories, sandboxes and pilots were practical means identified at meetings for moving from definitions to demonstrations:

> The key critical success factor in the action plan is an agreement at ESS level to embark on a number of concrete pilot projects. A real understanding of the implications of big data for official statistics can only be gained through hands-on experience, 'learning by doing'. Different actors have already gained experience conducting pilots in their respective organisations at global, European and at national level. The purpose of the pilots is to gain experience in using big data in the context of official statistics.[22]

Pilots were noted as ways to gain experience in identifying and analysing the potential of Big Data for statistical data production.

> [The] 'Sandbox' environment has been created to provide a technical platform to load Big Data sets and tools. It gives participating statistical organisations the opportunity to test the feasibility of remote access and processing; test whether existing statistical standards / models / methods etc. can be applied to Big Data; ... [and] 'learning by doing'.[23]

Repeated definitions of big data or the data scientist were thus insufficient to appreciate the implications for the profession of national statisticians. Beyond discursive claims, specific material–semiotic practices of doing things were recognised as necessary. As such, the latter were not separate from the former but together were part and parcel of the struggle to understand the implications of Big Data for national statisticians through their practising and testing of specific skills recognised as the domain of data science.

Differentiate

It was through demonstrations that discourses about the promise of big data led to more nuanced critiques and started to focus on differentiating the data scientist from the figure of the national statistician. This was exemplified in the description of the figure of the iStatistician by Walter Radermacher, the Director General of Eurostat. He set out this role in the context of a 'data revolution' and in relation to a genealogy of statistics beginning with its birth during the period of state formation in the first part of the nineteenth century, noting the shared etymology of state and statistics.[24] This he called the 'descriptive' era of Statistics 1.0. In the twentieth century came Statistics 2.0 with the move to mathematics, inference, surveys and sampling. Statistics 3.0 came later in that century with the introduction of new technologies and IT infrastructures. The twenty-first century was then characterised as the 'data revolution': big data, machine-to-machine communication and modelling and the era of Statistics 4.0.

The iStatistician, Radermacher argued, is the professional of Statistics 4.0. The classical profile of the statistician in earlier eras was that of a data gatherer and information generator who was invested in a 'data collection machinery'. In Statistics 4.0 that profile must move to less data generation to a focus on information and knowledge generation along with in-depth knowledge of both statistics and information technologies. That the iStatistician was chosen is an interesting strategic move. By 2016 the appropriateness of the term big data was in question. Although the term had always been debated, with people questioning the hype it generated, in 2015 the term big data was coming to be seen as unfashionable and other practices such as machine learning, the internet of things and AI were becoming more prominent. This was illustrated in the move of the UNECE big data project from a focus on big data to a focus on data integration. The rationale was that big data is insufficient to serve the purposes of official statistics and only when taken together and integrated with multiple and especially official data sources can their value be realised. This conclusion followed several years of experiments and pilots that individually revealed the limitations of data from mobile phones, search engine queries or social media sources.

The definition of the iStatistician proposed by the Director General marked out a similar distinction. Rather than focusing on data, his concern was the analytic skills required to manipulate high-volume datasets, deal with uncertainty and work with predictive analytics, machine learning and modelling. But in a move to further differentiate the statistician, he noted that skills are insufficient: only the iStatistician can generate trust and confidence in advanced analytics and produce high-quality products while at the same time dealing with political issues such as data privacy. Relationally then, the data scientist is distinguished as having specific analytic skills but lacking other competencies that are the province of the iStatistician.

Defend

At a meeting where a draft version of this chapter was presented, national statisticians offered that the skills – or cultural and embodied capital – to work with big data are not the dominion of one professional, whether named a data scientist or iStatistician.[25] Rather, a 'Da Vinci team' composed of professionals with different and complementary skills is necessary that combines knowledge of IT with soft skills such as communication, for example. They also noted that the creation of data scientist positions within NSIs is a matter of ongoing debate; some argued that what is required is the reskilling of national statisticians and not new positions. We suggest that their observations resonate with the competencies of the iStatistician and their emplacement in collectives, the offices of national statistics. Furthermore, they highlight that, while big data and data scientists are bringing into question the skills and competencies of national statisticians, they are also being mobilised to reinforce and defend existing values that they command such as trustworthiness, public accountability, civil service and democratic legitimacy. These principles constitute another repetition often asserted at international meetings in relation to big data: that the investments of NSIs in myriad forms of data and their capacities to secure the principles of official statistics ensure the relative advantage of national statisticians in the future:

> It is unlikely that NSOs [NSIs] will lose the 'official statistics' trademark but they could slowly lose their reputation and relevance unless they get on board. One big advantage that NSOs have is the existence of infrastructures to address the accuracy, consistency and interpretability of the statistics produced. By incorporating relevant Big data sources into their official statistics process NSOs are best positioned to measure their accuracy, ensure the consistency of the whole systems of official statistics and providing interpretation while constantly working on relevance and timeliness. The role and importance of official statistics will thus be protected. (UNECE 2013)

National statisticians, in other words, assert their authority to establish, but also to evaluate adherence to, the legitimate criteria for the production official statistics. The effects of big data are thus both disruptive and continuous. Data scientists are not 'taking over' or replacing national statisticians but they are being relationally reconfigured through a process of differentiation. As part of this, while requiring new skills, big data is also (potentially) reinforcing established values and norms for the legitimate production of official statistics. That is, struggles over the naming and defining of big data and professions are part of larger stakes in the production, consecration and institutionalisation of official statistics.

Conclusion

The production of official statistics involves practices where the uptake of big data is leading to changing valuations of the relative authority of skills, expertise and knowledge within the transnational field of statistics. Big data is an object of investment whose value is being produced by the competitive struggles of professionals who claim stakes in its meaning and functioning. Exactly how a new faction – the data scientist – and the remaking of another – the national statistician – relationally take shape and have consequences for how official statistics are generated, valued and trusted is yet to be known. We have elaborated this as a struggle that is happening through three kinds of practices that are very much connected to political struggles

over the legitimate exercise of what Bourdieu named symbolic violence: the power to name and make things. This is one meaning we
give to the politics of method: that the object of study and the professions that invest in them are being defined at the same time.

A final aspect of the politics of method concerns our own practice,
about which we draw three observations. First, ethnography has
enabled us to account for often undocumented practices involved in
the remaking and emergence of professions such as the formation of
a habitus. Second, a collaborative ethnography enabled us to trace
how these practices are transversal and happen across numerous sites
that are not of similar significance but fulfil specific roles in the formation of professions. Third, we emphasised the importance of documenting and interpreting not only discursive struggles but also
material-semiotic practices. As we have noted, many national statisticians are aware of the role of 'learning by doing' as evident in their
insistence on experimentation and demonstration. In that regard, we
also suggest that such practices allow them to be their own ethnographers: to observe each other and reflect on what their observations
mean for their profession.

Acknowledgements

The research leading to this publication has received funding from the Euro-
pean Research Council under the European Union's Seventh Framework
Programme (FP/2007–2013) / ERC Grant Agreement no. 615588. Principal
Investigator, Evelyn Ruppert, Goldsmiths, University of London.

Notes

1 A quick look on Google Trends shows that searches for the term 'data
   science' started increasing in frequency around 2012, and are still
   climbing.
2 Some, often academic, statisticians have publicly spoken out against a
   division between data science and statistics, arguing that statistics are at
   the core of data science and that the volume of data does not change that
   fact (cf. Meulman 2016).
3 The ethnographic fieldwork, which began in 2013, was part of an ERC-
   funded project, Peopling Europe: How data make a people (ARITH-
   MUS; 2014–19; CoG 615588) and involved a team of researchers: Evelyn
   Ruppert (PI), Baki Cakici, Francisca Grommé, Stephan Scheel, Ville

Takala and Funda Ustek-Spilda. This chapter has benefited from the insights of all team members, and is the result of ongoing collective work, conversations and analysis.

4   The fieldsites include NSIs and international statistical organisations: the Office for National Statistics of England and Wales; Statistics Netherlands; Statistics Estonia; Statistics Finland; Turkstat; Eurostat; and the Statistical Division of the United Nations Economic Commission for Europe.

5   The following draws on a working paper that we wrote with our colleagues. See Scheel et al. 2016.

6   The ISI was founded in 1885 but international meetings began in 1853. It has had consultative status with the Economic and Social Council of the United Nations since 1949. The IAOS has existed since 1985 and it is a specialised section of the ISI consisting of producers and users of official statistics.

7   Eurostat 2014. 'Big data – an opportunity or a threat to official statistics?' Presentation to the Economic Commission for Europe Conference of European Statisticians. Sixty-second plenary session, Paris, 9–11 April.

8   Fieldwork notes. From the opening address of Walter Radermacher, the Director General of Eurostat at the 'New Techniques and Technologies for Statistics (NTTS)' 2015 conference in Brussels, Belgium, an international biennial scientific gathering organised by Eurostat.

9   Eurostat 2015; internal document.

10 We only briefly summarise the key points for us of Austin and Butler on speech acts; for further elaboration see Isin and Ruppert 2015.

11 After 'matters of concern' (Latour 2004).

12 We are suggesting not that statisticians have a more or less embodied relationship with data compared to other professionals but that specific dispositions and their embodiment might be different. Studies of analytic practices in other fields point out that working with data also involves developing a sense for data (see, for instance, Myers 2014). When we refer to 'sensibilities' here, we primarily mean a sense of what dispositions are valued by this faction of the field and as part of how statisticians relate to data.

13 Fieldwork memo: European Data Forum 2015. Exploiting Data Integration, Luxembourg, 16–17 November.

14 Fieldwork memo: Q2016 conference: Eurostat Biannual Quality Conference, Madrid, Spain, 1–2 June.

15 UNECE 2013. 'What does "Big data" mean for official statistics?' Economic Commission for Europe. Conference of European Statisticians. Sixty-first plenary session, Geneva, 10–12 June.

16 See for example Kitchin 2013 and Mayer-Schonberger and Cukier 2013.

17 UNECE 2014a. 'How big is Big Data? Exploring the role of Big Data in Official Statistics.' Draft paper. UNECE Statistics Wikis. www1.unece.org/stat/platform/pages/viewpage.action?pageId=99484307 [accessed 4 March 2018].
18 UNECE 2016. 'Interim Report of the Task Force on the Value of Official Statistics.' Conference of European Statisticians. Sixty-fourth plenary session, Paris, 27–9 April.
19 European Statistical Services Committee 2011.
20 Fieldwork notes. February 2015.
21 Fieldwork notes. April 2014.
22 Fieldwork notes. October 2014.
23 UNECE 2014. 'Sandbox.' UNECE Statistics Wikis. www1.unece.org/stat/platform/display/bigdata/Sandbox [accessed 4 March 2018].
24 Fieldwork notes. From the opening address of Walter Radermacher, the Director General of Eurostat at the 'New Techniques and Technologies for Statistics (NTTS)' 2015 conference in Brussels, Belgium, an international biennial scientific gathering organised by Eurostat.
25 The meeting took place on 6 February 2017 at Goldsmiths, University of London.

References

Austin, J.L. 1962. *How to Do Things with Words*. Oxford: Oxford University Press.

Bigo, Didier. 2011. 'Pierre Bourdieu and International Relations: Power of Practices, Practices of Power'. *International Political Sociology* 5(3): 225–58.

Bourdieu, Pierre. 1984. *Distinction: A Social Critique of the Judgement of Taste*. Cambridge, MA: Harvard University Press.

Bourdieu, Pierre. 1988. 'Social Space and Symbolic Power'. *Sociological Theory* 7: 14–25.

Bourdieu, Pierre and Wacquant, Loic. 2006. *Reflexive Anthropologie*. Frankfurt am Main: Suhrkamp.

Burrows, Roger and Savage, Mike. 2014. 'After the Crisis? Big Data and the Methodological Challenges of Empirical Sociology'. *Big Data & Society* 1(1): 1–6.

Butler, Judith. 1990. *Gender Trouble: Feminism and the Subversion of Identity*. New York and London: Routledge.

Cukier, Kenneth. 2010. 'Data, Data Everywhere'. *The Economist*, 25 February. www.economist.com/node/15557443 [accessed 5 December 2017].

Desrosières, Alain. 1998. *The Politics of Large Numbers: A History of Statistical Reasoning*. Edited by R.D. Whitley. Cambridge, MA, and London: Harvard University Press.

Desrosières, Alain. 2001. 'How Real Are Statistics? Four Possible Attitudes'. *Social Research* 68(2): 339–55.

Dezalay, Yves, and Garth, Bryant G.. 1996. *Dealing in Virtue: International Commercial Arbitration and the Construction of a Transnational Legal Order*. Chicago: University of Chicago Press.

Dobbin, Frank. 2008. 'The Poverty of Organizational Theory: Comment on: "Bourdieu and Organizational Analysis"'. *Theory and Society* 37(1): 53–63.

Donoho, David. 2015. '50 Years of Data Science' presented at the Tukey Centennial workshop, Princeton, NJ, 18 September. Available at: http://courses.csail.mit.edu/18.337/2015/docs/50YearsDataScience.pdf [accessed 4 March 2018].

European Statistical Services Committee. 2011. 'European Statistics Code of Practice for the National and Community Statistical Authorities'. Luxembourg: Eurostat.

Eurostat. 2014. 'Big Data – An Opportunity or a Threat to Official Statistics?' Presentation to the Economic Commission for Europe Conference of European Statisticians. Sixty-second plenary session, Paris, 9–11 April.

Franssen, Thomas. 2015. 'How Books Travel: Translation Flows and Practices of Dutch Acquiring Editors and New York Literary Scouts, 1980–2009.' PhD Thesis, University of Amsterdam.

Gehl, Robert W. 2015. 'Sharing, Knowledge Management and Big Data: A Partial Genealogy of the Data Scientist'. *European Journal of Cultural Studies* 18(4–5): 413–28.

Halavais, Alexander. 2015. 'Bigger Sociological Imaginations: Framing Big Social Data Theory and Methods'. *Information, Communication & Society* 18(5): 583–94.

Halford, S. and Savage, M. 2010. 'Reconceptualizing Digital Social Inequality'. *Information, Communication & Society* 13(7): 937–55.

INSEE. 2016. 'In October 2016, the French Business Climate Is Stable'. *INSEE: Economic Indicators*. Available at: www.insee.fr/en/themes/info-rapide.asp?id=105&date=20161025 [accessed 4 March 2018].

Isin, Engin and Ruppert, Evelyn. 2015. *Being Digital Citizens*. London: Rowman & Littlefield International.

Kitchin, Rob. 2013. 'Big Data and Human Geography: Opportunities, Challenges and Risks'. *Dialogues in Human Geography* 3(3): 262–7.

Kitchin, Rob. 2014. *The Data Revolution: Big Data, Open Data, Data Infrastructures and Their Consequences*. London: Sage.

Latour, Bruno. 2004. 'Why Has Critique Run out of Steam? From Matters of Fact to Matters of Concern'. *Critical Inquiry* 30(2): 225–48.

Loukides, Mike. 2010. 'What Is Data Science?' O'Reilly Media. Available at: www.oreilly.com/ideas/what-is-data-science [accessed 4 March 2018].

Madsen, Mikael Rask. 2011. 'Reflexivity and the Construction of the International Object: The Case of Human Rights'. *International Political Sociology* 5(3): 259–75.

Madsen, Mikael Rask. 2014. 'The International Judiciary as Transnational Power Elite'. *International Political Sociology* 8(3): 332–4.

Mayer-Schönberger, Viktor, and Cukier, Kenneth Neil. 2013. *Big Data: A Revolution That Will Transform How We Live, Work and Think*. London: John Murray.

Meulman, Jacqueline. 2016. 'When It Comes to Data, Size Isn't Everything'. *STAtOR* 17(2): 37–8.

Muniesa, Fabian and Linhardt, Dominique. 2011. 'Trials of Explicitness in the Implementation of Public Management Reform'. *Critical Perspectives on Accounting* 22(6): 550–66.

Myers, Natasha. 2014. 'Rendering Machinic Life'. In *Representation in Scientific Practice Revisited*. Edited by Catelijne Coopmans, Janet Vertesi, Michael E. Lynch and Steve Woolgar. Cambridge, MA: The MIT Press, 153–77.

Naur, Peter. 1974. *Concise Survey of Computer Methods*. Lund: Petrocelli Books.

Pasquale, Frank. 2015. *The Black Box Society: The Secret Algorithms that Control Money and Information*. Cambridge, MA: Harvard University Press.

Patil, Thomas H. and Davenport, D.J. 2012. 'Data Scientist: The Sexiest Job of the 21st Century'. *Harvard Business Review*. https://hbr.org/2012/10/data-scientist-the-sexiest-job-of-the-21st-century [accessed 4 March 2018].

Ruppert, Evelyn. 2012. 'Seeing Population: Census and Surveillance by Numbers'. In *Routledge International Handbook of Surveillance Studies*. Edited by K. Ball, K. Haggerty and D. Lyon. London: Routledge, 209–16.

Ruppert, Evelyn, Law, John and Savage, Mike. 2013. 'Reassembling Social Science Methods: The Challenge of Digital Devices'. *Theory, Culture & Society*, Special Issue on The Social Life of Methods, 30(4): 22–46.

Saari, Matti. 2016. 'Statistics Finland – Preliminary Population Statistics'. Statistics Finland. http://www.stat.fi/til/vamuu/index_en.html [accessed 4 March 2018].

Savage, Mike. 2010. *Identities and Social Change in Britain since 1940: The Politics of Method*. Oxford: Oxford University Press.

Scheel, Stephan, Cakici, Baki, Grommé, Francisca, Ruppert, Evelyn, Takala, Ville and Ustek-Spilda, Funda. 2016. 'Transcending Methodological Nationalism through Transversal Methods? On the Stakes and Challenges of Collaboration'. *ARITHMUS Working Paper* No. 1. Goldsmiths College, University of London.

UNECE. 2013. 'What Does "Big data" Mean for Official Statistics?' Economic Commission for Europe. Conference of European Statisticians. Sixty-first plenary session, Geneva, 10–12 June.

UNECE. 2014a. 'How Big Is Big Data? Exploring the Role of Big Data in Official Statistics'. Draft paper. UNECE Statistics Wikis. www1.unece.org/stat/platform/pages/viewpage.action?pageId=99484307 [accessed 2 December 2016].

UNECE. 2014b. 'Sandbox'. UNECE Statistics Wikis. www1.unece.org/stat/platform/display/bigdata/Sandbox [accessed 2 December 2016].

UNECE. 2016. 'Interim Report of the Task Force on the Value of Official Statistics'. Conference of European Statisticians. Sixty-fourth plenary session, Paris, 27–9 April.

3

Becoming a real data scientist: expertise, flexibility and lifelong learning

Ian Lowrie

'How do I spend my time, as a student?'

Kyrill, a graduate student at the new Higher School of Economics (HSE) department of computer science, repeated my question back to me. He seemed not overly impressed at its incisiveness, but probably wanted to be polite and give a real answer.

'Well, I guess I learn, you know? I also teach, some. And I spend a lot of time with computers.'

He paused, thinking it over for a while as I placed my coffee order with the waitress in what he had laughingly called an 'American-Style café, you know, with hamburgers and doughnuts for breakfast.'

'Really though, it is learning, like, all the time. I am only a graduate student, so even when I am teaching, I am still learning. Learning to teach. I could say that I am also learning how be not just an average guy, but to be a real data scientist [laughs].'

During my fieldwork with Moscow Data scientists, I was told that learning to be a 'real data scientist' meant becoming an expert in a range of programming languages, software environments, mathematical approaches and statistical principles. For the majority of my informants, however, this accumulation of techniques did not alone put the 'real' in front of the 'data scientist'. They told me that a robust repertoire of timely skills was necessary but not sufficient for enacting data-scientific excellence. According to Vika, a graduate lecturer at the HSE, 'first, you should know mathematics. Then you must be familiar with the latest techniques, obviously. It is important to stay up to date.' 'However,' she went on, 'I think it is more important to be clever, to have a good approach to solving problems.'

In this view, the collection of technical and mathematical knowledge serves as a professional 'ground state' (Traweek 1988): a reservoir of fixed and essential competence from which to draw in the performance of more culturally valuable forms of data-scientific virtuosity. As we shall see, the ability to habitually and reliably perform data-scientific excellence requires that methodological knowledge be assembled alongside more diffuse forms of communicative and epistemological judgement and abstraction (cf. Bourdieu 1988; Halpern 2015).

This is not to say that the accumulation of techniques or excellence in fundamental mathematics is viewed as unimportant by data scientists. Quite the contrary: students, academics and professionals alike agreed that they should focus on staying 'up to date', while building and maintaining 'fluency' in mathematics. Although there was a hierarchy of value that privileged more ephemeral forms of 'creativity', 'judgment' or 'insight' above mere 'programming ability' or 'familiarity with techniques', my informants were quite aware of the recursive relationship between these two levels. As Vika explained further, 'of course, you must absolutely know what you are doing with the techniques, first. Otherwise you won't be able to do anything so interesting, right? This is why we focus on them in teaching.' It is impossible to make the gossamer distinctions of judgement separating 'interesting' from clumsy solutions to problems without having spent years hacking out code and building machines.

Certainly, this view was shared by students, who universally felt that traditional mathematics education in Russia was hopelessly out of date, overly focused on theoretical knowledge, and disconnected from the world of what Vika called 'practical engineering tasks'. When I asked them what was required of a good teacher, for example, virtually all of them followed Sergei, a Moscow State graduate student, in pointing towards 'familiarity with contemporary methods, above all else'. It wasn't that they disdained the commitment to theoretical knowledge and scientific rigour of traditional departments like those at Moscow State University or the Bauman School. Rather, they felt that for data scientists, as opposed to 'regular' mathematicians, such virtues could be achieved only through deep and frequent submersion in the messier, more practical business of building machines and solving real-world problems.

As a consequence, my informants spent a great deal of time learning how to do new things. They diligently studied for their university seminars, read papers, took online courses, sought out mentors, browsed peers' repositories on GitHub, participated in programming competitions and hackathons, surfed HabrHabr and StackOverflow and attended conferences, masterclasses, and meetups. Students, academics and professionals alike agreed that education should not be 'confined to the classroom', as Viktor – a junior professor at the HSE – put it: 'life is about learning, so your work should be about learning too. It's important to always seek out the best opportunity to improve. You can't just think that what I'm telling you in lecture is enough. There are always some people who know more than you, more than me, even.' The accumulation of skills during such itineraries, however, remained distinct from, if essential to, the cultivation of excellence. Rather, developing those skills forced students to *practise* the more capacious forms of judgement that were the ultimate hallmark of what Viktor called a 'mature scientific mind'.

The data scientists I met during my fieldwork spent a great deal of time learning and thinking about learning. In this chapter, I continue with a look at how they cultivate methodological skills, before turning to the more ephemeral forms of professional abstraction and expert judgement. In charting this educational nexus, my goal is to contribute a novel empirical perspective to the growing literature on the social study of algorithms and big data. This dynamic literature has brought critical perspectives to bear on algorithms themselves as the objects of second-order analysis (e.g. Kockelman 2013; Rieder 2015), studied the impact of algorithmic data handling on social life (e.g. Ochigame and Holston 2016; Just and Latzer 2016), and shown how it changes existing forms of expertise (e.g. Carlson 2015; Leonelli 2014). However, unlike anthropological studies of expertise, which often foreground the cultivation of skill (e.g. Marchand 2009; Traweek 1988), critical algorithm studies has paid surprisingly scant attention to how data scientists learn their craft. This is an unfortunate lacuna, given both how methodologically fruitful studying education can be for understanding skilled practice, and the central practical and ideological role of learning within the data science community. This chapter works in this empirical gap, taking a direct look at how people learn to build, maintain and operate algorithmic infrastructure. Although it focuses on the Russian context, the goal is to generate laterally portable theory (Howe and Boyer 2016) that can illuminate data-scientific work in other milieux.

Learning

My fieldwork with Moscow data scientists focused on the collaborative formation of a new department of computer science by the Higher School of Economics, a massive state research university, and Yandex, a web infrastructure firm that my informants often called (with varying degrees of irony) 'the Russian Google'. In a national context where academic–industrial collaboration remains relatively rudimentary and intermittent (Bychkova, Chernysh and Popova 2015), the department's comprehensive integration of corporate and university personnel and objectives was viewed as 'innovative', 'highly experimental' or even 'a little scandalous' by both members and outsiders. As a participant observer of the Western academic–industrial milieu, I had expected that this collaboration would be focused on shaping a research agenda geared towards producing immediately useful knowledge and technology (as in Rabinow 1996 or, less optimistically, Mirowski 2011). However, most of those whom I interviewed were nonplussed (or confused) by the suggestion that industry priorities would have a role in shaping the scientific agenda. 'Is that how you do things in the United States?' one junior professor asked me. 'That seems like it would be an unpleasant arrangement for any serious researcher.'

Rather, the mixing of industry and academy in the department was designed to shape pedagogical practice. Russian mathematics and computer science education are heavily skewed towards the theoretical over the applied. While the 'truly elite' system of mathematics education in Russia has a history of producing world–class theorists, according to one Lomonosov professor its 'ossified' and 'outdated' curriculum and pedagogical style made it markedly 'less successful in producing data scientists of sufficiently high quality'. This was because, he argued, training data scientists of 'quality' required more than formal mathematical education: it demanded concrete engagement with 'the world of applied tasks', and training in 'the most contemporary methods, which often come from industry'.

The Higher School viewed its collaboration with Yandex as a way to self-consciously organise against the 'dusty', 'traditional' education of the elite mathematics departments. This collaboration was thorough and robust, ranging from the broadest institutional levels to the most capillary features of daily education in the department. Industrial partners were full participants in the academic council governing curriculum and evaluation; students worked on annual research and development projects (*kursovy raboty*) with the oversight of corporate mentors; many of the faculty were drawn directly from industry in order to teach methods courses; academic mentors aggressively encouraged their students to secure outside work; students were frequently invited to participate in faculty research collaborations with industry.

These educational tactics were motivated by an explicit pedagogical ideology. My informants felt that becoming a skilled data scientist required both a theoretically rigorous mathematical education and submersion in the messier world of data-scientific practice. 'It's important to get out and spend time learning how to do practical work, even if the goal is scientific excellence,' said Yuri, a senior HSE professor. Building bridges to industry was viewed as an expedient way to at once break out of the institutional formalism and inertia of the academy and also to 'bring real data and new techniques into the educational process'. Happily, the practical experience that this provided students also prepared 'our guys to get jobs in industry right away'. As a consequence, Yuri held that the classroom was 'only one stop' on an idealised itinerary of learning that included time spent in data centres, start-ups, internet forums, cafés, hackathons, academic conferences and corporate meeting rooms: the 'places where real problems are solved every day'.

As he explained, however, 'in the wild … it is hard to provide the proper educational support for young people'. These multiple scenes might be crucial for cultivating the various facets of a well-rounded body of data-scientific expertise, but did not themselves provide the necessary direction required of any 'regular (*normalnii*), reliable educational programme'. According to Yuri, 'some people might be OK on their own, without support. Self-educated. Most people need more help.' As much as possible, the department simulated such scenes and encounters for students in-house, through masterclasses, the *kursovy raboty* and various workshops. However, it also aggressively encouraged students to take part in outside activities. For Yuri and his colleagues, the department was, in this respect, a co-ordinating body, directing a plan of education as well as an itinerary of movement through a variety of professional scenes. Crucially, they taught skills, but they also taught a style of and attitude towards learning itself. As Yuri told me, he felt that he was obliged to teach students 'such-and-such set of useful methods', but that ultimately 'the most important thing for them is to stay interested, intellectually, and to know how to satisfy those interests … with proper seriousness'.

Methodological education

Early in my fieldwork, I asked Yuri what exactly it was that data scientists *do* that made them different from computer scientists or mathematicians. 'After all,' I said, 'you guys share much of the same mathematical or theoretical training.' Yuri thought for a moment, then laughed. 'Well, unlike those guys, you know, we actually solve problems!' Solving problems, for Yuri and his colleagues, usually meant developing machines that improved the function of existing sociotechnical infrastructures, made predictions about how complex systems would change over time, or classified data. Building and operating these machines required an array of methodological skills that ran from programming competence and hardware knowhow, through familiarity with specific algorithmic approaches and probability theory, to specific domain knowledge.

For virtually all of the data scientists I met, however, these disparate areas of methodological prowess were integrated within a form of intellection that Vika called 'mathematical thinking', and others called simply 'logic' or 'reasoning'. The ability to think clearly, propositionally and rigorously about the way that the various methodological components of any given algorithmic assemblage interact with one another, and to translate its outputs into useful knowledge, was held paramount. This was, in part, likely because virtually all of the data scientists that I met in Russia were excellent and comprehensively trained mathematicians, first and foremost.

Direct training in mathematics itself, however, was largely something that my informants described as *already* accomplished, prior to the educational activities in which they were more directly invested. In describing incoming undergraduate students, professors told me about how a local system of elite gymnasia and fiercely competitive olympiads fed an extremely talented pool of young mathematicians into the university system; in describing new graduate students and probationary workers, they somewhat contradictorily told me about the 'serious preparation' these latter received as *undergraduates* at not only the world-class mathematics and computer science departments of universities like Lomonosov but even 'common, regional universities'. Mathematical excellence was something that just seemed to float in the milieu, an ever-present background of competence against which the more dynamic figure of data-scientific education could emerge.

Certainly, most of my student informants were supremely confident in their ability to apply sophisticated mathematical theory to data-scientific problem solving. They were less confident, however, in their programming skills and ability to understand the practical demands of the problem domains in which they would operate as professional data scientists. 'I'm pretty good at discrete mathematics and [graph] theory,' one undergraduate told me, 'but I am still not so sure that I understand very much about how to analyse social networks. Practically, I mean. The best methods and their application.' Their professors and managers generally agreed with this assessment; as a consequence, the data-science education that I observed generally *relied* upon and *reinforced*, rather than introducing, mathematical skills and knowledge, using them to scaffold more specific and practical forms of expertise.

This was perhaps most directly observably the case in formal course work. Like many others at the HSE, a graph theory course that I observed was divided into two components: there was a lecture from a professor, followed by a lab session led by a graduate student teaching assistant. The lectures focused on explaining the mathematical and epistemological principles behind the algorithms used to study graph-theoretical problems, such as predicting the spread of disease or identifying clusters in social networks. In the laboratory session, students worked together on learning precisely 'the best methods and their application', using Jupyter Notebook to try out the various approaches discussed in the lecture session as they watched the teaching assistant run through his own analyses on the projector, while providing colour commentary and suggesting tips and tricks.

Given this format, we might already expect pedagogical attention and student enthusiasm to condense around what Fyodor, the lecturer, called the 'admittedly more engaging' hands-on components of the course. What was remarkable to me, however, was how much even the *lecture* component tilted towards the practical business of making algorithms work, rather than on probability theory. Instead of asking questions *about* the mathematics on display, students tended to use statistical principles as fixed points of reference for questions about the technical aspects of implementation. What questions there were about mathematics didn't focus on fundamentals, but rather on the nuances of particular approaches or distinctions between different iterations of a given algorithm. Rather than ask questions about mathematical principles, most students seemed to prefer using their laptops or phones to look up what one called 'missing information' on Wikipedia or Stack Overflow. Similarly, the homework Fyodor assigned eschewed proofs, instead focusing on 'trying to get students to do a little bit of real [programming] work'.

However, this was not the result of an intellectual privileging of the applied over the theoretical or scientific. When I asked Fyodor why he spent so much energy on practical aspects in lecture, instead of relying on his TA to teach them 'how to use the stuff [he] told them about', he laughed: 'Most of my students assimilate this "stuff I tell them about" very quickly, but only in principle. Intellectually, they are very good. They are often not so good at making it work.' Kyrill, the teaching assistant, agreed. 'We don't need to spend so much time here working on the principle of things. Many students really are very excellent, with some success in mathematical olympics … What they need from us is knowledge and experience about how to do real science.'

For Kyrill and Fyodor, doing real science was emphatically *about* the algorithms under study. As researchers, they worked to develop *new* algorithmic approaches. However, in a pedagogical context, the 'relatively well-characterised' algorithms that they were trying to teach students to use were more or less straightforward, intellectually. Learning to use them to solve real-world problems, however, required students to learn to operate within unfamiliar software environments, think carefully about how they implemented them in machine code, and develop competence in the selection of modular analysis and

visualisation packages. Practically, this pushed the curriculum at the
HSE beyond the 'mostly formal' approach to mathematics typical of
other elite departments.

Collecting techniques beyond the classroom

In their formal education, my informants learned to accumulate techniques and assemble them against a background of foundational mathematical knowledge. However, few students confined their learning
to the department: those with any passion for data science were vora-
cious consumers of knowledge, and their quest for new techniques
spilled out across other networks and communicative technologies.
They were constantly learning from their friends and colleagues,
websites and meet-ups, books and journals. Dima, a young developer
at Yandex and a PhD student at the Higher School, told me that
learning new things was 'the most enjoyable thing in the world'. He
described himself as 'constantly' learning techniques, because 'it's fun',
but also 'retty much required … for success in business, but to be a
good scientist, I think … A good scientist should be familiar with the
most current research in his field.' His advisers agreed; as Viktor old
me, 'If you don't want to continue to learn new things as a professional, you could easily be a business analyst … Data science requires
[one] to always stay current … I chose to become a data scientist
because I enjoy learning new things, and my students should be the
same … if they are [going to be] successful.'

In describing the lifelong learning that supported their success in
business and in science, my informants frequently pointed towards
their mathematical training as their primary resource for assimilating
new technical knowledge. Dima told me that his education in mathematics at a regional technical university 'wasn't actually all that
useful' in his day-to-day work, which 'was mostly just programming
boring solutions … to well-characterised problems'. He hoped to
move from a developer role into a machine-learning position, however,
where he thought that 'that [his] mathematics education will definitely be useful, for sure'. Rather than as a reservoir of knowledge,
this education provided the tools to learn: 'Once you have learned
the basic principles behind things, but also how to think carefully and
formally, it is very easy to assimilate [*osvoit*] new methods.' To prepare
for his career move, he was taking online courses from 'Western'

universities that he found 'extremely interesting, but extremely easy', and reading standard data analysis textbooks, which he was 'surprised' to find that he 'understood very well, because of [this] education'. This understanding was a direct result of fluency in what Dima called the 'formal language' of mathematics, which provided a 'consistent' and '"universal' frame through which to assimilate new methodological approaches.

Mathematics was also a 'language' in a more sociological sense. Data scientists work on disparate problems, with a huge range of algorithms, implemented in different software languages across variegated hardware. As a consequence, Yuri told me that it can 'sometimes it can be difficult to speak together ... at meet-ups or some seminars'. What made 'learning from each other ... a little easier', however, is that 'the level of mathematical knowledge is very high here in Moscow'. When communication about 'narrow problems requiring a lot of domain knowledge' or 'focused on the challenges of certain programming languages' broke down, Yuri said that the discussion often shifted register to the formal mathematical properties 'underlying' the matter at hand. As 'scientists,' he told me, 'we can communicate better when we put things in mathematical terms. [We] can put formulas up on the whiteboard, which we all understand.'

Dima and Yuri cast excellence in fundamental mathematics as the practical basis for a lifetime of skill accumulation and as a metalanguage for framing discussions of unfamiliar methods and approaches. They also, however, used it as a conceptual tool for thinking *about* learning itself. 'When I want to learn some new thing,' Dima told me, 'the easiest way is to break things down into formalisable components, and then put them back together in my brain.' In this, Dima and Yuri joined with many of their colleagues in viewing fundamental mathematical knowledge not as an end in itself, or even as a practical tool, but rather as the basis for a lifetime of learning new skills.

Abstraction and judgement

My informants felt that their mathematical competence allowed for the rapid and continual assimilation of new techniques over the life course. This process of accumulation alone, however, did not provide them with the deep practical experience required to function as competent data scientists: Vika argued that the capacity to 'think abstractly' was ultimately more crucial. Thinking 'abstractly', however, certainly did not mean a retreat from the concrete. Rather, my informants viewed abstraction as their professional form of engagement *with* the concrete: in engaging any particular problem, the competent data scientist must take a step back and think in comprehensive, systematic terms about both the concrete algorithmic assemblage at hand, the sociotechnical systems in which it is embedded and the repertoire of possible manoeuvres available to the analyst. Unlike mathematical and methodological knowledge, this capacity could not be the direct object of pedagogy. It was more a form of practical wisdom, slowly accumulated through experience carrying out data-scientific projects within functioning, 'real world' sociotechnical systems.

Most basically, data scientists needed to learn how to 'work from data to solutions'. When approaching a problem, Vika told me that it was necessary to begin by assessing the 'quality and type of data that you have … Business … will ask you … to provide such and such an outcome. But this is not always possible. Instead, it is much better to look at what data they have collected, to see what it will let you do, and then offer various directions to the client … [to] tell them what their data can, and what it cannot', achieve.

My informants felt that, rather than being structured primarily by strategic or scientific imperatives, the problem spaces of data-scientific inquiry necessarily emerged at the confluence of sociotechnical assemblages and the data which they produce.

Grigori, a wunderkind doctoral candidate and developer at Yandex Data Factory, put this in terms of striving to 'be as data-driven as possible, in all things'. Being data-driven, he told me,

> means only using those techniques that are most appropriate for a set of data, and for the task at hand. These two things are really the same. They *should* be the same. You can't have a task without data, as far as I am concerned. And in choosing how to resolve some task, that must be decided by the nature of the data in question, not simply what methods I am … most familiar with, or what the business has been doing in the past.

In its strongest formulations, 'data-driven' science has been animated by a dream of inquiry free from hypothesis-testing, which would instead allow immanent patterns in the data to emerge and shape scientific knowledge or business practice directly (see Kitchin 2014). Grigori was certainly touched by this epistemological dream, but formulated it as a robust professional maxim. More succinctly, Vika told me that it simply meant that 'you shouldn't use a hammer for a screw'.

However, despite Grigori's easy conflation of data and the 'task at hand', it is important to remember that there is no such thing as raw data (Gitelman 2013): that data is always the product of specific forms of recording within sociotechnical systems such as experimental, financial or manufacturing infrastructures. In systems-theoretical terms, the data handled by data science is second-order products of these infrastructures observing themselves or their environments. As such, practically speaking, it is crucial begin with an abstract, 'systems-based' understanding of the algorithmic assemblage under study as a functioning totality. For this reason, a truly 'data-driven' approach, limiting itself only to the immanent features of the data at hand, was *not* appropriate. In fact, Yuri dismissed such epistemological austerity as just 'messing around with the data', which might produce 'intellectually interesting … but not so useful' results. Knowing the goals of the systems that have produced the data at hand, understanding their internal function and identifying appropriate criteria by which to judge success or failure are crucial for 'choosing an appropriate approach [*podxodyashii podxod*]' to the 'improvement of system function'.

Whatever the dreams of a wholly data-driven analytics, data cannot univocally dictate the method of their analysis, especially because a corpus might be deployed to various ends; customer churn data might, for example, be used either to target advertising or to determine more efficient pricing models, which purposes would require different techniques to be applied. Vika explained that, for this reason, while she felt comfortable using 'training' data and its adjacent 'toy problems' to teach her students methods, they ultimately needed to work with 'real problems' to understand such 'critical but difficult distinctions'. Learning the forms of judgement required to operate 'in the wild' required actually putting in hours with lively data, produced by 'real organisations', and integrated with functioning infrastructure.

In other words, doing good data science requires learning to think about both the system under analysis and the range of techniques available to the analyst. One undergraduate, working in a data services start-up, compared himself to a trainer collecting and battling Pokemon:

> You go out and collect all your little guys, your algorithm-Pokemon. You train them, practise with them. You may have some favourites … but when you fight an enemy you must choose the best one, the right one for the job. You know, certain [enemy] monsters have weaknesses and you must choose the one with a strength that corresponds. You have to understand your guys and the other guys, totally. That's how you win!

In this ludic metaphor, delivered in English, the process of learning to think abstractly about data and systems is structurally and processually coupled to the process of accumulating techniques. Methods-monsters must be collected, but they also must be deployed frequently in real situations, in order to work out what they can and can't do, and how they function in specific types of battles.

For those working in the context of real organisations with 'actual demands' for 'productive solutions', it is imperative to constantly evaluate and expand one's stable of monsters. As Grigori put it, one's repertoire of algorithmic techniques 'must always be current … [because] our field changes very rapidly, and if you do not bring contemporary methods to your work, you will often find that your approach is not better than what those guys already have'. One of his colleagues chimed in to tell me that theoretical mathematicians 'had it easy', as they dealt in 'fundamental truths', which were essentially timeless, joking that 'number theory doesn't change that often'. The world of practical computing tasks, however, 'evolved very quickly', according to Viktor. As a consequence, 'our algorithms must be constantly improving, or we're out of a job'. For my informants, staying current was ultimately less about employing fashionable languages or architectures than about satisfying the continual, intellectual and practical demand to surpass the efficiency of previous algorithmic approaches (see Lowrie 2017). As Dima put it: 'If you can't do the best job, why bother?'

Further, even the most well-packaged methods-monster can't just be unleashed into computational infrastructure to do its work unsupervised. My informants were never content to allow the assemblages they built complete autonomy over their own output, at least until they had proved that they could work without continual 'tinkering' or 'interpretation'. As Zev, a kinetic 'independent machine learning consultant' from Israel, explained to me in English:

> people think that these things just work by themselves. That's the whole point of machine learning, right? Wrong! People don't have any idea how much time and knowledge it takes to, first of all, just get these things working, but second, to make sure that we know what their results mean for a specific company, [or] project. I won't say that we 'fabricate' results, but we definitely 'massage' them to make useful insights for [the] company.

Zev and his colleagues continually intervened into their machines at various stages to ensure that they produced what they called, variously, 'elegant', 'clear', or 'useful' results. Far from the fantasy of epistemological automation that haunts both the popular imagination and some academic commentary on these systems, algorithmic assemblages required the constant intermingling of human and non-human cognition to produce –'"seful insights'.

When trying to build machines that produced elegant and useful results, for example, my informants were guided as much by the practical demands of their clients or experimental systems as they were by scientific rigour: 'While we don't know the answers,' according to Yuri, when working on a concrete project, 'we definitely know the questions we are supposed to answer.' He told me that this meant that, rather than selecting algorithmic approaches solely on their scientific merits, 'Often times I will try a variety of equally bad approaches, until I find one that gives me a useful answer.' The 'usefulness' of this answer was dictated and evaluated by human judgements about scientific, business or infrastructural expediency, rather than formal epistemological criteria.

Experienced data scientists often also felt as comfortable tinkering with their datasets as they did tinkering with their models: removing outliers that would 'distract' learning machines from their core analytical goals, or packing them with more of certain classes of data that would purposely skew them towards learning particular features – and this all the while insisting that they strove to 'be as data-driven as possible'. However, my informants were insistent that such tinkering was not 'fakery', that, when done judiciously by a competent and 'sensitive' investigator, it produced *more* accurate and efficient machines than those that just omnivorously consumed all available data. 'Ian,'

Dima told me. 'It can't be "faking" if it works!' Efficiency, rather than truth, was the dominant criterion in these decisions (Lowrie 2017).

Further, even the most competently designed, well-tuned, fully automated algorithmic information processing machine must still contend with the communicative problems of feeding its results back into the broader sociotechnical assemblage within which it operates. This tends to become a deeply social communicative process; when machine insights needed to be translated into organisational action, my informants were often called upon to act as 'translators' or 'brokers' for data-scientific knowledge. Grigori told me that in the context of 'sufficiently scientific organizations', this could often be achieved simply by deploying the social currency and epistemological authority of data science itself: 'You can say, "just trust me" and if it works, you are OK,' he said laughingly. When working with '"ld-style firms', however, 'it is necessary to … communicate the results of your analysis very clearly, like, to show all of your work to the guy in charge, but very simply.' This can mean putting together 'slick powerpoints' and utilising sophisticated visualisation packages (indeed, many workshops and class sessions that I observed focused on transmitting precisely such skills). However, no technical tricks in the world could replace experience: as Grigori explained, more than 'fancy graphics', it is often more crucial to know 'how to talk like a businessman … [and] when to talk like a big nerd. Sometimes it impresses them, [but] sometimes it makes them angry.' It takes communicative skill and judgement to determine the appropriate method for integrating data-scientific knowledge with existing modes of analysis and decision-making.

Unlike methodological knowledge, which can be taught in the classroom, the abstraction, judgement and communicative skills required to perform data-scientific excellence are accumulated slowly, through constant submersion in the 'world of applied tasks'. Like the medical students discussed by Prentice (2012), data scientists cannot simply rehearse a series of specific tasks until perfection, but rather must use their task work across a range of interrelated but distinct domains of engagement to cultivate a series of transposable and durable orientations and approaches (albeit in this case towards systems and data rather than bodies). Unlike for these other professionals, however, there is no ready-made institutional home, such as the hospital, that would bring together a curated collection of opportunities for practising such tasks on 'real' cases. As such, data scientists must range beyond the university, engaging functioning organisations on their own terms, to develop their forms of expert judgement. However, far from troubling the coherence of the abstractions at the core of this judgement, their consistency across these various domains, and the academic-industrial divide, in fact serves as an oft-cited local proof of its coherence. As one of Grigori's trainees put it to me: 'We're all data scientists, after all. If I work in industry, or in an institute, I'm still trying to think in the same way.'

Conclusion

The industrial and academic data scientists whom I met in Russia were always working to accumulate new skills. They felt that staying up-to-date and expanding their domains of practical expertise were essential components of their role as scientists. However, they weren't interested in just *any* currently available methods. They were interested primarily in 'trending' skills, skills that they felt would become 'necessary to learn' for 'future specialists'. Choosing which skills to learn is about 'anticipating possible directions for the career', in Yuri's words, and trying 'to steer yourself towards them'. In this, my inform-ants were engaged in a form of futurological speculation that is a necessary component of any process of skill acquisition in contempo-rary market environments, whether at work or in universities (Wilson 2013).

In many respects, my informants' dual commitments to 'staying current' and developing 'broad toolkits' resonates with existing research on the role of skilled learning in contemporary knowledge capitalism. Certainly, these commitments are shared by many students and workers in late liberalism, where flexible selves with flexible skills (Urciuoli 2008) are told that they must take charge of their own 'lifelong learning' (Olssen 2006) in order to secure and maintain their place as active participants in the knowledge economy (Brine 2006). My informants were certainly participants in a globalising informa-tion economy, structured by many of the same neoliberal forces described by these scholars.

For Russian data scientists, however, the existential stakes of staying current were configured somewhat differently than for those with other forms of expertise, or those operating in in other more straightforwardly neoliberal environments. Since the collapse of the Soviet Union, the Russian political economy has been extremely volatile, with little stability at either the structural level or in specific domains of activity. The science system specifically has suffered a number of successive shocks and political crises in the decades since the collapse of the Soviet Union (Graham and Dezhina 2008; Dezhina 2014). Market and political forces alike have been extremely hard to predict, with entire sectors of development flourishing and dying out as the result of what one sociologist friend called the 'simple random caprice' of political intervention or changing economic conditions. Some expert communities have weathered this chaos better than others: those working in the so-called 'blackboard sciences' of theoretical mathematics and physics, for example, have been able to continue training excellent students and producing internationally important research. Those in applied sectors such as computer engineering, or big science fields such as particle physics, have been less successful.

Lately, information technology has been a limited exception to this general trend, in large part as the result of direct government investment in and support for ventures such as the HSE's new department. However, my informants felt that their fledgling sector was particularly vulnerable to political caprice or uncontrollable economic changes precisely *because* of its reliance on such support. When we turned to talk of the future, it was difficult for them to maintain confidence in even the existence of particular forms of work, such as internet advertising, or institutions, like the department, beyond the very near-term future. Despite a robust faith in their ability to predict which *techniques* would become professionally dominant in the near future, they were uncertain about the stability of the economic and institutional landscapes within which familiarity with such techniques would translate into capital and careers.

However, unlike other precarious workers, my informants were not exactly *forced* into lifelong learning or flexibility by the labour market. Quite the contrary: they were universally aware that they could have comfortably chosen to follow many of their peers into the static, 'tea-drinking' world of academic fundamental maths, where they could have taught 'the same old discrete mathematics textbooks from the seventies', and given 'the same lectures year after year'. Conversely, they could have gone into industrial careers as what one Yandex developer called 'traditional business analysts', who use 'off-the-shelf' approaches that 'have barely changed in twenty years'. Instead, many of my informants told me they chose data science as a career particularly *because* they were excited about the prospect of spending their careers in an 'unpredictable sector', constantly assimilating new techniques, building new collaborations and moving between different 'application spaces'. My informants experienced compulsory lifelong learning and methodological flexibility as intellectually challenging and exciting.

Of course, they were always aware that things could 'go south', as Grigori told me in English. What he and his colleagues could 'bank on' in this 'sometimes difficult climate', however, was their accumulated 'fundamental knowledge'. Most basically, this was mathematical fluency: 'If I understand what is going on in mathematical terms, I can always just learn new things … If my industry changes, that will always be possible, I think.' More specifically, however, the form of abstract reasoning and judgement proper to data-scientific expertise was itself viewed as laterally transferable beyond the specific domain of industrial data science. 'Even if I end up doing, you know, just business analytics or systems management,' one undergraduate at the Higher School told me, 'I will still be a more successful worker because of how I think about problems.' More than skills, data science is about a 'frame of mind', she told me, switching to English.

If mathematical fluency is a base upon which to build a route to the ultimate heights of data-scientific abstraction and judgement, the scaffolds along the way are made up of specific, concrete techniques. These techniques are themselves practically important for career success at any given moment, but do not exhaust either the professional identity or expert toolkit of the practising data scientist. When they imagine their ideal careers, my informants imagined a series of ever-more competent and ever-more flexible selves. This expansion of technical capability, however, was not valued as a response to the demands of a neoliberal workplace. Rather, their enthusiastic submersion in a lifelong process of methodological learning was part of a quest for scientific excellence; their accumulated techniques were valued not only as useful ends in themselves but as practical means for developing the more gossamer intellectual qualities and orientations of 'a mature scientific mind'. In their understanding, learning was a fundamentally scientific process that mediated between the empyrean, timeless forms of theoretical reason so valued in the Russian science system, and the flexible world of skills and techniques familiar to scholars of late liberal workplaces and universities.

References

Brine, J. 2006. 'Lifelong Larning and the Knowledge Economy: Those that Know and Those that Do Not – The Discourse of the European Union'. *British Educational Research Journal* 32(5): 649–65.

Bourdieu, P. 1988. *Homo Academicus*. Redwood City, CA: Stanford University Press.

Bychkova, O., Chernysh, A. and Popova, E. 2015. 'Dirty Dances: Academia–Industry Relations in Russia'. *Triple Helix* 2(1): 2–13.

Carlson, M. 2015. 'The Robotic Reporter: Automated Journalism and the Redefinition of Labor, Compositional Forms, and Journalistic Authority'. *Digital Journalism* 3(3): 416–31.

Dezhina, I. 2014. 'Russia's Academy of Sciences' Reform: Causes and Consequences for Russian Science'. *Russie. Nei. Visions* 77: 1–27.

Gitelman, L. 2013. *Raw Data Is an Oxymoron*. Cambridge, MA: MIT Press.

Graham, L. and Dezhina, I. 2008. *Science in the New Russia: Crisis, Aid, Reform*. Bloomington: Indiana University Press.

Halpern, O. 2015. *Beautiful Data: A History of Vision and Reason since 1945*. Durham, NC: Duke University Press.

Howe, C. and Boyer, D. 2016. 'Portable Analytics and Lateral Theory'. In *Theory Can Be More Than It Used to Be: Learning Anthropology's Method in a Time of Transition*. Edited by D. Boyer, J. Faubion and G. Marcus. Ithaca, NY: Cornell University Press, 15–38.

Just, N. and Latzer, M. 2016. 'Governance by Algorithms: Reality Construction by Algorithmic Selection on the Internet'. *Media, Culture & Society* 39(2): 238–58.

Kitchin, R. 2014. 'Big Data, New Epistemologies and Paradigm Shifts'. *Big Data & Society* 1(1): 1–12.

Kockelman, P. 2013. 'The Anthropology of an Equation. Sieves, Spam Filters, Agentive Algorithms, and Ontologies of Transformation'. *Hau* 3(3): 33–61.

Leonelli, S. 2014. 'What Difference Does Quantity Make? On the Epistemology of Big Data in Biology'. *Big Data & Society* 1(1): 1–11.

Lowrie, I. 2017. 'Algorithmic Rationality: Epistemology and Efficiency in the Data Sciences'. *Big Data & Society* 4(1): 1–13.

Marchand, T.H.J. 2009. *The Masons of Djenné*. Indiana University Press.

Mirowski, P. 2011. *Science-Mart: Privatizing American Science*. Cambridge, MA: Harvard University Press.

Ochigame, R. and Holston, J. 2016. 'Filtering Dissent: Social Media and Land Struggles in Brazil'. *The New Left Review* 99: 85–108.

Olssen, M. 2006. 'Understanding the Mechanisms of Neoliberal Control: Lifelong Learning, Flexibility and Knowledge Capitalism'. *International Journal of Lifelong Education* 25(3): 213–30.

Prentice, R. 2012. *Bodies in Formation: An Ethnography of Anatomy and Surgery Education*. Durham, NC: Duke University Press.

Rabinow, P. 1996. *Making PCR: A Story of Biotechnology*. Chicago: Chicago University Press.

Rieder, B. 2015. 'What Is in PageRank? A Historical and Conceptual Investigation of a Recursive Status Index'. *Computational Culture* 2. http://computationalculture.net/what_is_in_pagerank/ [last accessed 21 February 2018].

Traweek, S. 1988. *Beamtimes and Lifetimes: The World of High Energy Physicists*. Cambridge, MA: Harvard University Press.

Urciuoli, B. 2008. 'Skills and Selves in the New Workplace'. *American Ethnologist* 35(2): 211–28.

Wilson, R. 2013. 'Skills Anticipation: The Future of Work and Education'. *International Journal of Educational Research* 61: 101–10.

4

Engineering ethnography

Kaiton Williams

Data here and there

In Oakland, California, a man brushes past me as I exit my neigh-
bourhood market. 'Data', his T-shirt informs me, 'is the new bacon'.
In Kingston, Jamaica, I sit in a nondescript meeting room for a pitch
on the potential at the crossroads of agriculture and information
technology. 'Data', I read on the screen, 'is the new oil'.

I hadn't travelled to Jamaica to focus on data in particular, whether
as oil or bacon, product or substrate. I came to work within its community of technology developers and to trace the lines between island
actions and Silicon Valley ideas. Over the last five years, in sync with
global currents, the community has been growing, powered by an
ecosystem of training programmes, competitions and incubators that
now dot the Caribbean. The data metaphors, however silly they might
seem, draw attention to the anticipatory and revolutionary representations of technology and its development within these spaces.

Earlier treatments of the arrival and use of the internet in Trinidad
and Tobago (Miller and Slater 2000) and the cellphone in Jamaica
(Horst and Miller 2006) showed how new innovations were chan-
nelled into long-established national and personal projects of freedom.
The internet in particular took on a utopian representation that conjoined personal and market freedom with ideas of global mobility and
identity, giving it 'a symbolic totality as well as a practical multiplicity'
(Miller and Slater 2000: 16). The same can be said about today's

growing flow of data, powered by mutual improvements to internet services and mobile devices.

The internet was once the domain of the desktop while the mobile offered an etiolated version. Over the last decade, however, smartphones have dramatically risen in power and fallen in cost. They are now the default computing platform for billions, creating new markets for entrepreneurial developers, and have shifted the dominant model for software to online services accessed through browsers and mobile apps (Lison 2015). Mutually supporting infrastructures for the development of these products have also been improving rapidly. Cloud computing and Infrastructure as Service platforms such as Amazon Web Services, Google's App Engine and Microsoft's Azure have made it easier and cheaper to build web applications and then scale them up in complexity and across the globe.

This has been a boon for Jamaican developers.[1] They could now compose globally available software and services from these components without leaving the island. While the nation might be at the margin of the global economy, a combination of how-to guides, templates, open-source programming libraries and a tapestry of internet services and APIs now provides the potential for international reach and parity at a small fraction of what it would have cost a decade ago.

Data wended its way through these new conduits. It also powered crime,[2] provided security[3] and offered the basis for better governance.[4] At the mobile innovation programme where I worked as a technical trainer, and the start-up accelerator where I was a consulting engineer, cohorts of largely black, future-focused teams worked on a wide range of products. Many organised themselves around flows of information; for a few others, data was the product. Like the 'new oil', it was something that they needed to uncover, refine and shape for market. Some focused on agriculture, hoping to use drones to gather information on soil and crop health. Others built market information systems that would co-ordinate the buying and selling of produce and prevent theft. Others yet were digitising, securing and circulating medical and court records.

In this chapter, I examine how local start-up entrepreneurs navigate the mythologies of data and the realities of its production as part of an attempt to build software for a global market. I reflect on long-term engagement with VideoLogs, a team working to provide businesses with 'emotionally intelligent' analysis of customer feedback, focusing on their production of a data service through flexible alignments of 'black box' cloud computing systems. I show how data science is strategically distributed and reassembled through this effort, and highlight the opportunities and risks that arise within an entrepreneurial entanglement of self, product and market. By placing today's efforts against earlier attempts to develop a national data processing industry, I show how representations of data are incorporated into both the construction of new products and the ongoing project of building a nation and a state.

I also reflect on how this engagement has expanded my ethnographic practice. I arrived in Jamaica after a decade spent as a systems engineer in Silicon Valley's internet services industrial complex, and amid an auto-ethnographic study of self-tracking – an inquiry into developing relationships with popular health and fitness tools and an attempt to discover and improve myself through the data they provided (Williams 2015). Data science and ethnography offered me new forms of engagement with the world and new languages with which to describe it.

Punctuated by frequent commutes between countries, my time in the field expanded my original concern beyond a qualitative versus a quantitative relationship. It provided an invaluable forum for an examination of the relationships between engineering and ethnography, participation and observation, big data criticism and small data production. Further, I grew up on the island, and my arrival, as a return, was the beginning of an exploration of my citizenship and the attendant complications of being a native ethnographer: a Jamaican studying Jamaicans but also an engineer studying other engineers, an analyst immersed in my own relationships with data while studying actors developing their own.

Is the data world flat?

This is not the first moment when data offered powerful possibilities for Jamaica and its citizens. While the Big Data and machine-and-metrics-based decision-making that mark today's technology landscape might be new to the Caribbean, data processing is not. In the 1980s many of the countries in the region began to embrace the Informatics and Business Process Outsourcing (BPO) industry as a new stage in their decades-long effort for 'industrialisation by invitation' (Lewis 1950).

That programme began after the Second World War as an effort to create a new manufacturing base that could supplant plateauing agricultural production and employ a growing population. Regional leaders, believing that it would be difficult for their small states to develop their own industrial prowess, established programmes that offered tax incentives, industrial plants and reduced regulations to multinational corporations and foreign investors. In Jamaica, this focused on the assembly of garments, the mining of bauxite and intensifying the production of sugar.

BPO, when it arrived, would centre on telemarketing, customer service and a wide range of data entry chores. These included transcoding audio to text; digitising a wide range of paper documents; processing forms and claims; and handling exceptions in automated systems such as airline ticketing transactions (Skinner 1998; Schware and Hume 1996). These tasks required a combination of mundane -keying in- and contextual human decision-making.

In Jamaica, the imperatives for this transition to a service industry were rooted in the economic declines of earlier industrialisation bases and a combination of local political ideologies and the foreign requirements of structural adjustment policies. These latter policies, associated with economic stabilisation loans from the IMF and the World Bank, resulted in shifts that prioritised open markets, foreign investment and privatisation. At the same time, companies in the US were increasing externalising their information and 'back office' services, in synchronisation with the rise of commoditisation and 'electronification' technologies (Hepworth 1990).

This made attracting the outsourcing of data work a logical solution across the Caribbean – a switch to less tangible and more fluid forms in response to deepening collapses in commodity exports as globalisation increased and preferential trade agreements vanished. The hope was that a services industry, and informatics and data processing work more specifically, would re-create lost advantages while providing much needed foreign exchange to service loans (Mullings 2004). The labour cost differentials made Jamaica a viable target for this work. What these new technologies made possible, the vulnerable economic state of affairs in Jamaica made profitable.

Jamaican planners saw a mutual benefit. With their trainable, English-speaking populace and the region's geographical and cultural proximity to the United States, the local data processing industry would grow alongside the efficiency demands of American businesses, simultaneously achieving America's industrial informatisation and Jamaican national development goals (Schware and Hume 1996). Multinational firms would employ and 'upskill' citizens while facilitating technology transfers that would establish a vibrant local data industry (Intex 1992).

Enclaves and ambiguous spaces

In Jamaica, these companies were established within export-processing, 'Offshore' Free Zones. Firms in the zones were exempted from taxes on profits, imports and exports using legal systems and often the same buildings that had catered to previous industrialisation efforts. Jamaica Digiport International, the main data processing site in the island's second city of Montego Bay, provided uninterruptible power and a satellite earth station, allowing companies to skip over the island's ailing physical infrastructure and much of its regulatory system (Skinner 1998).

In the garment industry, partly finished items would be transported to the island, stitched together, and put back on ships. This pattern would repeat as the zones transitioned to data processing work. Raw data would arrive at the nearby airport in paper form or electronically via satellite. It would then be processed and returned via satellite or flown by freight, encoded on to tapes or disks.

The BPO industry quickly occupied an ambiguous space that the companies manipulated to maximum benefit. Although labour-intensive and zoned in the offshore industrial sector, its symbolic links to white-collar computing gave the jobs higher status than those in the garment manufacturing industry. The air-conditioned environments were a distinct shift from those in temperate factories and this shift in atmosphere was part of what Freeman (2000) describes as the 'informatics language': a technical data discourse of cleanliness, accuracy and individualisation that was a source of symbolic capital used to foster identity and maintain discipline.

Both sets of workers were paid by the volume and quality of the work they produced, but in the BPO industry this new commodity was 'information' – abstract and flexible. This combination of new technologies and imaginaries also represented a new arena for the creation and manipulation of workers' identities (Freeman 2000; Mullings 1999). Operators were also encouraged to see themselves as white-collar employees, in the hope that this would circumvent the development of a 'militancy characteristic of organized industrial workers' (Pearson and Mitter 1993: 61). In Freeman's account in particular, both the industry and the largely female workforce worked to stabilise the 'pink collar" notion of an Informatics professional's attire and comportment as a prerequisite to continued employment, reproducing through separate lines of thought a merging between colonial and digital values. A worker perceived as careless or sloppy in her appearance could not be counted on to produce quick, accurate data.

Flattened fantasies

The field's relatively low cost of entry also attracted local companies – early variants of today's start-ups. Working with data meant agility and the ability to act without the hurdles that had stymied entrepreneurs before. These local, subcontracting companies were run by 'black, middle-class professionals' (Mullings 1998) who thus far had not have been able to own the means of production given the hegemony of minority ethnic elites in the more capital-intensive industries that had supplanted the plantation economy (Pearson and Mitter 1993; Reid 1980).

But, while they had early successes in winning contracts, these achievements were short-lived. The government's goal for the industry was to secure external investment and foreign exchange, and the resulting incentives, tilted towards foreign firms, limited the success of locals by excluding them from the Free Zones,[5] the benefits of reduced taxes and the vital lower cost and higher bandwidth satellite connections (Mullings 2004; Skinner 1998).

This state of affairs continued even though a plurality of data processing firms were locally owned. While creating a wider data and knowledge economy was the dream, these decisions on incentives reflected pragmatic choices for state management. Despite early gains, these small local firms had trouble accessing the continuing capital and resources they needed to ensure a steady flow of processing jobs and to make the infrastructural improvements needed to transition to higher-level services such as software development.

The utopian data vision was also dashed on a national scale. Hoped-for technology transfers failed to materialise and even the larger foreign firms offered only basic data entry and processing services. As Jamaica was attempting to increase investment in the industry, the technological advances that first enabled the externalisation of processing destabilised the industry. Continuing improvements to informatics such as optical character recognition and online transaction processing reduced the need for paper-based data conversion and the processing of forms and claims. At the same time, lower-priced competitors arose in the Philippines, Bangladesh and China (Mullings 1998) – now more readily accessible following improvements to telecommunication networks. The industry's drive to the bottom meant that firms would use the production and locational flexibility of data work to relocate quickly, circumnavigating any regulatory regimes and requirements unfavourable to them (Hepworth 1990).

VideoLogs and new data identities

The BPO industry has yet to fulfil national data and knowledge economy dreams but it has not disappeared. Now focused primarily on call-centre services, it has actually grown in recent years but is dominated by foreign firms. Local tech entrepreneurs are drawn instead to the ecosystem of training programmes, competitions and conferences now facilitated by the government and InfoDev, the World Bank's global programme for innovation and entrepreneurship.

Pablo and Clive are two of the developers navigating this new territory. Their current product, VideoLogs,[6] is an online service for Customer Experience Management. It offers subscribing companies the ability to quantify and track the emotions of their customers via a more engaging alternative to common 'Rate your experience' follow-up surveys. In their view, these forms are tedious and customers are unlikely to complete them. When submitted, the combination of rating scales and blank text boxes make them a poor carrier for the customer's emotional response.

Instead, companies who signed up with VideoLogs could solicit responses from their customers via prompts sent through email, SMS or bots for chat apps like Facebook's Messenger. Customers could reply to those prompts via smartphone by combining text, emoji 'tags' and a video or selfie. These responses would be uploaded to the platform and then distributed to a network of machine-learning systems that would produce an emotional score chart from detected facial expressions, sentiment analysis of what was said, and a range of other signals.

A customer, asked for feedback on a recent flight, might respond with a 15-second video. Text would be extracted from the video's audio channel, mined for relevant keywords, and run through sentiment analysis for an overall assessment as positive or negative and an emotional score. The video would be broken down into a series of frames or windows, each of which would be also assigned an emotion, this time on the basis of the customer's facial features. Overall, the video might be scored with high confidence as 'angry' but sections would be marked according to other found emotions such as 'sadness' or 'disgust', allowing for undercurrents of probable emotions.

The platform was also designed to aggregate these results, combining emotions derived from a customer's emoji choices, facial expressions and word choices into a 'heartbeat' which companies could use to track their customers' feelings over time. This was imagined to be a richer alternative to the Net Promotor Score (NPS) – a common but contested (Keiningham et al. 2008) measure of customer loyalty that focused on providing companies with the 'One Number You Need to Grow' (Reichheld 2003). Where the NPS was based on 0–10 score to a single question, 'How likely is it that you would recommend our company to a friend?', they believed emotions were a better indicator of engagement, and the heartbeat would bring these to the surface.

From product first to vision first

VideoLogs was the result of several pivots as the team worked out their product–market fit: the relationship between what they could build and what the market would respond to. They knew that their product would remain centred on the potentials of data and machine-driven insights but each adjustment focused on a slightly different domain.

Their previous product allowed event attenders to exchange contact information and track interactions via a combination of mobile app, bluetooth-based beacon devices for tracking locations indoors and a mesh of online services. Attenders could sign up to use the app as a passport for entry to events, to store and exchange contact information with people they met and to provide feedback on the gathering. Event planners would pay to use the platform for organising events and would be able to access analytics on attenders.

To build VideoLogs and its vision of a world of business relationships built on emotional data, Pablo and Clive changed their approach. They had invested significant development effort into their earlier product before engaging with customers, only to find that Jamaican companies did not respond as they had hoped. Now they would develop the product only after they had sold the vision.

This new approach reversed that risk and introduced another. They had invested months of work earlier but did not find 'traction' – proof of market demand. This time there would be less investment in a data *product* and more effort spent on articulating a data *vision*. But they might attract customers without being able to produce the matching system.

It was through this process that they concluded that neither product would be viable within Jamaica. Though they didn't sell directly to individual end-users, they needed data-savvy businesses with customers who would be likely to use such a system. In their experience, Jamaican firms lacked the fluency in, and synchronisation with, the connected, data-driven world they imagined for their product and its users.

To give their company the best long-term chance, they also needed funding sources that understood this vision. This meant globally connected venture capitalists who were versed in the internet and in mobile platforms while keeping abreast of industry trends in analytics and machine learning. This was about more than money; these funders could provide mentorship and access to a network that would help them win early customers and grow. This largely ruled out the sources of venture capital they might be able to access in Jamaica.

Data moves more easily than its developers

As a result, they looked to Silicon Valley, which held sway as market, funding source, potential new home and philosophically resonant environment for many young Jamaican entrepreneurs. Moving there from Jamaica, however, meant several hurdles: immigration, certainly, but also institutional and cultural. Despite claims of digital technology's global reach and the Valley's language of disruption, the industry centred there continues to be plagued by poor diversity.[7]

They were developing at the margin of the margin. In Jamaica, they drew themselves as ahead of the market. When viewed from the Valley however, Jamaica was in the periphery and so were they. This double-consciousness was an important part of the decisions they made as they worked on the product and on the company they had formed around it. It informed how they framed themselves as a data analytics firm, how they chose their marketing messages and even how they articulated their personal identities.

The intermediating qualities of the internet and the language of data and analytics had offered them an opening. They could defer to the identities of VideoLogs' methods, not theirs as its developers. A cartoon from the *New Yorker* magazine in 1993 symbolised this opportunity, depicting a dog using a computer while explaining to another that 'On the Internet, nobody knows you're a dog.'[8]

It didn't matter, in many cases, that they hit 'Release' while seated in a café in Kingston. Though they made plans and wrote code while on the island, they used the same development and co-ordination tools as other engineers located in the Valley and distributed all over the world. The resulting service they made was accessible to anyone through a globally distributed platform.

This opening had limits, however. For small teams, initial sales and agreements are often built on and nurtured through personal relationships. As they work to find new customers and grow their company, founders often craft intertwined stories of self and product, delivered in personal and engaging terms. While this arc has come to be expected, particularly in how previous failures are articulated and then recuperated within a larger entrepreneurial journey, these personal revelations have different consequences for entrepreneurs who fail to fit the expectations of potential customers or funders.

These presentational strategies had been popularised by the largely white tech founders who make up the Valley's understood default culture. Self-presentation affirmed their neutral belonging; their racial identity was hegemonic and unmarked (Eglash 2002). On the other hand, being black or Jamaican was pregnant with potentially alienating meaning that interpellated their claims to the data-savvy tech entrepreneur identity.

Other, more foundational, choices can be read through this lens as well. They realised their vision by knitting together a fabric of APIs and services from cognitive computing platforms such as Microsoft's Cognitive Services, IBM's Watson or Google's Cloud Machine Learning Services. These metered Big Data platforms offered a range of tools for needed tasks in computer vision – recognising people and objects in videos – and natural language processing. Ostensibly, this helped them fulfil VideoLog's promised features. But by connecting and curating them in turn, this compilation also leveraged the authority of the established firms that offered them.

Though the company's ethos was to directly link customers and businesses through a rich channel of emotional information, data and its analysis presented the chance to construct an intermediary identity. Deferring to the neutral realm of data science, and the functional machine-learning approaches aligned with it, offered an inclusive avenue for product and corporate development. It was a world vision that they knew the US market had responded to, but they also knew that trust in their ability to deliver that vision would be adjudicated along racial lines. Self-exposure then held few benefits.

Their adroit use of marketing strategies reflected this tacit understanding. They used their blog and social media to set out the company's direction in an official yet relatable and fun tone saturated with well-cited charts and statistics on their methods. The VideoLogs website reflected popular start-up design trends – minimalist design cues, sans-serif typefaces and a restrained palette – but, unlike their closest competitor, their 'About Us' page did not include their photos or personal information and they adroitly sidestepped the issue of location by using a legitimate address in California.

At best, revealing or focusing on their identities might attract attention from customers or funders specifically interested in supporting diversity in the industry. But they might also alienate potential customers at a time when every opportunity mattered.[9] Another *New Yorker* cartoon, this time from 2015, highlights the ramifications of this new personal and more social landscape. Two dogs, seemingly older and world-weary versions of the pair in the 1993 cartoon, watch their owner use a computer. One, turning to the other, asks: 'Remember when, on the Internet, nobody knew who you were?'[10]

Data reassembled

Despite its promises for a new direction in Jamaica, data processing in the Free Zones became a metonym for the larger enclave in which the country continues to be positioned. Firms arrived surrounded by utopian promises of a democratic, emergent global knowledge grid wherein newly digitised information would 'reduce gaps in vital knowledge worldwide' (Dizard 1989: 16) but data, and the control of its processing, retraced politically and economically asymmetrical lines between countries meant to be the core and those to be maintained at the periphery. Jamaica's economic straits and its structural adjustment to open markets and deregulated spaces married well with these data-driven processes of externalisation.

Working with data did not usher in a new era in the island's industrialisation. Mullings (2004) argues that the intangibility of data work, and the fluidity it enabled, made the nation more vulnerable to exclusion and marginality. The countries whose raw data flowed into Jamaica were reluctant to distribute the wealth and expertise that emerged from processing it, while the compartmentalisation and architecture of the industry's global processing pipeline made it difficult for local companies to participate as equals and build a vibrant Jamaican industry. Jamaica, it seems, was designed to be a dominion of the global knowledge community, not an equal member (Skinner 1998).

BPO painted the picture of Jamaican technological possibility in strokes of cheap labour and low complexity (Anderson and Witter 1994). Pablo, Clive and the other entrepreneurs who move through the island's tech ecosystem are working to break through those enclaves of the past and paint a new image. Here, data offers yet another direction, this time united with internet infrastructures understood as emerging from, and responsible for, Silicon Valley's successes.

Empowered by these new systems, Pablo and Clive are revisiting the BPO formula. VideoLogs is a reconfiguration of the assembly lines of human data processors into a loosely coupled bricolage of distributed services and databases. Instead of managing their own servers and building their own machine-learning models, they outsource those concerns to cloud computing firms, echoing, through new materials, what BPO management firms were able to do through subcontracted global labour.

This explosion and rearrangement is providing them with a measure of control that had been denied to a previous generation of entrepreneurs. By outsourcing elements of their analysis, their advantage emerges in agility and flexibility not domain expertise in statistical methods, computer vision or computational linguistics. This integrative, generalist approach emphasises work at the seams (Vertesi 2014): making multiple local alignments between heterogeneous infrastructures in order to produce a processing pipeline and a (seemingly) seamless experience for their customers.

Their approach is closely linked to newly emerging technical capabilities in online services and Big Data but it is also a reflection of capabilities and modes of being that extend beyond the screen. The hope for the blossoming start-up ecosystem and the services industry that preceded continues to be that opportunities in the digital and knowledge economy will compensate for losses in traditional modes of production and energise the productivity and creativity of citizens. Drawing on multiple lines of analysis, Freeman (2007) argues that this shift in modes of production has demanded a flexible, autonomous subject who can thrive within the precarious flows and frequent reorientations as the static hierarchies of previous economic formations fade.

This embrace of flexibility is revealed in Pablo and Clive's identification of data opportunities. Flexibly aligning and loosely coupling newly emerging forms of computational services have helped them secure a niche at the nexus of product and market demand. It drives their curation and then tactical deployment of computational power and authority in order to fulfil their vision and modulate to concerns about their identity.

However, the failure of a previous generation's effort to territorialise a data-processing industry is a reminder of the attendant impermanence of and risk in a niche founded on the possibilities and shifting priorities of external platforms. It demands an interrogation of the supposed revolutionary ordering of today's algorithmic and data-driven opportunities, not just for society at large but also for those who attempt to build on it from the industry's margins.

New conduits offer new opportunities but, in also accelerating the hyper-mobility of capital, also increase marginalisation and inequality. In the face of these demands, entrepreneurs like Pablo and Clive continue to find ways forward, meeting the challenges of development by finding niches and seizing on approaches and patterns that had excluded them before – advancing their own visions through tactical conjunctions and flexible alignments. They too are then entrepreneurial projects: under constant renovation, inextricable from the risk of the market, hinged on emerging innovations and new hopes for data.

Conclusion: native lines and knots

These lines trace a year of transit within and between California, my adopted home, and Jamaica, my first home, made strange again through fieldwork. The lines emerge from a continually morphing dataset that includes not just my geographic location but other signals collected in the pursuit of self-knowledge through numbers: data on sleep, diet, exercise and more. The lines also connect sites of tech development, pursued in locations that stretch beyond where the island meets the sea, tracking long talks and vital check-ins held on the move with entrepreneurs while driving through Kingston and San Francisco.

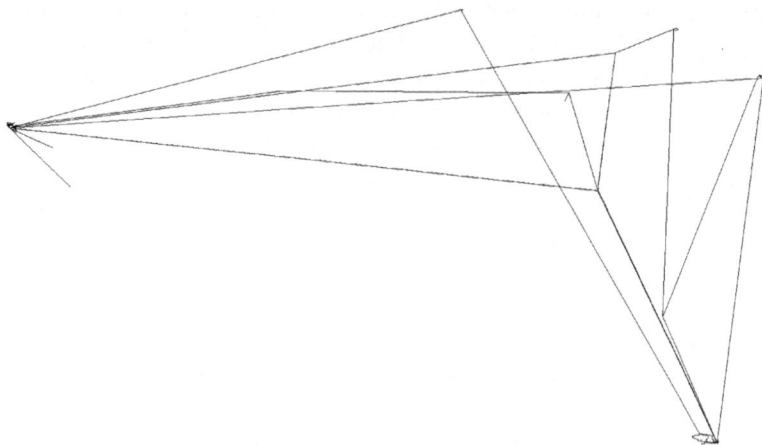

Figure 4.1 A year of field lines

The lines represent a knitting together of roles in the field: fellow islander, engineer, Valley denizen, data practitioner – never just an ethnographer. I tried to put all these identities to use: approaching the data world they were venturing into as both critical scholar and engineer of its infrastructure; helping teams who were looking abroad for customers and funding by connecting them with the Valley networks I could muster; working alongside others as an engineer and designer. With the impetus of my university affiliation and my Fortune 100 work history, I became an asset that could be and was often deployed on the 'About Us' slide of a pitch deck[11] as a technical adviser, product manager or board member.

How should I frame all these points of connection? This map view suggests a network. Dealing with similar spatial and temporal complexities in her study of internet use in Ghana, Burrell (2009), drawing on work from Marcus (1995) and Strathern (1996), defined her fieldsite as a network 'composed of fixed and moving points including spaces, people, and objects' (Burrell 2009: 189), thus eliding the imprecision of broad, territorial boundaries that were ill-suited for containing the institutions, places and people that influenced internet use. As a network, my fieldsite could stretch across sites in Jamaica and California, containing online and offline spaces and helping alleviate my tension about when, and where, I was 'in the field'.

However, Ingold argues that the common network model depends on an inversion, where each element is 'turned in upon itself prior to its integration into the network' (2011: 70). The network model paints people and places as points, and lines as the relations between them. Instead, he suggests an alternative structure that would reject the network's key distinction between things and their relations: 'Organisms and persons, then, are not so much nodes in a network as knots in a tissue of knots, whose constituent strands, as they become tied up with other strands, in other knots, comprise *the meshwork*' (emphasis mine) (Ingold 2011: 70).

'Things', Ingold argues, 'are their relations.' This restructures inquiry from relations *between* to relations *along* enmeshed ways of life. This knotting together – a progressive intermeshing rather than points of connection between distinct and separable points – reflects that I was always somewhat in the Valley, even in Jamaica; always an engineer, even as an ethnographer; always sceptical about data's potential, even while trying to capture it myself. Shifting from *between* to *along* underscored our intra-action (Barad 1998) and mutual constitution. My presence was as fundamental a part of their journey – reflected in my place in pitch decks – as theirs was to the construction of my research and my renewed relationship with Jamaica.

But it raised the spectre of 'going native': the putative danger for an ethnographer to become too involved in the community under inquiry and thus lose the requisite distance for objectivity. The ethnographic researcher is expected to be both external observer and somewhat native. Pre-existing nativity however is treated differently from the nativity achieved in the field – the achievement on which ethnographic authority has traditionally hung (Bunzl 2004). This has long haunted researchers from the communities they study, positioning them as 'native first and ethnographer second' and their work as less valid or virtual (Weston 1997: 171). This, as Weston continues, denies the native ethnographer 'the option of representing herself as a complex, integrated, compound figure'.

Scholars working from a Black feminist and a Caribbean perspective (Slocum 2001; Harrison 1997; Bolles 2001; Ulysse 2007) have all examined how researchers of colour have embraced nativity to argue that being inside a region or community can provide valuable insights. However, Narayan (1993), deconstructing the category of native as constraining, argues that the distance between us and those we study varies more with context than it does with ethnicity or geography, and that achieved closeness through long-term interaction is more valid and may provide greater insights than closeness conferred by birth. Everyone, in this formulation, can be native in some way.

But the viability of this deconstruction hinges on gatekeeping and power structures beyond the individual ethnographer. Weston argues that it risks 'glossing over the power relations that historically have marked particular people as particular sorts of hybrids' (Weston 1997: 182). Not everyone has control of their definition.

And as Slocum (2001) points out, there are also political reasons we might have for choosing to make parts of our identity relevant and seen at any moment: reasons for choosing to be seen as a Jamaican or an engineer, an entrepreneur or an ethnographer, or as deeply saturated in data ourselves. She argues that, no matter how socially constructed, our identity traits have implications for the people we study, for how we perform that inquiry and for the communities with which we align ourselves.

At first, my self-tracking work felt different from my work within the Jamaican tech community. It was drawn around the practices and tools of the Quantified Self, and that discourse seemed largely driven by, and focused on, white, metropolitan and Western concerns not largely black postcolonial conditions. And, as an auto-ethnographic exercise, the scale and orientation were also markedly different: focused inwards instead of out, directed at my own experience rather than at those of others or at national outcomes.

Over the years, I developed strategies for managing the transition between the two projects and between California and Jamaica. When I travelled to conferences along lines traced in this image, I would hold one project as an aside as I presented work from the other. To ensure that I was always driving on the correct side of the road and operating the turn signals instead of the windshield wipers, I would steer only with my left hand in the US and only with my right in Jamaica.

This uneasy ambidexterity provided a commonality beyond shared nationality or technical capability. The developers I worked with juggled the demands of day-to-day life in Jamaica and the require-ments of building software and services for the global market, all while making their own trips to the Valley and other start-up hubs across the globe. For many young black Jamaicans seeking their way in a society that remains shaped by the inequities of slavery and colo-nial rule, technology development symbolised by the flexible recon-figuration of services and data flows has become an attractive avenue for navigating the country's hierarchy and the world beyond it.

But while the Valley's tech culture might offer radical breaks from the island's stratified socioeconomic order, to be taken seriously as targets for patronage requires a realignment of the world's view of them and of the country. Here are new poises to adopt and fresh challenges to hurdle. It is here that a command of data and its flows has offered the most potential.

Across the Jamaican tech ecosystem, data and new subjectivities are being forged in tandem and I attempted to attend to the journey of entrepreneurs like Pablo and Clive through a research approach steeped in my own mutual constitution and data saturation, hoping to unite the strengths of data literacy and ethnography to attend to the sociotechnical mobilities of data and the people who work on it. One hope of many is that, through a sensitivity to data and its possibilities, we could both make conduits – across borders of nation, history and flesh – to new approaches to life and new forms of knowledge. Data promised to provide answers to many questions. What are people really feeling? What's going on in my body? Who are we and what can we be?

Notes

1 I use 'developer' and 'entrepreneur' interchangeably to reflect the slip-page used by my informants. While 'tech-preneur' and the hyphenated 'start-up' are used by the local media and government officials to describe this union of technology development and business interests, this did not reflect usage within the community. The ungainliness of the term surely contributed to their avoidance but more significantly, it signals a distinction between the Valley and the island that they would prefer to avoid.

2 Karyl Walker (2012) 'Lotto Scammers Living Large', *Jamaica Observer.* www.jamaicaobserver.com/news/Lotto-scammers-living-large_ 11448148 [accessed 15 February 2017].

3 Samuel Lee, Sandra Moscoso and Dave Oakley (2014Open Data on the Ground: Jamaica's Crimebot.' The World Bank. https:// blogs.worldbank.org/opendata/open-data-ground-jamaica-s-crimebot [accessed 15 February 2017].

4 Rochelle Williams (2016), 'Free Government Data Online.' Jamaican Information Service. http://jis.gov.jm/free-government-data-online/ [accessed 15 February 2017].

5 This segregation was also to follow the requirements of IMF policies that considered incentives to local businesses as a form of market intervention 'reminiscent of earlier import substitution strategies' (Mullings 2004: 290).

6 Pablo, Clive and VideoLogs are all pseudonyms.

7 Anna Wiener (2016), 'Why Can't Silicon Valley Solve Its Diversity Problem?', *New Yorker.* www.newyorker.com/business/currency/why-cant-silicon-valley-solve-its-diversity-problem [accessed 20 January 2017].

8 Peter Steiner, *New Yorker,* 5 July 1993, p. 61.

9 Studies such as Ayres, Banaji and Jolls (2015) have demonstrated the negative effects of perceived racial identity of sellers within online purchasing behaviour. See Fairlie and Robb (2008) for a wider examination of the relationships between race and entrepreneurial success.

10 Kaamran Hafeez, *New Yorker,* 23 February 2015, p. 115.

11 A deck of slides made to present the company's fundamentals to investors. The contents vary but they typically outline the problem the company is trying to solve, key members of its management team, and business model and financial projections.

References

Anderson, Patricia and Witter, Michael. 1994. 'Crisis, Adjustment and Social Change: A Case Study of Jamaica'. In *Consequences of Structural Adjustment: A Review of the Jamaican Experience*. Edited by Elsie LeFranc. Kingston: Canoe Press, 1–55.

Ayres, Ian, Banaji, Mahzarin and Jolls, Christine. 2015. 'Race Effects on eBay'. *The RAND Journal of Economics* 46(4): 891–917.

Barad, Karen Michelle. 1998. 'Getting Real: Technoscientific Practices and the Materialization of Reality'. *Differences: A Journal of Feminist Cultural Studies* 10: 87–126.

Bolles, A. 2001. 'Seeking the Ancestors'. In *Black Feminist Anthropology: Theory, Politics, Praxis, and Poetics*. Edited by I. McClaurin. New Brunswick, NJ: Rutgers University Press, 24–48.

Bunzl, Matti. 2004. 'Boas, Foucault, and the "Native Anthropologist": Notes toward a Neo-Boasian Anthropology'. *American Anthropologist* 106(3): 435–42.

Burrell, Jenna. 2009. 'The Field Site as a Network: A Strategy for Locating Ethnographic Research'. *Field Methods* 21(2): 181–99.

Dizard, Wilson P. 1989. *The Coming Information Age: An Overview of Technology, Economics, and Politics*. New York and London: Longman.

Eglash, Ron. 2002. 'Race, Sex, and Nerds: From Black Geeks to Asian American Hipsters'. *Social Text* 20(271): 49–64.

Fairlie, Robert W. and Robb, Alicia. 2008. *Race and Entrepreneurial Success: Black-, Asian-, and White-Owned Businesses in the United States*. Cambridge, MA: MIT Press.

Freeman, Carla. 2000. *High Tech and High Heels in the Global Economy: Women, Work, and Pink-Collar Identities in the Caribbean*. Durham, NC: Duke University Press.

Freeman, Carla. 2007. 'The Reputation of Neoliberalism'. *American Ethnologist* 34(2): 252–67.

Harrison, Faye. 1997. 'Ethnography as Politics'. In *Decolonizing Anthropology*. Edited by Faye Harrison. Arlington, VA: Association of African American Anthropologists, American Anthropological Association, 88–110.

Hepworth, Mark E. 1990. *Geography of the Information Economy*. New York: Guilford Press.

Horst, Heather A. and Miller, Daniel. 2006. *The Cell Phone: An Anthropology of Communication*. Oxford: Berg.

Ingold, Tim. 2011. *Being Alive: Essays on Movement, Knowledge and Description.* New York: Routledge.

Intex. 1992. 'Jamaican Information Services Sector Study'. Alexandria, VA: Intex.

Keiningham, Timothy L., Aksoy, Lerzan, Cooil, Bruce, Andreassen, Tor Wallin and Williams, Luke. 2008. 'A Holistic Examination of Net Promoter'. *Journal of Database Marketing & Customer Strategy Management* 15(2): 79–90.

Lewis, W.A. 1950. 'The Industrialisation of the British West Indies'. *Caribbean Economic Review* 2(1): 1–51.

Lison, Andrew. 2015. 'From Shrink Wrap to Services: The Universal Machine and Universal Exchange'. In *There Is No Software, There Are Just Services.* Edited by Irina Kaldrack and Martina Leeker. Milton Keynes: meson press, 57–72.

Marcus, G.E. 1995. 'Ethnography in/of the World System: The Emergence of Multi-Sited Ethnography'. *Annual Review of Anthropology* 24(1): 95–117.

Miller, Daniel and Slater, Don. 2000. *The Internet: An Ethnographic Approach.* Oxford: Berg.

Mullings, Beverley. 1998. 'Jamaicas Information Processing Services: Neoliberal Niche or Structural Limitation?' In *Globalization and Neoliberalism.* Edited by Thomas Klak. Lanham, MD: Rowman & Littlefield, 107–22.

Mullings, Beverley. 1999. 'Sides of the Same Coin?: Coping and Resistance among Jamaican Data-Entry Operators'. *Annals of the Association of American Geographers* 89(2): 290–311.

Mullings, Beverley. 2004. 'Globalization and the Territorialization of the New Caribbean Service Economy'. *Journal of Economic Geography* 4(3): 275–98.

Narayan, K. 1993. 'How Native Is a Native Anthropologist?' *American Anthropologist* 95(3): 671–86.

Pearson, R. and Mitter, S. 1993. 'Employment and Working Conditions of Low-Skilled Information-Processing Workers in Less Developed Countries'. *International Labour Review* 132(1): 132–49.

Reichheld, Frederick. 2003. "The One Number You Need to Grow". Harvard Business Review, December 2003, https://hbr.org/2003/12/the-one-number-you-need-to-grow [last accessed 21 February 2018].

Reid, S. 1980. 'Economic Elites in Jamaica: A Study of Monistic Relationship'. *Anthropologica* 22(1): 25–44.

Schware, R. and Hume, S. 1996. *Prospects for Information Service Exports from the English-Speaking Caribbean.* Washington, DC: World Bank.

Skinner, Ewart. 1998. 'The Caribbean Data Processors'. In *Global Productions.* Edited by Gerald Sussman and John Lent. Cresskill, NJ: Hampton Press, 57–90.

Slocum, K. 2001. 'Negotiating Identity and Black Feminist Politics in Caribbean Research'. In *Black Feminist Anthropology: Theory, Politics, Praxis, and Poetics*. Edited by I. McClaurin. New Brunswick, NJ: Rutgers University Press, 126–49.

Strathern, M. 1996. 'Cutting the Network'. *Journal of the Royal Anthropological Institute* 2(3): 517–35.

Ulysse, Gina A. 2007. *Downtown Ladies: Informal Commercial Importers, a Haitian Anthropologist, and Self-Making in Jamaica*. Chicago: University of Chicago Press.

Vertesi, Janet. 2014. 'Seamful Spaces: Heterogeneous Infrastructures in Interaction'. *Science, Technology & Human Values* 39(2): 264–84.

Weston, Kath. 1997. 'The Virtual Anthropologist'. In *Anthropological Locations: Boundaries and Grounds of a Field Science*. Edited by James Ferguson and Akhil Gupta. Berkeley: University of California Press, 163–84.

Williams, Kaiton. 2015. '"An Anxious Alliance'. In *Proceedings of the Fifth Decennial Aarhus Conference*: 121–31.

Part II

Knowing data

5

'If everything is information': archives and collecting on the frontiers of data-driven science

Antonia Walford

Whereas there have been many critiques of the sorts of massive, automatic and invasive 'social' or 'personal' data collection that has come to characterise a great deal of commercial big data knowledge production (boyd and Crawford 2012; Dalton et al. 2016; Kitchin 2014), there has been less critical attention paid to the 'data deluge' that has been occurring in the natural sciences. The vast amounts of data that ostentatiously 'big' science projects such as CERN are churning out have been remarked upon in the popular press, but it is not only in such spectacular experimental settings that data is becoming remarkable in science. In the environmental sciences, for example, the increasing efforts to 'instrument the earth' (Lehning et al. 2009: 45) – that is, establish environmental sensor networks in even the most inhospitable habitats of the planet – and to make the data thereby collected available globally, have heralded a shift 'into data' as well, even if a less voluminous, vertiginous one.[1]

The relative lack of attention to the 'data-fication' of the environment notwithstanding (although see Gabrys 2016; McNally et al. 2012), the embracing of technological panaceas for environmental crisis has been a concern in the critical social sciences for some time. A good example is the overt effort in such quarters to resist what could be called 'techno-fixes' when it comes to working out how to approach climate change (Hulme 2014; Szerszynski 2010; see also Jasanoff 2003), but this is also related to the work of scholars such as Anna Tsing and Donna Haraway on the need to recognise more broadly the profound intertwining of global capitalism with such technological regimes that now inform environmental governance (most recently see Tsing 2015; Haraway 2016). Indeed, transforming environmental phenomena, such as carbon, into numbers – or data – is clearly one way in which they can be controlled, evaluated and traded on the market (Lippert 2015; Verran 2012).[2]

In this chapter I want to approach the acceleration of quantification practices in the environmental sciences, and the imaginaries that go with it, slightly differently. Rather than home in directly on the commodification of the environment that might be occurring through these new technological practices, I want to focus attention on another key critical trope which has been employed to shed light on these data-driven landscapes. Within science, the problem of vast amounts of data is often framed as an urgent need for data storage solutions; and, as a result, there has been an explosion of databasing initiatives. It is therefore perhaps of no surprise that one of the most prevalent tropes in the critical discourse on new scientific data practices is *the archive*. I argue, however, that some of the new database initiatives that are emerging in the environmental sciences are transforming this trope in ways that need to be critically attended to.

In the second part of the chapter, I want to turn to another important practice that is crucial to understanding data infrastructures and the worlds they produce, and yet has received much less critical attention than database archives, namely *collecting*. As itself a form or trope, collecting provides a different critical imaginary from that of the archive, sensitising us to another set of conflicting forces: the simultaneity of appropriation and transformation. Reading some historical insights about collecting as a pivotal aspect of colonial conquest (Jasanoff 2005) back into contemporary scientific data practices re-orients my analysis towards data collection 'as a means of self-fashioning' (Jasanoff 2005: 7), that occurs along the tangled, contingent frontiers of knowledge production. In conclusion, I want to ask what these investigations can tell us when turned back on the practice of ethnography itself.

Database/archive

The archive has become perhaps most well-known as a 'protean category' (Waterton 2010: 646) in the thought of Michel Foucault and

Jacques Derrida and has been extensively explored in anthropology, history and cognate disciplines.[3] As Elizabeth Povinelli summarises, the archive can be understood from a Foucauldian perspective as a hegemonic instrument of (state) power which nevertheless contains within it its own undoing in the form of the subaltern voices that it works (more or less successfully) to suppress (2011: 151; see also Zeitlyn 2012). Derrida, whom I shall concentrate more on here, also famously focused on the archive as a form of power –both to 'command' (to ordain the law) and to 'commence' (to lay claim to the origin of nature/history) (Derrida 1995: 1). Thus, the archive does not just passively catalogue the world, it also enacts or performs the world in certain ways. But at the same time, for Derrida, the archive is always working 'against itself' (1995: 14): to archive or save the trace of the thing is also to forget the thing itself; to memorise, copy or repeat is to endlessly undo the possibility of the origin. The archive 'sheds its signs as it deposits them there, as a snake sheds its skin' (Nora 1989: 13); that is to say, 'we classify in order to be able to forget', as Geoffrey Bowker puts it (2008: 21).

The archive, in a Derridean understanding, is also always posing the question of the distinction between the internal and the external,[4] as it seeks to conceal that which it does not capture or contain. Thus we can also discern that the archive is always haunted obsessively by the idea that *something* exceeds it (including the capacity to archive itself). For Derrida, the archive was then not a place but a principle – the *drive*[5] to archive: 'Thus archival power depends not only on the ability to shelter the memory of its own construction so as to appear as a form of rule without a command but also on a certain inexhaustible suspicion that somewhere another, fuller account of this rule exists' (Povinelli 2011: 151). This drive, this 'archive fever' (*mal d'archive*),[6] then is constituted by both the archive's totalising aspirations and repetitious quest for the origin, and its corollary undoing: the archive negates itself through the very act of archiving, as there is no inside that does not imply an outside; no origin that is not also a copy; no saving of a name that is not the loss of the thing named. Derrida did not shy away from the contradictions of the archive (of course); this was, in fact, the point: 'history must be preserved; history can never be preserved' (Boulter 2011: 12).

Derrida's work on the archive has provoked extensive reflection in the critical social sciences, which it is beyond the scope of this chapter to discuss. Instead, in this section I want to draw out the ways in which these archival analytics have intersected with the interests of those studying informational practices in the sciences. These have for the most part centred, as I have mentioned, on the role of databases.[7]

The title of this chapter – 'If everything is information'– comes from Geoffrey Bowker's *Memory Practices in the Sciences* (2008). Bowker has been tracking the informational practices in the natural sciences for many years, including the role of databases in emergent forms of scientific knowledge production. As he notes, since the 1980s there has been a shift in how modern scientific work handles the information it produces. Previously, scientific papers, and the arguments they contained, acted as the archive of scientific knowledge. However, in contemporary scientific practices, Bowker draws our attention to the way in which 'increasingly, the database (the information stored) is seen as an end in itself' (2000: 643). Bowker gives us the example of the Human Genome Project, in which the end product was not a set of papers but the database or 'map' itself.[8] Such cartographic ambitions suggest for Bowker that these databases are a direct continuation of the drive for the imperial archive: to govern the furthermost reaches of the 'natural empire' (Bowker 2008: 121).

Bowker also draws our attention to how these databases do not so much conserve as create the world in a certain form, through practices of naming and classification. One of the most pressing concerns therefore that resurfaces in reading scientific databases as archives is how this classification and ordering enact a certain topography of remembering and forgetting. In terms of biodiversity, as Bowker points out, this may be a matter of life and death for the organisms chosen to be preserved and those left by the wayside. But a more profound ramification that he draws out is the extent to which the performativity of this totalising logic might lead to its own ultimate logical conclusion: that the archive can take the place of the Earth altogether. As physical collections are being replaced by digitised collections, which are much easier to maintain, we 'get right back to the archives embedded in the earth itself' (Bowker 2008: 135), so that the conservation of species in 'nature' becomes a question of the conservation of species *in silico*. The potential then is for the archive to enact the world in its own image: nothing will be saved that is not in the database, if/then the database becomes all that there is.

However, this totalising enactment is also countered, as 'every archive is partial, and every partial archive has its own anxieties: incompleteness, redactions, mis-filings, duplications, obfuscations, ignorance, secrets' (Jardine and Kelty 2016). Framing databases in science as archival practices in this context means drawing attention not only to their totalising imaginaries but simultaneously to the partial pasts and incomplete futures that the sciences are enacting and perpetuating, even as they purport to represent the entire Earth. Returning to Derrida's contradictory formulation of the archive, it is not just the partiality of the archive which is important, but the tension that it enacts between conservation and destruction. In the critical analysis of biodiversity databases, this is configured as the capacity of the database infrastructure to render the world in its own image, and the capacity of the world to escape that rendering. Thus we can also see an echo of the Derridean tension emerge in the ways in which databases have been approached analytically; as Boris Jardine and Chris Kelty remark, 'at one and the same time we fear' what is 'rendered possible by our accumulations, and we insist on the impossibility of its power' (Jardine and Kelty 2016).

However, there is another important aspect of contemporary environmental science database initiatives which deserves attention, namely the emphasis on the data being 'reusable'. The point of many such databasing programmes in the environmental sciences is, in fact, exactly that data is always kept 'alive', in a format that others can use. Thus there is an imperative for data to be shared, reused and constantly circulated, and not just stored (Bowker 2008: 120). This necessity for data to be endlessly reconnected is an important extension of the archival imaginary, I will argue, that collapses the tension between totality and partiality, such that the latter cannot be evoked as a counter to the former. The database, in such a framing, is totalising exactly because it is infinitely partial.

Connectivity/relationality

Connectivity, reusability and inter-operability of data have become the keystone in recent database practices that are emerging within the environmental sciences. One particularly striking example of this in the Earth Observation sciences (which are centred on satellite data, or remote sensing data) is known as the Group on Earth Observation

(GEO). The GEO, according to their website, is partnerships of 103 nations, the European Commission and 95 participating organisations 'that envisions a future wherein decisions and actions for the benefit of humankind are informed by coordinated, comprehensive and sustained Earth observations and information'.[9] To this end, the GEO community is creating a 'Global Earth Observation System of Systems (GEOSS) that will link Earth observation resources world-wide across multiple Societal Benefit Areas'.[10] This System of Systems is essentially a vast distributed database, which will link up hundreds if not thousands of different remote sensing databases around the world, and make the data within them accessible and available.

On one of the demos on the GEO website, called 'GEO in Action', we are confronted by the slogan 'Countries have borders. Earth Observations don't', and told that 'it is only in the last few decades that we have the tools to observe the entire planet ... By combing [*sic*] data over time, or by comparing data from different sources, intelligent decisions can be made about human development, wildlife protection and the effects of climate change'.[11] Then, in demonstration of what observing the entire planet might look like, we are guided through a series of data visualisations, starting with a section called 'Feed the World', which displays data on global crop yield, and then a series of other data visualisations of crop farming monitored from space. We are subsequently introduced to data about the location of fish shoals in the Indian Ocean, Inuit communities, gas reserves, ice sea coverage, where to place renewable energy stations, Tunisian river flood control, microscopic phytoplankton, alongside citizen science data on Japanese knotweed in the UK.[12] It is a vertiginous display, swooping between scales and levels and entities, and connecting everything through that movement. As the press statement for the GEO 2015 summit in Mexico City reads: 'GEO commits to unleash the power of open data to address global challenges.'[13]

Certainly, one can read archival totalising aspirations into such discourse that surrounds the GEOSS – there is no talk of the exclusions, frictions, subjugations or forgetting that such a databasing initiative will enact. However, it is also necessary to pay attention to how this archival form is reconfiguring 'the enlightenment panoptic project of assembling all knowledge in one place' (Waterton 2010: 648). The database-as-archive that Bowker explores seeks to represent and conserve the entire Earth; it is however inevitably partial because it can never take account of everything. But by putting reusability and interoperability at the heart of the archive, initiatives like the GEOSS profoundly change the relationship between the 'part' and the 'whole', and the 'inside' and the 'outside'. As data about Inuit communities, marine chlorophyll, global temperature, Japanese knotweed and so on is 'mashed up' together, the sensation of totality is created out of not so much a sense of encompassment but the potential for constant and generative variation. Data collected for one purpose can be endlessly repurposed, and put into relation with any number of other datasets, in a form of dynamic data-driven hyper-relationality. The 'drive' to archive here is not motivated by a self-defeating nostalgia for what is lost, nor the repetitive posing of the question as to what is inside or what is original, so much as an anxiety for infinite relationality. This is why these database initiatives are in part constituted by Open Data programmes, in order to make the data widely available: the data must be given 'multiple forms of scientific as well as financial, social, and political value' (Leonelli 2013: 10).[14] This folding of the archive into notions of infinite connection and reusability is, I suggest, one of the characteristics of data-driven science.

One of the effects of this potential for proliferating connectivity is to 'collapse' the inside and the outside of the database in a specific way, such that, as Tahani Nadim points out, a 'corollary of issues (poverty, sustainability, public health, food security, etc.)' are made 'thinkable and doable primarily through environmental Big Data' (2016: 1). Here it is possible to hear echoes of Bowker's concerns that the database might take the place of the world it seeks to conserve. But it is important to recognise that the totality that inheres in the GEOSS as archive is one that lies not in its contents but in its connections. Its capacity to simultaneously capture and perform the world lies in the power of making potentially infinite connections between as many different data repositories as possible, and generating new forms of data in the process that become fodder for its drive for connectivity. As it functions exactly by continuously relating and separating its multitude of disparate parts, partiality, in a sense, here comes to stand for totality.[15]

Collecting/frontiers

As I have demonstrated, the totalising claims of archives – including databases – have traditionally been challenged by critical social scientists on the grounds of their inevitable partiality and thus their capacity for self-negation. Likewise, for the GEOSS, one could demonstrate all the other means by which data might be able to move into new contexts, which lie outside of its frenetic database dynamics – informal exchanges between researchers over coffee, for example (see Hilgartner and Brandt-Rauf 1994; cf. Walford 2012). However, I would like to suggest another way into thinking critically about these databasing initiatives. Databases are only one part of heterogeneous data infrastructures – and they would not exist if the data which they contain was not collected in the first place. Data collection has slipped out of view as a site for analytical enquiry, in part because of its increased automation within the Earth Observation sciences, Genomics and other Big Data scientific disciplines. By drawing attention back on to collecting, I want to move away from the archival tension between the total and the partial, and towards examining the tension between the internal and the external as a generative space in which we see a dialectic of appropriation and transformation being enacted.

Because of the colonialist provenance of the archive, I want to take my lead in investigating 'collection' from historian Maya Jasanoff, whose book *The Edges of Empire* is an attempt to reread colonial expansion – and particularly British colonial expansion between 1750 and 1850 – as itself a practice of collecting. She does so by focusing on the perspective of the collectors of artefacts and objects who populated the edges of empire, asking (in her words) how 'real people' experienced imperial expansion from within. She writes:

> I do not interpret collecting as a transparent or programmatic expression of imperial power, the playing-out of an 'imperial project'. Rather, the history of collecting reveals the complexities of empire; it shows how power and culture intersected in tangled, contingent, sometimes self-contradictory ways. Instead of seeing collecting as a manifestation of imperial power, I see the British Empire as itself a kind of collection: pieced together and gaining definition over time, shaped by a range of accidents, and intentions. (2005: 6)

Like Jasanoff, I want to argue that, in order to understand these new data-driven landscapes in science, we need to pay attention not only to their archival tendencies but also to the contested spaces in which data collection happens, shaped by accidents as much as intentions, coloured by liminality, contingency and uncertainty. We might think of these spaces of data collection as 'frontiers', though it should be noted that I do not use the languages of 'frontiers' in order to bolster the much-criticised analytic of the centre and the periphery (Anderson 2002; Harding 1994; cf. Appadurai 1986) – quite the opposite. That a database might be considered a 'centre', and that data collecting is understood to happen on a 'frontier' or 'edge', implies something about the emphasis which using an archival analytic places on exactly such a centre–periphery framework. Rather, I wish to ask whether, in analysing databases, we must consider them as part of much larger relational systems in which the frontier is itself central.

In order to explore this, I would like to present some of my own ethnographic work with researchers and technicians involved in the Large Scale Biosphere Atmosphere Experiment in Amazonia (LBA) – a long-term scientific programme, led by the Brazilian partners, to investigate the role of the Amazon forest in the global carbon cycle. The LBA would be in what Tony Hey calls the 'long tail' of data-driven science (2016), and, like many observational science programmes, certainly does not produce the quantities of data that genomes or particle physics does. But having erected a 300metre tower in the middle of the Amazon forest to complement its network of other measuring stations and micro-meteorological towers throughout the Amazon forest, the LBA has increasingly large amounts of data that it has to deal with, and participates in what might be thought of as global data infrastructures that manifest the same sorts of dynamics of connectivity and reusability that I have already outlined.[16] However, exactly because the LBA data does not get close to the petabytes of data being produced by CERN, or in genomics, it focuses our attention away from the problem of storage, and back on to collecting. In the vein of Jasanoff's compelling historical narrative, I want to pick out a few collecting characters from my fieldwork, in order to think through how collecting, as both practice and trope, might re-orient our analyses of data-driven environmental science.

The first example I want to take is the one that perhaps most obviously corresponds to the sorts of settings that Jasanoff explores in her book. The LBA often had foreign (*estrangeiro*) researchers – non-Brazilian researchers – who came for periods of time (weeks to months) to collect data at the LBA's research sites in the Amazon forest. Whilst I was at the LBA, two of these were Peter and Robert.[17] Robert was interested in measuring volatile organic compounds

(VOCs), and brought with him an incredibly sensitive and expensive instrument called a Proton Transfer Reaction Mass Spectrometer (PTR-MS), in order to do so. This instrument suffered considerably on the way over from the US, and arrived quite damaged in Manaus, but Robert tended to it constantly and very devotedly. A little shed next to one of the LBA's towers in the forest had to be converted into a temperature-controlled environment, festooned with insulation, wires and tubes, for the PTR-MS to be ensconced in. Peter likewise needed to tend almost constantly to his instrument, known as a Picarro. It needed to be kept at a constant temperature in order to be able to measure gas concentration, so he spent a long time trying to work out how to let air circulate within the protective casing of the instrument so it did not overheat in the tropical humidity, without allowing the bees in to make their waxy hives in it.

Both Peter and Robert stayed only a relatively short period of time at the LBA, though this is normal for foreign researchers doing what are called 'campaigns', or data collection drives. But, as Robert pointed out to me on several occasions, it takes a particular sort of scientist to venture out into the forest to collect their own data in these difficult conditions; many of his colleagues are pushing for automatic data collection and data sent directly to their laptops. But as it is generally unusual for the 'top' (*top*) Brazilian scientists involved in the longer-term projects of the LBA to venture much to the LBA research sites, it was of some amusement to the local data collectors and technicians at the base camp that several foreign, high-status researchers – like Robert and Peter – actively wanted to go out into the forest, sleep in a hammock, eat the same thing every day, get sunburnt, bitten, wet, stung, damp and sleep-deprived. In fact, one foreign researcher insisted on sleeping in his own tent just outside the main base camp in the forest, which left the local data collectors completely bemused, especially as there were always rumours circulating of jaguar sightings.

Both Peter and Robert obviously revelled in being 'in the field'. Nevertheless, this sense of exciting exploration that they both felt when out collecting their data was given a different cast when considered in the light of some of the hushed conversations circulating around the LBA. I had several conversations with people about data being taken without permission by foreign collaborators, and some of the more senior researchers at the LBA quite bluntly stated that they saw the data as an Amazonian resource that was being funnelled to the global North with nothing coming back in return. These conversations would also often turn to various famous cases of biopiracy from the Amazon – the acaí berry being one of the most common I heard. Very few of the foreign researchers could speak Portuguese, which often exacerbated the sense of separation, and there were glaring economic discrepancies between the foreign researchers and the local people who were employed long-term at the LBA research base camp in the forest. Many of the foreign researchers I spoke to were sensitive to this; as one said to me, he struggled very much with feeling like a scientific imperialist when he was out in the LBA research sites. This sensitivity was in part because most of the foreigners knew that, when they moved out from the air-conditioned environment of the LBA headquarters in the city of Manaus to the LBA base camp in the forest, they always needed the help and support of the local people who knew their way around the forest, how to work the capricious infrastructures and how to speak the language. As a result, they did attempt to reciprocate. Robert was involved in the supervision of a graduate student at the LBA, and allowed others to use the PTR-MS, and Peter was giving talks and technical support (and, in the end, the use of the data he collected). Nevertheless, the multifaceted discrepancies between foreign researchers and local technicians became exceedingly obvious when out at the LBA research base camp.

The second characters I want to think about are the data collectors, who do all the manual labour at the research base camp, and most of the data collection for the long-term projects the LBA runs, such as collecting hydrological data, as well as the meteorological data from the LBA's towers. They are all local people from Manaus, generally with low educational levels, and were often kept on short contracts, which meant that they did not qualify for social security from the LBA. They were moved from project to project almost willy-nilly – although, if you are a 'trusted' data collector, you might be given more long-term work. Generally financially precarious, the data collectors were resentful that they were not given more stable contracts for the crucial work that they did. But at the same time, many of them told me that they did this work because they loved being in the forest. They would tell me avidly about how best to collect the data, how to make the machines do what you want them to do, what they have learnt doing the job, the people from other countries whom they have met through the data collecting. There was also a very strong sense of community between the data collectors that had grown out of sharing so much time with each other, out in the middle of the forest. I would often hear them say things like 'we're all family here', or 'we're brothers' (they were mostly men). This often contributed to the extent to which the foreign researchers appeared, and indeed felt, even more out of place when they came to do their data collection campaigns.

The third set of characters around data collection I want to think about are the data processors, or 'curators' as I came to think of them, who 'cleaned' the data (this was how their work was described: *limpar os dados*). The two I spent the most time with both have master's degrees in micrometeorology, and were originally data collectors, before graduating on to data processing. They were responsible for the quality control of the data that had been automatically collected by the instruments on the tower, which was sent in real time to the LBA HQ in Manaus – so, although they harvested this data, they did so from a computer screen, not from an instrument in the forest. They spent hours and hours with the data, making it ready for either storage or circulation, carefully teasing out the errors and flaws in the data, standardising it and making it available for use by other researchers. As I was told, they had to learn how to 'woo' (*namorar*) the data, get to know it intimately. But though they worked endlessly trying to give the data the coherent shape it needed for others to use it, when I was there they almost never published themselves. Unless they could publish with it, they were very aware that they would never become anything more than data curators, despite their master's degrees. Unlike the data collectors, being given credit by those who used the data they painstakingly cleaned was therefore of the utmost importance. Their liminal position was a direct function of their truncated relationship to the data that they created and cared for, but could not carry forward into what might be considered scientific knowledge (cf. Walford 2012).

The final set of characters I want to briefly touch on are the instruments themselves. The LBA uses a range of instruments to collect the data, from lowly water beakers which the hydrology data collectors carry with them, to pluviometers that sit on the top of the towers to measure rainfall, to high-tech spectrometers that are installed for brief periods of time for data collection campaigns. These instruments seem to lie at the smallest scale of data frontier that I encountered in my fieldwork, and I would like to dwell here on how they function. Let us take humidity of the air, for example, which the LBA measures continuously using an instrument called a hygrometer. The property of the environment – humidity – has a relation to a property of a material inside the hygrometer. Originally, for example, there was a human hair fixed inside hygrometers,[18] because human hair expands and contracts according to humidity in the air. In these original instruments, a stylus was attached to the hair, with its tip resting on a revolving drum of paper. As the hair lengthened and contracted, it caused the stylus to move up and down, recording the change on the revolving drum of paper (Knowles Middleton 1969: 81–132). This provided a continuously varying line that could then be 'read' using a scale. The modern electrical hygrometers that are installed on the towers have a semi-conductor in them rather than a hair, but the principle is basically similar. As was explained during a short course the LBA technician gave in electronics, it is the conductivity of the semi-conductor that is affected by the property of nature in question. Lithium chloride is a common semi-conductor in electric hygrometers, as its resistance (how much current is let through it) changes depending on the amount of water it has absorbed from the air. The conductivity of the substance is therefore correlated with the relative humidity of the air. Most of the instruments that are on the LBA towers convert one property into another property in this way using semi-conductors; and this basic idea holds also for the high-tech instruments such as the PTR-MS. The PTR-MS works on the principle of mass spectrometry, which relies on the fact that, if you subject a moving object (in this case a molecule) to a sideways force, how far it is deflected from its original path depends on its mass, as long as the speed and the size of the force are known. Charging the molecules from the air sucked in to the PTR-MS, and then subjecting them to an electro-magnetic field, will mean they are deflected differently depending on their mass. These charged molecules then hit a detector at different times and places, generating a current.

One could say, therefore, that these instruments all work by transforming one property into another continuously and analogically. The data is then created by reading this continuous property generated in the instrument against a scale. Without wanting to go further into the technical details, then, this can be understood in the same way as we might read a thermometer; as Paul Edwards notes, '[Y]our act of reading the thermometer transforms a continuous, infinitely variable analogue quantity into a discrete number, such as 75° F: a set of digits, which vary discretely or discontinuously' (2010: 105). Of course, this is how the instruments ideally are understood to work; when out in the forest, there are all sorts of problems and accidents. The instruments can get damaged, dirty or stolen; they become decalibrated, or a power surge kills their battery. They get struck by lightning, or bees get stuck in them. They need to be constantly tended to, in order to make sure they are performing correctly. And even when performing correctly, they function with a certain amount of observational uncertainty, which comes as standard from the factory calibration process. As what might be thought of as the very edge of scientific data collection, they are in a constant state of uncertain relationship with the forest.

Transformation/appropriation

Collecting data happens in all sort of different ways at the LBA, by many different people and by many different instruments. So the first point to make is that this particular data frontier is not in fact easily imagined as a line or a boundary. It is an unevenly textured surface, constituted by all sorts of interfaces and relations, and shaped by social and political seams that are thrown into stark relief. This particular frontier is shaped by discourses of colonial exploitation of Brazil by outsiders; but also exploitation which occurs within Brazil itself, by the economically rich but relatively resource-poor Southern region of the resource-rich but economically poor Northern Amazonian region. These relations become exceedingly obvious when on this frontier, and in such a space data collection becomes analogous with other forms of extraction, and can be understood as appropriation, exploitation and capture. But, as Jasanoff points out, there are also all sorts of complex alliances and relations that emerge at the colonial frontier. Peter and Robert know that they have to forge relations with the local people in order to get their work done; they are aware of their privileged position as rich North Americans; and they tried to develop a relationship, more or less successfully, with the local people whom they relied upon. What is interesting is the contrast between the solidity of some of these alliances and relations and the ephemerality of others.

The second point I want to draw out is that collecting data is a struggle, because it involves continuously managing the shifting edges at which the transformation of the forest into data can happen. The instruments are the main means by which these edges are forged – but, even when the instruments are functioning as intended, the edges that they implement are not hard and fast lines or cuts. They are, in the first instance, analogical relations between the properties outside the instrument and the properties inside. The external and the internal here interpenetrate; the outside and the inside of the instrument are in continuous relation with each other, and not until the continuously varying current that the instrument creates is put against a scale does any sort of discrete separation occur. This porosity of boundaries is another theme that runs through Jasanoff's description, such that 'all empires were precarious, porous, multicultural and multilingual, and that of all the political orders ever devised they, more than any other, defy simple description or heavy abstraction' (Pagden 2006). This seems, metaphorically at least, to be an apt description of the micro-frontier of data collection, which relies on the boundary between the instrument and world being permeable and fluid, albeit in controlled ways. Added to this, however, is that the instruments very rarely function as they are intended to when taken out into the forest. There are always accidents and unforeseen events that have to be countenanced, when the relation between the forest and the instrument slips out of control. There is therefore a precariousness to these micro-frontiers of scientific data collection, which speaks to the continuous necessity to make and remake relationships with the forest.

The third point, related to the last, is that, at the same time as endlessly building frontiers or edges in order to collect data, this process also involves 'self-fashioning', as Jasanoff puts it (2005: 7). Jasanoff draws attention to how collecting, as a practice that characterised those who lived on colonial frontiers, was a means for self-transformation. She takes, for example, the famous figure of British colonial power, Clive of India, who was commandeer-in-chief of British India and established the military and political supremacy of the East India Company in Bengal in the eighteenth century. When back in the UK, however, he used the wealth he had amassed to procure fine houses, beautiful art and stylish furnishings, as "'[l]ike most imperial collectors, Clive, the son of a Shropshire lawyer, was an outsider to metropolitan power structures. He was provincial, middle-class, and nouveau riche. As a collector, he set out to make up for all that' (Jasanoff 2005: 33). Jasanoff finds Clive of Britain, the man he was trying to invent on his return, as of much interest as the Clive of India of countless history books. Although I do not want to draw this analogy too precisely, there is something arresting in thinking about data collection as a form of self-fashioning; that the frontier and the self are therefore made at the same time. Whether it is Robert and Peter reinventing themselves as scientist-explorers in the forest, or the data curators who are prevented from realising their scientific subjectivities through their truncated relationship to data – it seems clear that there is the potential on these data frontiers for reinvention and self-transformation that demands attention.

This self-fashioning also often involved, in Jasanoff's telling, an intimate involvement with the 'other' (2005: 309). This might be useful to characterise not the relations between the different people involved in collecting the LBA data but rather the relations between people and the data they collect. The fourth point then is how data collecting often involves relations of affect and intimacy with the data, and with the forest. Again, we see this with the data curators, and with the data collectors. In the case of those out in the forest, this is clearly a bodily experience of learning how to work in the forest, and a sense of intimacy with the instruments, and idiosyncratic data platforms. But it is also the case for the data curators, who stay in the office but still create relations of attachment to the data, relations that they then must truncate in order to make the data available for other researchers to use. This is an observation which is not limited to the earth systems sciences which often involve 'venturing out' into the world. Mike Fortun has in fact shown affect to be an important aspect of working with massive datasets in a very different scientific setting, namely genomics (Fortun 2015). Fortun argues that it is with the rise of new Big Data genomics – immense and ever-expanding databases with higher degrees of interconnection; increasing sequencing rates; bioinformatics on the up and up – that the amount of emotional excitement and intense engagement that scientists feel increases. He points to the 'deep connections between what is almost always troped as an overwhelming "'avalanche", "flood" or "rush" of data found in contemporary postgenomics and other fields in science ... and the creative, tacit epistemic virtues that I call "care of the data", the adroit, artful and cautious handling of large data sets that permit both multiple interpretations and multiple errors' (Fortun 2015: 36). This relation between data, care and intense engagement is also played out at the LBA research sites, as those involved with caring for the data construct intimate relationships with it that have reciprocal effects on their own identity.

Data collecting in the LBA, and other environmental sciences, often involves venturing out into the forest, or 'the field' as it was called; it involves a change in bodily disposition in order to be there – you eat different things, sleep differently, move differently. Data collection in these circumstances involves an intimate, often affective relationship between the data collector, the forest and the data that can be transformative in different ways. Collecting data is hard work – frogs fall in instruments and bees make homes in them, lightning burns cables, it is incredibly humid and wet. Collecting data requires a constant careful handling of how much of the forest gets in to your instruments, and how much is kept out. But it is exactly because the data from these remote areas of the Amazon is so difficult to collect that it is very valuable to the scientific community at large, and can lead on to successful scientific careers. The fact it emerges from this endlessly-negotiated frontier is in fact what, in part, lends it transformative power. So, when you collect data, you are in the middle of 'frontier-building', which is at the same time, a practice of *self-transformation*. Data collection, in this case, is both an appropriation and a transformation. I suggest that we need to examine to what extent such frontiers inhere in many spaces and aspects of data-driven science – not just, as I have done here, out in the Amazon forest but in data centres and laboratories all over the world. This can help us to rethink both the claims made by Big Data initiatives in the sciences such as the GEOSS, at the same time as rework the critiques which we have traditionally drawn upon, by moving away from the centre/periphery and part/whole hierarchies that archival analytics rest on. We might imagine rather that data infrastructures are riddled with 'frontiers' that have no centres, marking not an overarching hierarchy but a form of relating at a contested, porous boundary. The data deluge in science, then, might be recast not as a vertiginous increase in volumes of data but an increase in the contested and contingent relational frontiers where data collection happens.

Conclusion: collecting/ethnography

To briefly conclude, I will reflect on the extent to which this focus on collecting and frontiers might contribute to reframing the antagonistic relationship between the data of the data–driven sciences – both natural and social – and the ethnographic data of qualitative social sciences such as anthropology. Ethnography also involves collecting data, storing data and circulating data; but it has traditionally been framed as 'small', born of the result of intimate, personal and social relations nurtured between the ethnographer and their fieldsite, and in opposition to the vast, automatically collected and decontextualised datasets of big data that are emerging in the quantitative social sciences. The use of big data in the social sciences has therefore prompted a certain amount of resistance that draws upon decades of contestation between the qualitative and quantitative sciences (see Seaver 2015 for the case of anthropology). However, it has also caused some scholars to question the role of the qualitative social sciences, because Big Data is claimed to be able to reveal 'more' about the social than previous methods (Savage and Burrows 2007); and it has prompted yet others to try to come up with ways of bringing together 'small' or 'thick' data and 'big' data, as if the one fills in the gaps left by the other (Wang 2013). These oppositions, and their suggested solutions, are often drawn on the assumption that big data lacks relationality and social context (but therefore has greater generalisability and explanatory 'power') – and this is a characterisation that is easy to make when approaching data as a phenomenon that by definition bears no relation to its collection. But by bringing the focus back on to the collection, we might begin to see how conflicting relationalities cannot but be woven into any dataset; relations of stark inequality as well as relations of intimacy; macro–global relations as well as micro–local relations. It might even be argued that from this perspective, no data is in fact inherently 'big' or 'small'. The question then becomes under what conditions, and through what social, technological and political means does data become either – and indeed, whether there might be more than one way to be both.

There are also other consequences to draw out, as the question that my analysis thus far has not approached is how exactly the relations that are created on these porous data frontiers of data-driven environmental science play out in the subsequent ways in which the data becomes an actor in the world. Rather than suggest that these relations are simply expunged, as is often argued, we might instead do well to reflect upon how this is also a question that anthropology has invested a great deal of time in exploring. Indeed, how to understand the relationship between the field and the desk (Strathern 1999), between ethnography and anthropology (Ingold 2014), continues to exercise the anthropological imagination; and, practically, how one writes the relations one experiences in the field into a text, and to what extent this process is an appropriation or a transformation, is a conundrum that anthropologists face daily. Comparing anthropology to data-driven knowledge production from this perspective will also serve to remind anthropologists that ethnographic data collection also happens on frontiers, and ones that historically have been shaped by relations of colonialism and exploitation. But it might also make us think about the extent to which there might be many different frontiers throughout the anthropological infrastructure; that there are many relations between the field and the desk that play out at different stages of knowledge production, and which constitute a form of self-transformation as well. It might be that by focusing comparatively on the different forms of data collection, and the different contours and spaces of the frontiers on which this collection happens, we can begin to find new critical questions to ask of both data-driven science and anthropology.

Notes

1 As Tony Hey, Chief Data Scientist at the UK Science and Technology Facilities Council, points out, the areas of science where there has been the biggest data 'explosion' are astronomy, which produces millions of data-dense images of galaxies; and particle physics, with programmes like CERN generating petabytes of data. Genomics has also seen a data boom, doubling the amount of data it produces every six months. Tony Hey, Lecture, 2016: www.youtube.com/watch?v=R-OyGXgKC38 [accessed 20 May 2017].

2 The extent to which 'science' is complicit in these processes of commensuration and commodification of nature is still being debated, not least

within science itself; this has perhaps been nowhere more obvious than in the public/private controversies around the Human Genome Project (for example, see Reardon 2016).

3 Archivists themselves are also engaging in unpicking its critical potential; for example, Cook and Schwartz 2002.

4 'Where does the outside commence? That is the question of the archive' (Derrida 1995: 12).

5 Derrida derives this from Freud's principle of the 'death drive' (Derrida 1995).

6 Derrida defines archive fever as 'to have a compulsion, repetitive, and nostalgic desire for the archive, an irrepressible desire to return to the origin, a homesickness, a nostalgia for the return to the most archaic place of absolute commencement' (1995: 91).

7 A more extensive examination of the place and effects of archives across the social and natural sciences is addressed in the volume edited by Lorraine Daston, *Science in the Archives* (2017). My examination here could be thought of as a specific ethnographic exploration of what she describes in that volume as the 'wild-eyed fantasies' that 'shimmer through the arcana of data: dreams of immortality, gigantism and omniscience' (Daston 2017: 3).

8 There are also more recent examples, such as the Human Cell Atlas, which seeks to map every single human cell in every single human tissue, announced in October 2016. www.humancellatlas.org/ [accessed 22 May 2017].

9 www.earthobservations.org/geoss.php [accessed 10 October 2016].

10 www.earthobservations.org/wigeo.php [accessed 20 May 2017].

11 http://geoss.maps.arcgis.com/apps/MapJournal/index.html?appid=085c f926a2464132846286829864de1f [accessed 29 June 2016].

12 http://geoss.maps.arcgis.com/apps/MapJournal/index.html?appid=085c f926a2464132846286829864de1f [accessed 29 June 2016].

13 www.doi.gov/blog/geo-commits-unleash-power-open-data-address-global-challenges [accessed 20 May 2017].

14 This ability for the data to be endlessly recontextualised and revalued has led some critics to describe these processes as a form of commodification (for example, see Leonelli 2013).

15 One might also imagine then that these databases themselves refigure certain other archival logics, which it is beyond the scope of this chapter to discuss. For example, if the archive, as colonial trope, has traditionally been understood to be about commanding territoriality, the here and now, then these database configurations are more oceanic in their material imaginaries (cf. Seaver 2015). Likewise, if the archive has traditionally temporally indexed a form of memorialisation (albeit one that

forgets), one could argue that here we have another temporality which strives to keep everything constantly in the present.

16 Such as 'fluxnet', a 'network of regional networks' of meteorological flux towers. See https://fluxnet.ornl.gov/ [accessed 20 May 2017].

17 I have used pseudonyms throughout.

18 As it was a standardised instrument, it was stipulated that the hair had to be blonde (Knowles Middleton 1969: 85).

References

Anderson, W. 2002. 'Introduction: Postcolonial Technoscience'. *Social Studies of Science* 32(5/6): 643–58.

Appadurai, A. 1986. 'Theory in Anthropology: Centre and Periphery'. *Comparative Studies in Society and History* 28(2): 356–61.

Boulter, J. 2011. *Melancholy and the Archive: Trauma, History and Memory in the Contemporary Novel*. London: Continuum International Publishing Group.

Bowker, G. 2000. 'Biodiversity, Datadiversity'. *Social Studies of Science* 30(5): 643–83.

Bowker, G. 2008. *Memory Practices in the Sciences*. Cambridge, MA: MIT Press.

Boyd, D. and Crawford, K. 2012. 'Critical Questions for Big Data'. *Information, Communication & Society* 15(5): 662–79.

Cook, T. and Schwartz, J.M. 2002. 'Archives, Records, and Power: From (Postmodern) Theory to (Archival) Performance'. *Archival Science* 2: 171–85.

Dalton, C.M., Taylore, L. and Thatcher, J. 2016. 'Critical Data Studies: A Dialog on Data and space'. *Big Data & Society* (January–June): 1–9.

Daston, L. 2017. 'Introduction: Third Nature'. In *Science in the Archives*. Edited by Lorraine Daston. Chicago: Chicago University Press, 1–14.

Derrida, J. 1995. 'Archive Fever: A Freudian Impression'. *Diacritics* 25(2): 9–63.

Edwards, P.N. 2010. *A Vast Machine*. Cambridge, MA: MIT Press.

Fortun, M. 2015. 'What Toll Pursuit: Affective Assemblages in Genomics and Postgenomics'. In *Postgenomics: Perspectives on Biology After the Genome*. Edited by Sarah S. Richardson and Hallam Stevens. Durham, NC: Duke University Press, 32–55.

Gabrys, J. 2016. 'Practising, Materialising and Contesting Environmental Data'. *Big Data & Society* (July–December): 1–7.

Haraway, D. 2016. *Staying with the Trouble: Making Kin in the Chthulucene*. Durham, NC: Duke University Press.

Harding, S. 1994. 'Is Science Multicultural? Challenges, Resources, Opportunities, Uncertainties'. *Configurations* 2(2): 301–30.

Hey, T. 2016. 'The Fourth Paradigm: Data-Intensive Discovery and Open Science'. Guest Lecture given at the University of South Australia. www.youtube.com/watch?v=R-OyGXgKC38 [accessed February 2018].

Hilgartner, S. and Brandt-Rauf, S.I. 1994. 'Data Access, Ownership, and Control: Toward Empirical Studies of Access Practices'. *Science Communication* 15(4): 355–72.

Hulme, M. 2014. *Why We Disagree about Climate Change: Understanding Controversy, Inaction and Opportunity.* Cambridge: Cambridge University Press.

Ingold, T. 2014. 'That's Enough about Ethnography!' *Hau: Journal of Ethnographic Theory* 4(1): 383–95.

Jardine, B. and Kelty, C. 2016. 'The Total Archive: Preface'. *LIMN* 6. https://limn.it/preface-the-total-archive.

Jasanoff, M. 2005. *Edge of Empire: Conquest and Collecting in the East 1750–1850.* London: Harper Perennial.

Jasanoff, S. 2003. 'Technologies of Humility: Citizen Participation in Governing Science'. *Minerva* 41: 223–44.

Kitchin, R. 2014. *The Data Revolution: Big Data, Open Data, Data Infrastructures and Their Consequences.* Thousand Oaks, CA: Sage Publications.

Knowles Middleton, W.E. 1969. *Invention of the Meteorological Instruments.* Baltimore: Johns Hopkins Press.

Lehnig M., Dawes N., Bavay M. et al. 2009. 'Instrumenting the Earth: Next-Generation Sensor Networks and Environmental Science'. In *The Fourth Paradigm: Data-Intensive Scientific Discovery.* Edited by Tony Hey, Stewart Tansley and Kristin Tolle. Redmond, WA: Microsoft Research, 45–51.

Leonelli, S. 2013. 'Why the Current Insistence on Open Access to Scientific Data? Big Data, Knowledge Production, and the Political Economy of Contemporary Biology'. *Bulletin of Science, Technology, Society:* 33(1–2) 6–11.

Lippert, I. 2015. 'Environment as Datascape: Enacting Emissions Realities in Corporate Carbon Accounting'. *Geoforum* 66, 126–35.

McNally, R., Mackenzie, A., Hui, A., and Tomomitsu, J. 2012. 'Understanding the '"Intensive" in "Data Intensive Research"': Data Flows in Next Generation Sequencing and Environmental Networked Sensors'. *International Journal of Digital Curation* 7(1): 81–94.

Nadim, T. 2016. 'Blind Regards: Troubling Data and Their Sentinels'. *Big Data & Society* (July–December): 1–6.

Nora, P. 1989. 'Between Memory and History: Les lieux de Mémoire'. *Representations* 26: 7–24.

Pagden, A. 2006. 'C is for Colonies'. *London Review of Books* 28(9): 30–1.

Povinelli, E. 2011. 'The Woman on the Other Side of the Wall: Archiving the Otherwise in Postcolonial Digital Archives'. *Differences: A Journal of Feminist Cultural Studies* 22: 146–71.

Reardon, J. 2016. 'The Genomic Open'. *LIMN* 6. https://limn.it/the-genomic-open.

Savage, M. and Burrows, R. 2007. 'The Coming Crisis of Empirical Sociology'. *Sociology* 41(5): 885–99.

Seaver, N. 2015. 'Bastard Algebra'. In *Data, Now Bigger and Better!* Edited by Tom Boellstorff and Bill Maurer. Chicago: Prickly Paradigm Press.

Strathern, M. 1999. *Property, Substance and Effect: Anthropological Essays on Persons and Things.* New York: The Athlone Press.

Szerszynski, B. 2010. 'Reading and Writing the Weather Climate Technics and the Moment of Responsibility'. *Theory, Culture & Society* 27(2–3): 9–30.

Tsing, A.L. 2015. *The Mushroom at the End of the World: On the Possibility of Life in Capitalist Ruins.* Princeton: Princeton University Press.

Verran, H. 2012. 'The Changing Lives of Measures and Values: From Centre Stage in the Fading "Disciplinary" Society to Pervasive Background Instrument in the Emergent "Control" Society'. *The Sociological Review* 59(s2): 60–72.

Walford, A. 2012. 'Data Moves: Taking Amazonian Climate Science Seriously'. *Cambridge Anthropology* 30(2): 101–17.

Wang, T. 2013. 'Big Data Needs Thick Data'. *Ethnography Matters.* http://ethnographymatters.net/blog/2013/05/13/big-data-needs-thick-data [accessed 12 May 2017].

Waterton, C. 2010. 'Experimenting with the Archive: STS-ers as Analysts and Co-constructors of Databases and Other Archival Forms'. *Science, Technology, & Human Values* 35(5): 645–76.

Zeitlyn, D. 2012. 'Anthropology in and of the Archives: Possible Futures and Contingent Pasts. Archives as Anthropological Surrogates'. *Annual Review Anthropology* 41: 461–80.

6

Baseless data? Modelling, ethnography and the challenge of the anthropocene

Hannah Knox

While this book is about the implications of a phenomenon that has broadly come under the heading big data, my recent research on data practices among planners and environmental scientists has made me increasingly sceptical that the central challenge that transactional or 'found' data poses derives from its 'bigness'. In this chapter I turn away from a concern with bigness in order to reflect on another facet of data. I am interested in a concern that emerges within the practice of modelling unstructured data – or what I call here the challenge of 'baseless data' – and how this might reframe conversations about the relationship between ethnography and data science. The chapter unpacks how the modelling of found empirical data in the context of climate science begins with the issue of how to create a baseline. I then reflect on the way in which this relationship between data and baseline reaches its limits in the analysis of social phenomena, opening up a space for ethnography to enter in. Dwelling in this problem of the limit of quantitative modelling and the opening it potentially provides for ethnography to enter the discussion, I then develop a 'symmetrical' (Latour 2007) analysis of contemporary ethnography and its own conditions of possibility for responding to and fashioning data to create a model of social worlds. In conclusion I turn ethnography back on the question of how numerical data might elicit insights into social relations, by asking whether an attention to particular kinds of data-in-itself might provide a 'contact-zone' (Haraway 2008) from which collaborative work into anthropocenic (and other hybrid socio-technical) relationships might proceed.

From big to thin to modelled: critiques of data and the place of ethnography

Since Chris Anderson announced in *Wired* magazine in 2008 that big data signalled the future of scientific analysis and the 'end of theory' (Anderson 2008), there has been considerable discussion within the social and natural sciences about the continued relevance of conventional methods of research and analysis in the face of new forms of data. Anderson audaciously claimed that big data signalled the end of the need for scientific models, opening up the potential for a direct form of knowledge production through the analysis of huge amounts of actually existing data. No longer would science or the social sciences have to depend on statistical approximation to make knowledge claims – instead all they would have to do would be to map the masses of data available from which they would be able to discern actual tendencies, trends or patterns.

In anthropology, responses to this and similar claims about the promise of big data have primarily been to defend the utility of ethnography in the face of big data. Perhaps the least surprising response has been the argument that ethnography as a method of description is necessary for filling in the gaps that even the most totalising data analysis leaves behind (Burrell 2012). Tricia Wang's reflections on her experience of using ethnography in corporate research with Nokia adds a further nuance to this argument when she suggests that the value of ethnography in the face of big data is not that it is somehow 'small' and thus able to fill the gaps left behind by big data, but rather that it is 'thick' and as such it is able to provide explanations for that which big data can only describe at a surface level (Wang 2013).

Other responses to the relationship between big data and ethnography have focused less on what ethnography can add to big data analytics and more on what cultural analysis has to say about big data as a phenomenon. Boyd and Crawford's (2012) now seminal paper in *Information, Communication & Society* outlines an approach to big data that highlights the social, cultural and technological dimensions of contemporary data analysis. In an attempt to cut through the rather

epochal claims made by people like Anderson, they situate data analytics in a *longue durée* of computational methods for social research.
Focusing in particular on transactional data produced by social media
and internet-based technologies, boyd and Crawford illustrate that
data analysis not only holds the potential to produce new knowledge,
but opens the way to a transformation in the very criteria by which
knowledge claims are made and assessed.

Within anthropology a number of scholars have begun to explore
ethnographically and theoretically what this transformation in knowledge might actually look like. Paul Kockelman for example has
looked at the ordering principles of spam filters, analysing the algorithmic methods by which such filters work (Kockelman 2013). Char-
acterising spam filters as a specific kind of 'sieve', Kockelman situates
what might otherwise be seen as an arcane technical practice within
a culturally comparative framework that normalises and socialises
technical principles that are often treated as outside the domain of
ethnographic research.

Nick Seaver's work on music recommendation engines (Seaver
2015), and Eitan Wilf's (2013) work on the creation of a Jazz-
composing robot, likewise explore the principles at play in the development of such data-driven devices. In both these cases the principle
that lies at the heart of these technological artefacts is the promise of
being able to build meaning out of the relationship that exists between
discrete data streams. In both cases, categories or genres (of music)
are replaced by patterns or clusterings that derive from principles of
association. Whilst these ethnographic studies unravel some of the
ways of knowing that are created by contemporary data analysis, this
analysis of knowledge is also used to reflect back on anthropological
forms of knowledge production. In Wilf's study, for example, the
understanding of musical 'style' that emerges from his engagement
with a robotic composer is used to rethink the relevance of the idea
of style in the analysis of art forms as carriers of cultural meaning.

These recent ethnographic studies of data analytics have tended to
focus on data which is produced by networked consumer technologies (email, social media, website, search engines). As a result the
focus has been primarily on how a particular version of the social,
based on consumer preferences and consumption patterns (Savage
and Burrows 2007; Latour 2010), creates particular challenges to

social-scientific forms of knowledge production based on practices of post-hoc categorisation and classification. Yet big data analysis in fact extends far beyond consumer data. Interest in the possibilities afforded by new kinds of distributed data are found in fields as wide-ranging as genomics (Mackenzie et al. 2016), smart cities (Gabrys 2007, 2014) and environmental sciences (Fortun 2004). In these fields the challenges and possibilities associated with new forms of data extend beyond algorithmic methods for cross-referencing data points, and include such issues as the potential and risks of machine learning and artificial intelligence, the development of modelling techniques for predictive analytics and the development of methods for better visualising and communicating data from environmental sensors. If we have begun to develop some idea of how ethnographic knowledge is located in relation to the algorithms used in parsing and presenting consumer data, then the question remains what kinds of insights, and what kinds of new practices, might become possible when we consider the relationship between ethnography and data analysis in these other fields?

With this in mind, the aim of this chapter is to ask what kind of new openings for ethnography the practice of using data for the purposes of climate modelling generates. In climate science, data practices are focused not on using the granularity of sensory environmental data to provide individualised information but rather on using this data as a means of improving the modelling of systems at different geographical scales. Rather than finding an enthusiasm for 'big data' in itself, or an attempt to create correlations to predict individual behaviour, what we find in the climate sciences is the question of how to model systems that are capable of dealing with widely varying streams of data on both social and natural processes. The challenge faced by climate scientists is how to analyse and understand sensory and descriptive data by developing models of complex ecosystemic relations. If the problem of big data produces ethnography as small, and the problem of thin data produces an opening for ethnographic thickness, this chapter considers what kind of opening for ethnography is produced when we consider data as something that is oriented towards the practice of modelling ecosystems both in their current form and in their future manifestations. The chapter proceeds through a description of an encounter between ecosystem modelling and ethnographic description, which allows us to unpack the specific relation that each has to different kinds of data. In conclusion I consider how both data modelling and ethnography might be changed by this encounter.

Modelling in practice

This chapter draws on research that I conducted with a project that was based at a university in the north of England that was working to bring climate science and social science together in order to provide advice to local authorities and other local actors on how to adapt to future climate change. The project was established in 2011 and aimed to apply a 'socio-technical approach' to climate change adaptation with a view to providing a blueprint for cities and urban policy-makers of how to adapt to future environmental challenges. Several people were employed on the project, including a physical geographer, a quantitative social scientist, a policy expert, a junior qualitative social researcher and two senior professors who came respectively from a natural science and a social science background. During the course of the project I became involved in their work and contributed to some of the project research. This chapter emerges, ethnographically, out of the experience of both researching and being incorporated into the project as a representative of a particular kind of 'social' in the context of this sociotechnical approach. This particular position in the project is something I will return to later.

Modelling a local climate future

The central aim of the climate adaptation project was to create a local picture of future climate change that could be useful for policy-makers. This entailed the production of new kinds of descriptions of how changes in the climate would affect particular locations so that policy-makers in cities and regions could make informed decisions about how best to adapt to these predicated changes (Hebbert, Jankovic and Webb 2011). It was this framing that provided the rationale for the 'sociotechnical approach' (Guy and Shove 2000). In the context of this project, this specifically meant combining analyses and projections of local climate based on available empirical data with analysis of social conditions in the same locations.

The first challenge of the project was how to produce adequate projections of future climate for a particular city or region. Climate models work on the basis of modelling a global climate system (Edwards 2010) and have not conventionally been developed with a local or regional scale in mind (Hebbert, Jankovic and Webb 2011). Projections about future climate change are usually described in terms of different average temperatures over land and sea for large geographical areas. These averages tend to be described as a range of scenarios that are likely to occur under different social, economic and environmental conditions, and are often discussed in terms of high, medium and low (carbon) emission scenarios (Nakicenovic et al. 2000). In the climate adaptation project however, there was an awareness that, if this knowledge was to be useful, it needed to be scaled to the level at which administrative decisions were actually made – that is from the global to the nation, the region, the city or even the building.

Improvements in climate models over time have meant a gradual increase in the 'granularity' or level of geographical specificity for projections, achieved by incorporating new data into climate models. By the late 1990s climate models had developed to be able to provide projections of average future climatic conditions for grid squares of 250–500km (Edwards 1999). By 2009 models had improved in terms of the scale of climate projections that they could produce, but still operated as a relatively crude tool for projecting the effects of future weather and climate for scales that actual policy decisions about provision of local services, urban planning, construction etc. could be based upon. They were unable for example, to deal with significant local weather patterns such as the heat-island effect often associated with large urban areas, or the effects of concreted surfaces on projected flood risk (Jankovic and Hebbert 2012). A key issue that physical scientists working on the climate adaptation project were trying to resolve was how to scale large models to specific local circumstances by incorporating locally found weather data into climate models (Hebbert and Jankovic 2013).

The Chester Zoo Case Study

To explore how they did this, I turn my attention to one specific project that was under way during my fieldwork, called the Chester

Zoo Case Study. Chester Zoo is an attraction in the UK and, as it is primarily out-of-doors, weather was expected to play a big part in the way in which the Zoo is visited and used and so it made an ideal case study for climate adaptation.

Eleanor, the main scientist working on the project, was trained in physical geography but over the past few years she had been developing an expertise in local climate modelling. She had been brought into the project because of her experience of using a database produced by an organisation called the UK Climate Impacts programme (UKCIP). This database had been produced to localise global climate predictions within the UK. In 2009 a new version of the database, UKCP09, had been released which provided probabilistic projections of likely weather changes at a scale of tiles of 25km sq. (as opposed to 100km sq. in the 2002 version of the model). Eleanor's work involved further specifying the local relevance of this model by correlating data projections provided by UKCP09 with data parsed from specific weather stations near to Chester Zoo.

Collating this data required considerable work. It had originally been hoped that a weather station located at Hawarden in North Wales near to the Zoo would provide the local data but this weather station had closed in 2004, six years before the end of the time series that Eleanor was collecting data for. In order to make the data model work Eleanor had had to find a new source of data to fill in this gap. Nine miles away, and 33m higher in elevation on the edge of the Dee Estuary, Eleanor had managed to locate another weather station at Ness Gardens in the Wirral and planned to use this data instead for the final six years. Comparison of data between the two weather stations during the years when they overlapped showed that there was little difference in recorded temperature, although there was a slight difference in rainfall. Eleanor dealt with this by using a 'deterministic transfer model' to compare two sets of data so that the Ness Gardens data could be altered to stand in for Hawarden's missing data.

The linking of observational data with global models is central to the work of climate modelling. Naomi Oreskes et al. (1994) have shown that environmental modelling always raises the question of empirical validation and that incorporating local data into larger models is a central way in which this validation work occurs. Importantly Oreskes et al. point out that models like climate models are not truth claims about the way in which the world is, which can be objectively validated, but rather representations whose robustness is established by demonstrating correspondences between the model and the world described in observational data (Oreskes et al. 1994). Modelling takes place precisely when data is not sufficiently 'total', that is when there is a 'lack of full access, either in time or space, to the phenomena of interest' (Oreskes et al. 1994: 644). When the models are oriented towards policy ends, they suggest 'the burden is on the modeller to demonstrate the degree of correspondence between the model and the material world it seeks to represent and to delineate the limits of that correspondence' (1994: 644).

Using observational data to make deterministic predictions is actually just one of a number of ways of dealing with data gaps in predictive modelling. Other ways of filling in such data gaps that are used in climate modelling include the use of stochastic models whereby random noise is introduced into models into order to enable projections to be made, or, more recently, Bayesian techniques. These allow for changes in the data that is being generated over time to reflect back on the very process of modelling itself (see introduction and also Kockelman (2013) for a more in-depth discussion of Bayesian modelling techniques). In the case of the Chester Zoo Case Study, however, it was observational weather data that was used to validate the model. This observational data was brought into relation with the global model by using intermediate statistical models that would help the scientists demonstrate the robustness of the deterministic predictions that they wished to make (e.g. rainy weather reduces visitor numbers). The reason for using statistical models to align collected data and already modelled data derived from the problem of how to establish truth claims on the basis of information collected from different sources. The problem with distributed, found data is that it is not sufficiently clean, stable or formatted. Statistical modelling is a technique that aims to turn otherwise random numbers into a stable empirical baseline (Arnold 2013).

Baseless data

The problem of the lack of a baseline is not something that just afflicts environmental science but has also been noted as a problem in big data analysis (Ørberg 2014). Just as Eleanor's work was oriented to crafting a stable set of data out of the available points of data she had at her disposal, so other data scientists are also often charged with devising methods of making predictive assertions on the basis of distributed and messy data. Whilst ethnographers of data science have focused on the way in which correspondences are established between different data points, a practice which seems to do away with the notion of the baseline, data modelling techniques that produce models of systems rather than individual preferences absolutely depend on the establishment of a baseline from which change can be measured. Oreskes et al. (1994) for example, point out, in their discussion of how empirical data gets incorporated into models, that scientists who aim to develop numerical models that demonstrate analytical principles do so in order to generate a 'benchmark' against which other empirical cases can be compared.

This problem of creating a baseline when dealing with found environmental data well predates more recent pronouncements about big data. A paper by Dayton et al. (1998) for example, discusses the problem of how to detect ecosystemic changes in kelp forests and deployed the idea of the 'sliding baseline' to point out that 'the definition of a meaningful benchmark' for measuring change in these kinds of ecosystems 'is impossible' (Dayton et al. 1998: 309). Similarly, in a 1995 communication about fisheries research, a parallel point was made about the way in which each generation of scientists who study fisheries starts with a different baseline from that of the previous generations owing to differences in the environments being observed – a phenomenon termed the 'Shifting Baseline' (Pauly 1995; see also: McHarg 1971).

The work of climate modellers like Eleanor is not about creating data *de novo* then, but rather about spending considerable time working with data that is, to quote Paul Edwards, 'spotty, inconsistent, poorly calibrated and temporally brief' (Edwards 1999: 453) in order to turn it into a form that is consistent with global models. Given that climate modelling relies on this approach to data, it is not surprising that Eleanor used the solution that she had come up with to smooth the local observational data in order to calibrate the global climate model for local circumstances. When explaining her research to me, she stressed that dealing with data inconsistencies was a common activity that was necessary when conducting this kind of study that relied on historical data that had been produced without the intention of it being used for the kind of modelling work that Eleanor was involved in. Managing to do this was in itself an achievement and allowed the project to make assertions about projected changes in weather that it would not have otherwise been able to do.

Chester Zoo project: modelling the social

Whilst the modelling of future climatic conditions was a key part of the Chester Zoo project, the purpose of the analysis was to try to understand the impact of changing weather on local zoo visits. Once projections of the local climate had been developed, the next job was to align these with description of local social conditions. If the first challenge facing this group was one of scaling environmental data to the local level, the second challenge they faced was how to bring into the same frame of analysis an understanding of social practice. As we will see, the methods available for approaching and analysing social data were heavily informed by the analytical presuppositions that informed the modelling of natural scientific data. This would eventually have ramifications for my own capacity to articulate the value of ethnographic knowledge in this kind of research. But to understand why a tension existed between the data-driven modelling of the climate scientists and the understanding of social analysis that I came to the project with, we need first to look in more detail at the way in which social data was treated and the analytical commitments this form of analysis entailed.

If on the one hand the Chester Zoo project was about better understanding the likely future of the climate of the area within which the zoo was located, the purpose of this understanding was to predict the impact of changes in weather on the zoo itself. This was analysed specifically in terms of the impact of weather on visits to the zoo and involved a parallel 'social' analysis of historical data on visitor numbers.

What was intriguing to me, however, was that this social analysis proceeded on exactly the same basis as the modelling of climate data. Visitor numbers were treated as a dataset that could be analysed in terms of their internal systemic properties. On this basis, probabilities of projected changes in visitor numbers as a result of climate change were able to be made.

This cast into stark light the epistemological commitments of mod-elling. Using modelling as a way of conducting social analysis estab-lished the requirement whereby facts about past visitor numbers became the basis upon which assumptions were made about people's motivations for going to the zoo. Take for example this description of the findings of the project:

> The zoo was closed for 41 days during the foot-and-mouth epidemic of 2001. This natural experiment allows us to make *inferences* about the robustness of *visitor intentions*. After the period of closure, there was a recovery back to usual visit levels. The equivalent of 28 days' worth of visits was permanently lost, suggesting there was only a slight compen-sating 'bounce-back' for visits missed during closure.
>
> *Perhaps* the decision to visit a zoo is planned within the family ahead of time. This is consistent with evidence below and suggests the timing of zoo visits *may be postponed* if the weather is inclement on the chosen day, for up to two weeks, but not for much longer. (Aylen et al. 2014: 185, emphasis added)

Later in the paper, the authors shed light on how this form of argu-mentation is constructed, when the analytical presuppositions of the argument are spelled out in detail. The authors state:

> Hypotheses are tested using a 'general to specific' approach to model evaluation advocated by Hendry (e.g. Davidson et al. 1978; Gilbert 1986). This involves estimation of a very general model for visit levels, encompassing a wide range of weather and visitor related explanatory variables, and testing successive restrictions on these variables using specification tests. (Aylen et al. 2014: 188).

On the basis of this form of analysis, the finding of the project was that visitors seemed to be affected by short-term decisions based on local weather, but also by 'habit' in a way that is consistent with long-run changes in use of leisure time in the UK. Surprisingly, despite the very rigorous use of statistical technique to stabilise the numbers, no evidence was provided for this striking concluding claim. To this anthropologist this form of argumentation seemed very bizarre. In spite of precision of analysis, the supporting evidence for social claims seemed to be absent.

We saw earlier how new data analytic techniques have opened up various analytical spaces within which ethnographic methods have been able to be re-enter – in both the traditional guise of small and thick data, and in new understandings of how ethnographic knowledge is constructed. What kind of opening then, does this attention to the practice of modelling offer to our understanding of the continued or transformed role of ethnographic knowledge? To explore this I now turn to consider the place of ethnographic knowledge in the climate adaptation project.

Ethnography in a sociotechnical analysis

As mentioned earlier, during the course of studying the climate adaptation project I was called upon to bring my ethnographic expertise to bear on the project. Whilst social modelling was justified as an approach in the Chester Zoo report, there was also a sense in the climate adaptation project as a whole that some of the researchers were not confident that they knew how to do social research 'properly'. In an initial conversation with Julia, one of the members of the project, she confided in me that they were finding it challenging to know how to incorporate the social side into their sociotechnical analysis. As I seemed to be a bona-fide qualitative social researcher also employed at the time at the same university as the climate adaptation project, Julia invited me to come and help out with one part of the project that aimed to understand the social dynamics of how people inhabited commercial buildings in the city.

My involvement in the project as an ethnographer provided a productive vantage point from which to experience the tension between different kinds of data and their role in knowledge production. It also gave me cause to reflect on how both modelling and ethnography might be done differently and ultimately led to the writing of this chapter. Incorporating ethnographic methods into the sociotechnical project was not straightforward, and caused me not only to defend my methods but also to reflect more deeply on the epistemological commitments of qualitative social science and the reasons why there is often a failure to engage with modelling practices directly in our work.

One example of this tension came in an early meeting over coffee with Alan, one of the lead academics on the project, about the possibility of doing some ethnographic research with the adaptation

project. Alan talked about how he was interested in finding out more
about the different perspectives of people in the project and what their
understanding was of what they were working on. Alan, who himself
was well-versed in the literature from science and technology studies
on sociotechnical systems, was keen for ethnographic research to be
included. He was aware of the tensions I am describing here, and
said that he wanted to better understand the conflicting conceptions
of what the project was trying to do as it tried bringing the social
and the technical together. Enthused by this support for ethnography
and a shared interest in the tensions between different pragmatic and
epistemological positions within the project, I responded by saying
that even these kinds of conversation like the one he and I were
having were ethnographically illuminating. Alan seemed somewhat
perturbed by this aside and stressed to me that, for these interviews
with his project members to 'count', they would have to be proper
interviews and not just chats over coffee. Leaning back in his chair
with an air of authority and in the spirit of support, Alan advised
me: 'you can't just go to the British Sociological Association and
present a paper on the basis of a chat over coffee!' I assured Alan that
I would do some proper, recorded, interviews, which I did, alongside more informal conversations, but this comment continued to
trouble me.

As things progressed, I found a similar attitude towards qualitative
research replayed in the day-to-day work of the adaptation project.
The week following my conversation with Alan, the question of the
status of interviews as data came up again in a meeting about the
research project on buildings and climate adaptation. As I mentioned
above, my involvement in the study of buildings was to provide a
kind of robustness to the qualitative side of social research, but what
I hadn't realised initially was that there was already a junior research
assistant, whom I will call Angus, working on the project who had a
background in qualitative research himself. During the course of one
of the group meetings it soon became apparent that Angus was held
in some suspicion by Julia, the person who had been charged with
bringing a 'social' perspective to the research and who had invited
me to participate. Whilst responsible for the 'social' side of the sociotechnical analysis, Julia's background was not in qualitative social
research but was rather in quantitative methods and social network
analysis.

In the meeting we discussed how to plan for a series of interviews with managers and employees of commercial buildings in one UK city. The aim of the interviews was to understand how people were living in and using the buildings and how they were affected by heating, cooling and lighting. I suggested that we ask people to show us around the buildings either as they were being interviewed or afterwards. Julia was sceptical about this suggestion as she couldn't see how we would be able to record the interview successfully if we were walking around. I said that it was possible to keep notes, or that one person could talk and the other person could record but Julia was still concerned as she couldn't see how it would tally with our list of interview questions. She said that for her it was essential that everything was recorded because, if not, how could we mitigate the inevitable corruption of the data that would come with our own practices of interpretation?

When I was talking to Angus later in the project, just before doing one of our recorded interviews with the building managers, he expressed frustration at the way social research was approached in the project by both Julia and Eleanor. He told me that, like Julia, Eleanor had also told him she was concerned with the influence of the researcher on the interviewee in these social interviews, and with the interpretative power of the researcher in social research, and she was worried that Angus was not using the right methodological tools to get the right kind of data. Like Julia, Eleanor was concerned to make sure that the truth of the data was not influenced by personal assumptions. As if to indicate the implicit influence of the ongoing questioning of the validity of social research as a method of data production, Angus told me that he had woken in a panic the night before after having dreamed that he had forgotten his voice recorder for the interview we were about to conduct!

At the time I saw this distinction between the physical and quantitative geographers and Angus and myself as simply a reproduction of the division between C.P. Snow's 'two cultures' of art and science or between quantitative and qualitative approaches. However the backdrop of a need to reconcile climate science and social science, and the evident difficulty of even explicit attempts to do this within a framework of a 'sociotechnical' analysis, opened up for me the question that I have been exploring in this chapter and that Snow's characterisation doesn't entail – what if the phenomena being studied (in this case climate change) might have the capacity to force us to reimagine these 'two cultures' and their epistemological relation? What, for example, might happen if qualitative principles could be deployed to engage quantitative data rather than just providing the foundation for critique? Might the mixing-up of the social and natural provoked by anthropogenic climate change be the prompt for a mixing-up of the methodological divisions that we can see still endures between positivist natural science and interpretivist social science? One way I suggest we might do this is by thinking more expansively about how to engage data analytically.

Baseless data and ethnographic claim-making

As we saw earlier, climate modelling provides us with a particular response to the problem of the shifting or absent baseline, one that I have argued might help us think not only about climate modelling but also about other contemporary (big) data practices. As we have seen, inconsistencies in found data are dealt with by being stabilised through statistical techniques in order to produce a *general set of conditions* out of which specific projections can be made. As I have illustrated, this work requires on the one hand verification of the model itself, and on the other validation in relation to empirical data. How then does this contrast with the way in which ethnography produces knowledge?

Ethnographers, like climate scientists, are used to working with data that is 'found, unstructured, messy, inconsistent and spotty' (Edwards 1999: 453). However, unlike the data scientists we encountered earlier, ethnographers do not require the establishment of a stable empirical baseline to make knowledge claims and do not deploy statistical techniques to create this baseline.[1] This is not to say that there is no definitional work that ethnographers do – they certainly work carefully to think about the boundaries of their 'field' and how these are established and to familiarise themselves with theoretical and empirical discussions that might help in their understanding of the social phenomena they encounter. None the less ethnographers use neither strictly experimental methods nor statistical models to produce a general baseline from which social change can be measured.

As a method that works without baselines or benchmarks as such, but that still manages to make robust claims, how then does ethnography manage to make truth claims? How does it produce descriptions and suggestions? What kinds of descriptions can it and can it not provide? And what can an understanding of the similarities and differences between ethnography and data science teach us about where the social and the technical might overlap in productive ways? To answer these questions I turn my attention around to focus upon the method of description that I have deployed in this piece so far to make my argument.

Ethnography is a descriptive method that aims to explain phenomena in terms of the relationships that constitute them (Strathern 1991). Unlike data science, the ethnographic method does not propose to describe general causal relationships but rather aims to describe the kinds of relations through which social phenomena get held together. If in climate modelling knowledge claims are made, as we have seen, by enacting a move from the general to the specific, I suggest that, in contrast, ethnography is a method of description and analysis that starts with the specific and builds up to the general relationally. For contemporary anthropology the general tends to emerge after the 'fact'. This is the reason why anthropologists spend so much effort rendering themselves naive in order to relearn the connections and terms of reference that are relevant to the setting which we study (Coffey 1999).

We can see this in the construction of this text. In my description I started from the detail of Climate Adaptation and Chester Zoo projects, folding in quotation, description, citation and argumentation so as to demonstrate an entangled web of relations that created not a baseline but rather what anthropologists have variously called 'webs of significance' (Geertz 1973), a meshwork (Ingold 2011) or a nexus of relations (Gell 1998). Ethnographic description aims to create an epistemological 'web' which 'catches' relations and holds them, provisionally, in the particular relational configuration in which they are found. The result of ethnographic approaches that start from the impossibility of knowing everything at play in a social or natural situation is to deploy a method of capturing a scattered complexity and casting it across a descriptive surface.

This is crucially important for understanding how ethnography, as opposed to future-oriented predictive models, operates as a method for making claims about social change. The way in which ethnography discerns change is not to measure deviation from a stabilised baseline or norm, but rather to pay attention to the repatterning of a relational nexus where the things held together *and* the way of describing that holding together are both open to the potential that they might be transformed. This is somewhat similar to Barad's concept of 'intractivity' where both the measure and the things measured are understood to change in the practice of measurement (Barad 2007). Change is not linear or causal then, but is rather produced both through the re-weaving of the web that ethnography spins that catches relations and holds them in tension, and, simultaneously, a change in the things being caught. Ethnography thus always entails forms of description that will change in relation to the things that are being described. What then, might the implications be for a reinvigorated relationship between data science and ethnography?

The problem with much of the discussion about the relationship between data and ethnography to date is that ethnography has been held up as a 'richer', or 'deeper' form of description that does not suffer from the reductions and abstractions of numerical data (Ingold 2007). In this framing, ethnography and data science are treated as if they operate on the same ontological plane, with ethnographic knowledge being deeper and better (from the perspective of qualitative social scientists) than descriptions based on numbers. Ethnographic descriptions are implied to be more 'real' than numerical abstractions. However if we take the relational understanding of ethnography that has been put forward here as our starting point then I suggest that we might find ways in which ethnography might be understood not as more or less real than numerical descriptions, but as operating with a different relational understanding of reality and validity. What differentiates ethnographic description from computer models of eco-systems is not the proximity of the story that is told to an actually existing reality but the relational assumptions upon which claims to truth are made. This framing, I suggest, allows us to move beyond an opposition between those disciplines that deal in quantification or number and those that deal in qualitative data or text. It opens the way instead to considering whether numbers such as those derived from sensors and measurement devices that inform data science and climate science might actually be able to be incorporated into an ethnographic style of truth-making. Ethnography is a form of description that entails different epistemological parameters from data science, but that does not, *a priori*, have to reject the incorporation of numerical data into this analysis. Because of its epistemological commitments, ethnography will never be a method that uses data to establish general conditions before the fact. But there are, I suggest, ways in which we might be able to better incorporate data into our analysis of socio-technical entanglements, and this is by treating numerical data as we treat ethnographic facts – as points on a web that we respin through description.

An excellent example of the kind of ethnographic approach to data that I am advocating here is a recent project led by the design agency Folder called Italian Limes (www.italianlimes.net). Italian Limes is a design project that has been trying to use data to think across the social/natural divide. The project has been looking at the entangle-ment between climate change and the nation state as it is instantiated in the expansion and contraction of a glacier on the border between Italy and France. Starting not with modelled nature on the one side, and described politics on the other, this project started instead with the data produced by sensors placed along the French/Italian border on the glacier itself. The glacier is treated here neither as objective fact nor a descriptive representation but rather as something more akin to what Keck and Lakoff (2013) have termed a 'sentinel device' – a material device through which patterns of relations which are neither singularly social nor natural can be detected. In the Italian Limes project, the researchers designed a set of sensors that could be placed along the national border as it crossed over the glacier. The sensors were designed to wirelessly communicate their location to an exhibition device that could, in real time, for individual exhibition visitors, redraw the border at that exact point of time. In this sin-gular moment of interaction, visitors to the exhibition were invited to participate in the relationship between geological formations, the nation state, industrial carbon emissions, climate change and weather; meanwhile an archive of data about the shifting glacier or border was also generated.

Whilst this project is not what we might usually call ethnographic, I suggest that it works precisely in the mode of moving from the specific to the general that I have suggested ethnographic research also deploys. Interestingly, the Italian Limes project, which came out of a design and social and political science discussions, has since caught the interest of glaciologists who are more used to using model-based techniques and devices for measuring glaciers and predicting their movements.[2] Here it seems the Italian Limes project has opened up communication with glaciologists not by adding the social to their natural science but by approaching the question of what glacial movement might be able to elicit about social and political processes through a reinvention of data collection and its circulation. They have ended up devising completely new instruments and techniques and as a result are producing new forms of data that offer the opportunity of a new kind of conversation between glaciologists, designers, artists and political scientists.

To return in conclusion to the Chester Zoo project, what kind of equivalent form of data ethnography might have been possible in this project? One of the things that is interesting about the Italian Limes project is that the social and the natural were not two spheres of measurement that had to be brought together as independent and dependent variables, but were both instantiated in the same data trace. This has prompted me to think what might be an equivalent data trace at Chester Zoo that would have the potential to index both weather and the use of the zoo.

As a conservation organisation, Chester Zoo has been very active in trying to think about ways in which it can improve its environmental sustainability, and one of the things that it has done is to invest in a number of energy technologies such as solar panels and intelligent ambient control systems that measure thermostatic activity and use this measurement to predict energy needs. Energy is a profoundly promising sentinel device for observing relations that cross-cut and collapse the social and the natural. For example, data on the levels of energy produced and used by the zoo has the potential to open up a much more expansive and deeper set of issues about the relationship between changing weather and the zoo than techniques that model weather on the one hand, and visits on the other. There is a short video on the Chester Zoo website that showcases its work to improve energy efficiency at the zoo. In it the Environment and Facilities Manager points to the importance for the Zoo of not just reducing energy, or maintaining visitor numbers, but also of maintaining a number of different climates for the animals that they look after – something that is in itself intrinsically tied to visitor numbers.[3] Attending to energy data, we might start to see that the zoo does not only exist in a climate ecosystem that has the potential to affect visitor behaviour, but is generative, in a very literal sense, of multiple weather systems – humid, dry, warm, cold, temperate etc. – that are necessary both for the survival of the different animals and the zoo as an institution with visitors who come to see the animals in these managed habitats.

Working ethnographically with energy data from the zoo would not just be about approaching data analytics from an ethnographic perspective but could also be about creating experiments that establish forms of measurement and data analysis that might offer the opportunity to transgress divides that are often re-established by current data methods. This entails thinking beyond the use of data for establishing a relationship between different categories or 'universes' of things (see Dumit in Chapter 11 below), and instead identifying those sentinel devices that could most effectively index the complex webs of relations between otherwise separated worlds. Here the issue then becomes not the validation of a closed model by setting it alongside richer, thicker or deeper empirical evidence but rather the unravelling of relations that treat data-in-itself as a form of empirical evidence that allows us to trace and navigate, rather than measure and compare, transformations of both social and natural phenomena.

Notes

1 There are notable exceptions to this: for example see Helmreich 1999 for discussion of one such case.
2 Marco Ferrari, pers. comm.
3 https://youtu.be/Fp0P1ik55xo [accessed 4 July 2017].

References

Anderson, Chris. 2008. 'The End of Theory: The Data Deluge Makes the Scientific Method Obsolete'. *Wired*, 23 June. www.wired.com/2008/06/pb-theory [accessed 1 December 2012].

Arnold, Hannah. 2013. 'Should Weather and Climate Prediction Models Be Deterministic or Stochastic? Meeting Report'. *Weather* 68(10): 264.

Aylen, Jonathan, Albertson, Kevin and Cavan, Gina. 2014. 'The Impact of Weather and Climate on Tourist Demand: The Case of Chester Zoo'. *Climatic Change* 127(2): 183–97.

Barad, Karen Michelle. 2007. *Meeting the Universe Halfway: Quantum Physics and the Entanglement of Matter and Meaning.* Durham, NC: Duke University Press.

Boyd, D. and Crawford, K. 2012. 'Critical Questions for Big Data: Provocations for a Cultural, Technological, and Scholarly Phenomenon'. *Information Communication & Society: Special Issue: A Decade in Internet Time: The Dynamics of the Internet and Society* 15(5): 662–79.

Burrell, Jenna. 2012. 'The Ethnographer's Complete Guide to Big Data: Small Data People in a Big Data World'. *Ethnography Matters*, 28 May. http://ethnographymatters.net/blog/2012/05/28/small-data-people-in-a-big-data-world [accessed 4 December 2017].

Coffey, Amanda. 1999. *The Ethnographic Self: Fieldwork and the Representation of Identity.* London and Thousand Oaks, CA: Sage Publications.

Davidson J.E.H., Hendry, D.F., Srba, F. and Yeo S. 1978. 'Econometric Modelling of the Aggregate Time-Series Relationship between Consumers' Expenditure and Income in the United Kingdom'. *Economic Journal* 88(352): 661–92. ww.jstor.org/stable/2231972 [accessed 4 March 2018].

Dayton, Paul K., Tegner, Mia J., Edwards, Peter B. and Riser, Kristin L. 1998. 'Sliding Baselines, Ghosts, and Reduced Expectations in Kelp Forest Communities'. *Measuring Ecological Trends* 8(2): 309–22.

Edwards, Paul N. 1999. 'Global Climate Science, Uncertainty and Politics: Data-Laden Models, Model-Laden Data'. *Science as Culture* 8(4): 437–72.

Edwards, Paul N. 2010. *A Vast Machine: Computer Models, Climate Data, and the Politics Of Global Warming.* Cambridge, MA: MIT Press.

Fortun, Kim. 2004. 'Environmental Information Systems as Appropriate Technology'. *Design Issues* 20(3): 54–65.

Gabrys, J. 2007. 'Automatic Sensation: Environmental Sensors in the Digital City'. *The Senses and Society* 2(2): 189–200.

Gabrys, J. 2014. 'Programming Environments: Environmentality and Citizen Sensing in the Smart City'. *Environment and Planning D* 32(1): 30–48.

Geertz, Clifford. 1973. *The Interpretation of Cultures: Selected Essays.* New York: Basic Books.

Gell, Alfred. 1998. *Art and Agency: Towards a New Anthropological Theory.* Oxford: Clarendon.

Guy, Simon and Shove, Elizabeth. 2000. *The Sociology of Energy, Buildings and the Environment: Constructing Knowledge, Designing Practice.* London: Routledge.

Haraway, Donna Jeanne. 2008. *When Species Meet.* Bristol and Minneapolis, MN: University of Minnesota Press.

Hebbert, Michael and Jankovic, Vladimir. 2013. 'Cities and Climate Change: The Precedents and Why They Matter'. *Urban Studies* 50(7): 1332–47.

Hebbert, Michael, Jankovic, Vladimir and Webb, Brian. 2011. *City Weathers: Meteorology and Urban Design 1950–2010*. Manchester: Manchester Architecture Research Centre.

Helmreich, S. 1999. 'Digitizing "Development": Balinese Water Temples, Complexity and the Politics of Simulation'. *Critique of Anthropology* 19(3): 249–65.

Ingold, Tim. 2007. *Lines: A Brief History*. London: Routledge.

Ingold, Tim. 2011. *Being Alive: Essays on Movement, Knowledge and Description*. London: Routledge.

Jankovic, Vladimir and Hebbert, Michael. 2012. 'Hidden Climate Change – Urban Meteorology and the Scales of Real Weather'. *Climatic Change* 113(1): 23–33.

Keck, Frédéric and Lakoff, Andrew. 2013. 'Preface: Sentinel Devices', *Limn* 3. http://limn.it/a-dearth-of-numbers-the-actuary-and-the-sentinel-in-global-public-health [accessed 29 November 2017].

Kockelman, Paul. 2013. 'The Anthropology of an Equation. Sieves, Spam Filters, Agentive Algorithms, and Ontologies of Transformation'. *Hau* 3(3): 33–61.

Latour, Bruno. 2007. 'The Recall of Modernity: Anthropological Approaches'. *Cultural Studies Review* 13(1): 11–30.

Latour, Bruno. 2010. 'Tarde's Idea of Quantification'. In *The Social after Gabriel Tarde: Debates and Assessments*. Edited by Matei Candea. London: Routledge, 145-62.

Mackenzie, Adrian, McNally, Ruth, Mills, Richard and Sharples, Stuart. 2016. 'Post-Archival Genomics and the Bulk Logistics of DNA Sequences'. *BioSocieties* 11(1): 82–105.

McHarg, Ian L. 1971. *Design with Nature*. Garden City, NY: Published for the American Museum of Natural History by Doubleday/Natural History Press.

Nakicenovic, Nebojsa, Alcamo, Joseph, Grubler, A., Riahi, K., Roehrl, R.A., Rogner, H.-H. and Victor, N. 2000. *Special Report on Emissions Scenarios (SRES), a Special Report of Working Group III of the Intergovernmental Panel on Climate Change*. Cambridge: Cambridge University Press.

Ørberg, Rikke. 2014. 'Why Shifting Baseline Impacts Big Data Analysis'. SAS Guest Blog. https://blogs.sas.com/content/hiddeninsights/2014/03/17/guest-blog-why-shifting-baseline-impacts-big-data-analysis/ [last accessed 21 February 2018].

Oreskes, Naomi, Shrader-Frechette, Kristin and Belitz, Kenneth. 1994. 'Verification, Validation, and Confirmation of Numerical Models in the Earth'. *Science* 263(5147): 641–6.

Pauly, Daniel. 1995. 'Anecdotes and the Shifting Baseline Syndrome of Fisheries'. *Trends in Ecology and Evolution* 10(10): 430.

Savage, M. and Burrows, R.. 2007. 'The Coming Crisis of Empirical Sociology'. *Sociology* 41(5): 885–99.

Seaver, Nick. 2015. 'The Nice Thing About Context Is that Everyone Has
It'. *Media, Culture & Society* 37(7): 1101–9.

Strathern, Marilyn. 1991. *Partial Connections*. Savage, MD: Rowman & Littlefield.

Wang, Tricia. 2013. 'Big Data Needs Thick Data'. *Ethnography Matters*,
13 May. http://ethnographymatters.net/blog/2013/05/13/big-data-needs-
thick-data [accessed 29 November 2017].

Wilf, Eitan. 2013. 'Toward an Anthropology of Computer-Mediated, Algorithmic Forms of Sociality'. *Current Anthropology* 54(6): 716–39.

7

Operative ethnographies and large numbers

Adrian Mackenzie

I report here on a deliberately naive attempt to re-count a single number: approximately 29 million code repositories on Github at a particular point in time (late 2015). The number appeared in a research project primarily focused largely on transformations in the social life of coding, programming and software development amidst apps, clouds, virtualisation and the troubled life of code commons. In exploring 'how people build software' (Github 2015), the project explicitly sought to experiment with data-intensive methods, infrastructures and tools – cloud computing services such as Google Compute, data analytic and visualisation tools such as R, Python and IPython notebooks, large data stores such as BigQuery, streaming data from social media platform APIs (Application Programmer Interfaces), predictive models, especially in the form of machine-learning classifiers (support vector machines, Naive Bayes classifiers, random forests) – in making sense of what happens on Github en masse. Somewhat recursively (although I don't want to make too much of this recursion, since I do not think it amounts to a recursive public (Kelty 2008)), Github happens to be the *platform* that hosts the code development of many big data tools and infrastructures (hadoop, tensorflow, ipython, flow, d3.js, spark etc.). It also directly hosts all of the text, code, figures, intermediate results and configuration information for the research project I describe, including this chapter in various operational and executable forms (Metacommunities 2016a).

The approximate number 29 million will in this chapter serve as a synecdoche for big data in several ways. The number, a count of all the repositories on Github in late 2015, is a small part standing in for the whole. On the one hand, Github as a platform used by millions of people is a typical setting open to, affected by and shaped by big data practices. On the other hand, what happens on Github – coding, software development, configuration, modification and transformation of information infrastructures – shapes big data practices. Crucially, since open or publicly visible code repositories are shadowed by largely invisible private repositories that yield revenue for Github as a San Francisco-based business, it is inherently difficult to count all the repositories. 'All' here inevitably means 'some', but maybe that is always a problem for big data.

A focus limited to one big number (29 million), particularly one that presents itself as the total of all repositories, is inevitably narrow. The story of encounters with this single number might, however, evoke and exemplify the appeal, frustrations, hopes and material configurations associated with contemporary data practices that envision working with 'all the data' (Mayer-Schönberger and Cukier 2013). This number, one of a series of similar numbers, exists and exerts effects in different ways on counting and accounting. I'm interested in its composition, its instability, the 'stories,' imaginings and materialisations it authorises, and its practically problematic relation to big data infrastructures.

What kinds of engagement can we have with such numbers today amidst perhaps their deep transformation and re-materialisation in technologies?[1] Given so much computational counting, so many efforts to count all manner of things (species, clicks, stars, likes, cells and bitcoin transactions), and indeed strong injunctions to tell stories about such numbers, what can social researchers do? One key difficulty in developing an ethnographic sensibility around such numbers resides in the many detours, variations and differences they embody, not least for the social researcher who finds himself or herself trying to re-count them or account for them. These variations, shadings and shifting in numbers might be seen as the everyday frictions of ethnographic writing in its reflexive analytic mode, but they also spawn from the configured, infrastructural and operational complexity of ethnography as an experimental situated practice. As George Marcus suggests, 'experiment today is thus less about writing strategies and more about creating forms that concentrate and make accessible the intermediate, sometimes staged, sometimes serendipitous occasions of distinctively anthropological thinking and concept work' (Marcus 2014: 400). The chapter documents and practically re-enacts a series of operational queries – both in the technical sense of a statement executed by a database and in the sense of a question posed to a given state of affairs – concerned with large numbers and technical ensembles.

While I'm very drawn to attempts to count things and to weave counts into ethnographic writing, during this project I often wondered about how to count things whilst paying attention to their composition. Marcus enjoins ethnographers to 'make forms of processes' (Marcus 2014: 401). The problem is that, seen in a rather literal-minded way, counting is a process that very easily renders the form of a number. An ethnographic sensibility around numbers at a very minimum entails a double counting or re-counting. In the setting I describe (software development, distributed information and knowledge infrastructures), numbers and counts are sites of entanglement between device-specific materialities and collective imaginaries of order, totality, rank, inclusion, boundary and power. This double sense of numbers as both a calculatively ordered cutting-framing-summing-up form and as materially specific figuring of differences could well be understood in terms of what Lucy Suchman describes as a 'configuration':

> The device of *configuration* has two broad uses. First, as an aid to delineating the composition and bounds of an object of analysis, in part through the acknowledgment that doing so is integral not only to the study of technologies, but to their very existence as objects. And second, in drawing our analytic attention to the ways in which technologies materialize cultural imaginaries, just as imaginaries narrate the significance of technological artefacts. Configuration in this sense is a device for studying technologies with particular attention to the imaginaries and materialities that they *join together*, an orientation that resonates as well with the term's common usages to refer to the conjoining of diverse elements in practices of systems design and engineering. (Suchman 2012: 48)

While Suchman's examples of configuration come from software systems, I'm suggesting that a single number – 29 million repositories on Github – could be re-counted as a configuration. The argument is that even the listing, enumerating and counting of things in a single number can be seen as a configuration. Practically, a configured number, if such a curly term is permitted, will need to be counted in ways that hold together the two aspects Suchman highlights. A configured number might be integral to the existence of the 'technology', in this case the 'social coding' platform Github. At the same time, that number would, in its counting, call our attention to what is being materialised in terms of an imaginary and all that entails.[2]

Re-counting a capital number on a platform

On Github, two numbers have cardinal and indeed capital importance: the number of people using the platform, and the number of different code repositories stored there. I deal in this chapter only with the things – the repositories – not the people. The counting I undertake will focus on problems of copying, duplicating, and imitation of things – repositories – that render large numbers a moving substrate.

Software developers (coders, hackers, geeks, software engineers, software architectures, programmers, scientists etc.) turn to Github to find, deposit, discuss, collaborate, publish and tinker with code. Across a gamut of practices, rituals, organisational forms and inventions, they rely on an underlying set of protocols, tools and workflows that focus on the problem of versions and versioning of code called *git* (Straube 2016). Github, started in in 2007, epitomises and has indeed been central to – as the suffix 'hub' suggests – a mass of configurational events associated with the development of big data practices in association with large technical ensembles. Like many social media platforms, Github has grown tremendously in the last ten years to around 55 million software projects (March 2017; the current total of the 29 million that I focus on). Its growth flows from a variety of processes that are difficult to summarise or classify partly because the actors, topics or domains of coding are diverse, and partly because much of what flows through Github is both technically and socially 'innovative' in the sense in which Bruno Latour uses the term: '"innovative" means that we do not know the number of actors involved in advance' (Latour 1996: 72). (Again, a problem of counting appears here, albeit only in the limited form of 'not knowing in advance'.)

Given this massive confluence of coding, configuring, copying, collaborating and much playing around with repositories in some-times quixotic fashion (as we will see, many repositories are highly transient, and very many have a spam-like quality), Github, like many contemporary assemblages, seeks to describe itself through large numbers such as '55 million projects'. We might call them 'capital numbers' since they serve a vital function in attracting invest-ment (Github, with a market value of $2 billion, has received several hundred million dollars in venture capture (Gage 2015)), imbuing the platform with hub-like importance in contemporary techno-economies (see for instance, Quentin Hardy's writing about Github and 'open everything' (Hardy 2012)). They also, as I will suggest, directly lend weight to the injunction to 'tell stories with the [big] data'. Capital numbers in their sometimes daily changes and updates attest to an investment in being innovative and in open-ended pro-cesses of growth.

As Suchman's concept of a configuration suggests, capital numbers combine with cultural imaginaries of work, value, power and tech-nology in manifold ways. In June 2014, the Github 'about' page showed a photo of a women working in an urban office location, with lights and professional camera focused on her work. It described '6.1 million people collaborating right now across 13.2 million reposi-tories ... building amazing things together' (Github 2014). In late November 2015, the same page had a slightly more functional descrip-tion, and the image seems to be of a crowded press conference in China:

GitHub is how people build software. With a community of more than 12 million people, developers can discover, use, and contribute to over 29 million projects using a powerful collaborative development workflow. (Github 2015).

The numbers change over time alongside the composition of the actors involved (women coding and working at Github, a sore point for the company as a co-founder was involved in sexual harassment complaints; Chinese developers using Github, but also political activ-ists, leading to a denial of service attack on the Github, allegedly by the Chinese government). But the mundane yet sublime scale of these numbers (a 'community' of 12 million people? 29 million software repositories?) certainly forms part of an ongoing cultural, organisa-tional and financial capitalisation.

The litany of sense-making: enumerating the aggregate through events

In 2013, a year in which the injunction to do things with data was impacting social science research funders as well as many people in media, commerce, industry and government, my aggressively data-analytic ambition with respect to Github was to re-count the capital numbers – people and repositories – in some way. I planned to use data-analytic methods and infrastructures and code in all their stacked sophistication to count software projects on Github. In re-counting them, I imagined that I would capture something of their composition in all its heterogeneity and conformity, and show how their scale was an effect of specific dynamics of imitation. I felt disposed to contest the easy rhetorical slippages between 'code', 'open' and 'good'. The data-analytic practice would be both political and culturally worth-while since capital numbers are common in the capitalisation of social media platforms. It would be ethnographically recursive since my writing would be mixed with code in an experimental writing prac-tice derives from the sites – repositories – of the research.

Coding today takes place in increasingly complex associative infra-structures. How could I actually count software projects or people? Like many data scientists and digital sociologists, I turned to data published through the Github API (Application Programmer Inter-face). APIs were created not as a data resource for social scientists but for software developers working in convergence cultures (Jenkins 2004) where it is standard practice to connect different platforms, devices, and sites using code. APIs have great practical significance (Bucher 2013). In Github's case, data published through the API derives from acts of writing and reading code (although not only code – an extraordinary variety of other documents, texts, images, maps and other forms of data can be found on the platform). Actions are logged as developers write code and move that code in and out of repositories using the *git* version control system (Git 2014). Github seeks to figure coding as a social network practice based on a hub.

By common convention much API data from social media sites has an 'event' structure that links named actors and named entities to specific infrastructural locations (usually coded as a URL) at a par-ticular time (the 'timestamp'). While not all big data has this timestamp–actor–location–links texture, it is common enough to stand in as typical of the data that big data infrastructures and practices encounter. As Noortje Marres has persuasively argued, these data formats are not 'neutral' or in any way particularly good for social research, since they tend to pre-structure the kinds of engagement that one might have with the data (Marres 2012). Work needs to be done with and against the data format. A slightly recursive instance of this API-effect can be seen in event data for the project:

```
library(curl)
library(jsonlite)
con2 =
curl('https://api.github.com/repos/metacommunities/
    metacommunities/languages')
lang = fromJSON(readLines(con2), flatten=TRUE)
lang
## $'Jupyter Notebook'
## [1] 5316912
##
## $Python
## [1] 362165
##
## $TeX
## [1] 206395
##
## $R
## [1] 176827
##
## $Scala
## [1] 27835
##
## $Shell
## [1] 23630
##
## $JavaScript
## [1] 16699
##
## $'GCC Machine Description'
## [1] 15451
##
```

```
con3 =
curl('https://api.github.com/repos/metacommunities/
  metacommunities/contributors')
people = fromJSON(readLines(con3), flatten=TRUE)
people
## login id
## 1 rian39 526523
## 2 Milllss 4489313
## 3 rian32 885027
## 4 MatthewFuller 4973736
## 5 Goffinger 4973562
##      followers_url
## 1 https://api.github.com/users/rian39/followers
## 2 https://api.github.com/users/Milllss/followers
## 3 https://api.github.com/users/rian32/followers
## 4 https://api.github.com/users/MatthewFuller/followers
## 5 https://api.github.com/users/Goffinger/followers
##         following_url
##         repos_url
## 1 https://api.github.com/users/rian39/repos
## 2 https://api.github.com/users/Milllss/repos
## 3 https://api.github.com/users/rian32/repos
## 4 https://api.github.com/users/MatthewFuller/repos
## 5 https://api.github.com/users/Goffinger/repos

con4 = curl('https://api.github.com/repos/metacommunities/
  metacommunities/branches')
branches = fromJSON(readLines(con4), flatten=TRUE)
nrow(branches)
## [1] 30
```

In our/my case – I'm not sure how to report on the work I did with others in this project – I wanted to write code to gather, aggregate, clean, explore, visualise and model what has happening in repositories on Github. Code written for the research project itself exemplifies typical variations in action: languages and versions ('branches') abound.[3] The code vignette shown above summarises some of this (I return to the configurative events behind this summary below). APIs encourage code-dependent and automated engagement. They typically afford live or real-time observation of online processes. They also invite completionist ambitions: gathering all the data, all the events streaming in and out of the Github platform become imaginable and somewhat viable via APIs. The code vignette shown below, for instance, gathers the last few hundred events on the Github timeline, and is a typical starting point.

```
library(curl)
req = curl_fetch_memory('https://api.github.com/events')
print(rawToChar(req$content[1:1100]))
## [1] "[\n {\n \"id\": \"5774962987\",\n \"type\":
    \"IssueCommentEvent\",\n \"actor\": {\n \"id\": 719827,\n
    \"login\": \"fmueller\",\n \"display_login\": \"fmueller\",\n
    \"gravatar_id\": \"\",\n \"url\": \"https://api.github.com/users/
    fmueller\",\n \"avatar_url\": \"https://
    avatars.githubusercontent.com/u/719827?\"\n },\n \"repo\":
    {\n \"id\": 76853145,\n \"name\": \"zalando-incubator/zally\",\n
    \"url\": \"https://api.github.com/repos/zalando-incubator/zally\"\n
    },\n \"payload\": {\n \"action\": \"created\",\n \"issue\": {\n
    \"url\": \"https://api.github.com/repos/zalando-incubator/zally/
    issues/309\",\n \"repository_url\": \"https://api.github.com/repos/
    zalando-incubator/zally\",\n \"labels_url\": \"https://api.github.
    com/repos/zalando-incubator/zally/issues/309/labels{/name}\",\n
    \"comments_url\": \"https://api.github.com/repos/zalando-
    incubator/zally/issues/309/comments\",\n \"events_url\":
    \"https://api.github.com/repos/zalando-incubator/zally/issues/309/
    events\",\n \"html_url\": \"https://github.com/zalando-incubator/
    zally/pull/309\",\n \"id\": 224909677,\n "
```

The two lines of *R* code in the vignette (or *Gist*, as it would be called on Github) fetch the latest public – that is, visible to anyone – events from the API, and print them. (Private events have exactly the same format, but are available only through the API to authorised requests.) Rather than displaying them, big data practice would feed them all into some datastore awaiting further analysis.

What would it mean to count repositories using formatted, API data? The JSON (JavaScript Object Notation format; a format commonly used for social media data) records conjoin elements. The relatively simple PushEvent on Github shown in the data extract above documents how an *actor* calling themselves *6ijr* adds a file into a repository called *tbd-ace*. Note that the event also has various attributes

– it is a *public* event, it has a 'payload' (often much more complicated than simply *create README.md*) – and includes various indexical references or *ids* that link the event to other groups of people, organisations, repositories and images (*gravatar_id*). The intricate syntax of this data – many brackets, inverted commas, colons, commas – attests to a social configuration that orders actors, actions, places and times in discrete events in time. The list of components in the event data – actor, organisation, repository, payload gravatar, etc. – attests to the potential for the specific configuration of elements around a given repository to undergo rearrangements. New actors might be added; relations might appear between entities; the location of entities might shift, and forms of association ('organisations') might subsume or grow out of or around all of this. In short, each event in the timeline API suggests another small reconfiguration in the totality of elements comprising Github.

Imbuing numbers with importance

The ethnographic ambition to count or re-count capital numbers in the interests of understanding complex operational environments is not a lone wolf activity. Strikingly often, ethnographic research encounters parallel or similar ambitions associated with different actors. When our project started in 2012, we were clearly not the only people interested in using API data to understand the massive stream of event data converging on Github. A dataset purporting to contain the whole public event timeline of Github appeared in mid-2012. Ilya Grigorik, a 'Web Performance Engineer' at Google, launched a Github repository *igrigorik/githubarchive* linked to a website GithubArchive.org dedicated to archiving all the Github API public event data – the so-called 'timeline' – in one place (Grigorik 2012). Grigorik, or igrigorik, not only published all the data as hourly packages in a cloud-based data store but also copied that data to Google's newly launched cloud computing data analysis platform, *Google-BigQuery*. The Github timeline data was listed, along with all the words in Shakespeare and all the US birth name records, as one of three dataset exemplars that people could use to learn about Google BigQuery (Google 2016). Like the data on GithubArchive itself, the Google BigQuery copy of the Github public timeline data was updated hourly. Reaching back to 2011, it logs around four hundred million public events.[4]

The archiving, copying and transformation of Github event data into big data-ready format drew the attention of many people. The data was publicised through several 'Github Data Challenges' (2012–14). Working in different ways using data-analytic techniques and data visualisations, people re-counted events on the Github time-line in order to tell different 'stories' about Github's millions of repositories and people. These stories include many different configurations. 'Data challenges', hackathons and the like presented difficulties for my project of recounting the Github repositories. In some ways, the entries and projects that respond to the publication of the data threaten to supplant or render redundant the efforts of social researchers. They 'socialise' big data in multiple ways, albeit often retaining if not reinforcing aspects of its capitalisation.

For instance, the 'OpenSource Report Card' (http://osrc.dfm.io/) or dfm/osrc by Dan Foreman-Mackay (Foreman-Mackay 2014) is a prize-winning use of the timeline data (see Figure 7.1). It ingests all the data from the Githubarchive, counting what developers do, when

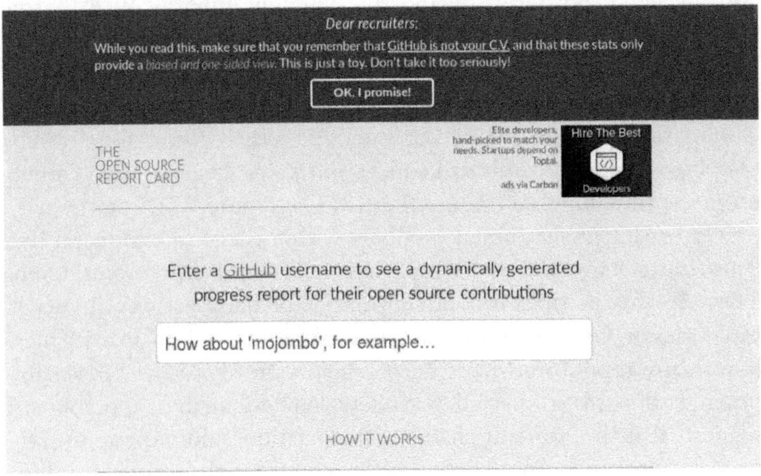

Figure 7.1 The Open Source report card

they do it and using what programming languages. With this data stored, it then builds a predictive model that allows it both to profile a given Github user in terms of the mixture of programming language they use and to predict whom that Github user might be similar to. Here the mass of events in the Github timeline are brought to bear on finding similarities between people, producing numbers and score to suggest similarities in coding work. Similarly, in response to the Github Data Challenge in 2012, people looked in the timeline data for feelings or 'sentiments' associated with different programming languages. Feelings associated with coding were mined by counting emotional words present in comments accompanying the Github events (Gómez 2012). The presence of words in these messages can be cross-linked with programming languages in order to profile how different programming languages elicit different emotional reactions.

Capital numbers were also *nationalised* or regionalised. People mapped coders and repositories by geographic location. The mapping of Github contributions by location performed by David Fischer (http://davidfischer.github.io/gdc2/#languages/All) is typical in that it too counts events, but this time puts the emphasis on the geography of the 'top' repositories, coders and their programming languages. As David Fischer puts it, 'this data set contains contributions to the top 200 GitHub repositories during the first four months of 2013 and plots the location based on what the contributor provided' (Fischer 2013).

Logistic narratives can be derived from data streams. People made live dashboards, a characteristic data-analytic visual form, for Github. Octoboard (http://octoboard.com/) animates changes on Github using the timeline data (Roussell 2015) (see Figure 7.2). Logistic narratives ornament the capital numbers with a range of peripheral live enumerations that point to the productive flow of actions on Github. They do this in the form of summaries of daily activity in major categories on Github – how many new repositories, how many issues, how many repositories have been 'open sourced' today. Like many other dashboards associated with social media analytics, octoboard suggests that the constant change in associations and projects in software development can no longer be known through leisurely rhythms of analysis, but is increasingly framed as a problem realtime, operational awareness of the flow of social actions.

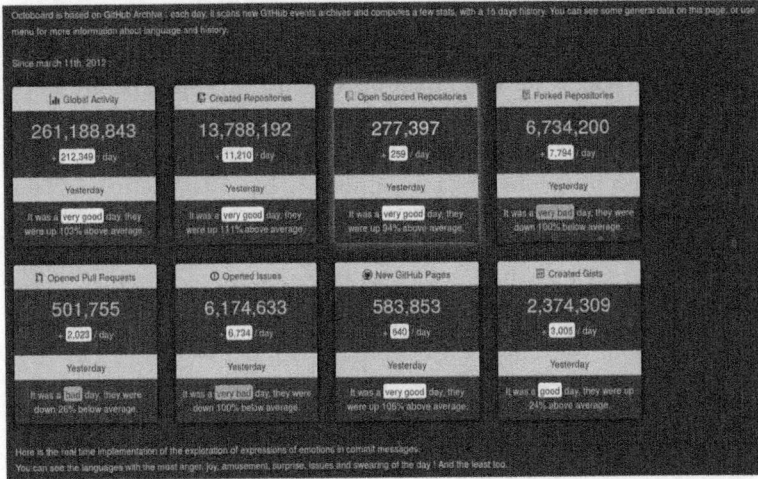

Figure 7.2 Octoboard: a Github dashboard

Looking slightly more widely, the Github timeline data has quickly become a favourite training tool for data mining textbooks that configure and convey the calculative agencies characteristic of capital numbers. In *Mining the Social Web: Data Mining Facebook, Twitter, LinkedIn, Google+, GitHub, and More*, Matthew Russell makes use of the Github timeline to demonstrate ways of using social network analysis to highlight the important nodes and links between repositories and users (Russell 2013). Finally and not least for my own projects, academic researchers in computer science and certain parts of management science, GithubArchive and the BigQuery publication of Github have been a boon because they permit relatively easy study technologically and economically important practices of software development. Academic researchers in fields such as software engineering do social network analysis in order to gauge productivity, reuse, efficiency and other engineering and management concerns (Thung et al. 2013). Like the many Github-hosted projects discussed above, they analyse sentiment (Guzman et al. 2014), collaboration and productivity (Dabbish et al. 2012) and geography (Takhteyev and Hilts 2010).

All of these re-countings enliven, animate, reactivate, localise and qualify the capital numbers. They configure the numbers in terms of work, geography, liveness and further accumulation by summing them up in different ways (realtime status updates and dashboards, networks of associations, geographies of work and affect) commonly found in contemporary data economies and as the outcome of big data practice. Many of the dashboards, maps, sentiment analyses and predictive recommendations are common in big data practice, and the fact that people using Github should so readily analyse Github itself using big data infrastructures such as GoogleBigQuery and other analytic devices is hardly surprising. Coders and software developers are, after all, key workers in the ongoing transformation of systems of controls and configuration associated with big data.

Acts of imagined accumulation

Given this vortex of work around the Github data, which I interpret both as symptomatic of big data practices and as a set of parallel 'storyfications' of the 'datafication' of Github, where would an ethnographic sensibility intervene? George Marcus in his account of prototyping ethnographic experimentation emphasises the ongoing relevance of 'images of moving through natural settings of social action' (Marcus 2014: 3). Is there any place or point at which analysis might ethnographically engage with the code-infrastructure-oriented practices associated with flows of data? Given my – and indeed 'our', since this project was a team effort, including statisticians and social theorists – propensity or somewhat unwitting interpellation as a white, middle-class, middle-age, relatively technically over-skilled male social researcher long drawn into information infrastructural transformations, the viable forms of ethnographic attentiveness to differences, slippages, experiential ambivalences and ambiguities were not obvious. Could writing queries for GoogleBigQuery GithubArchive dataset, developing data analytic and visualising code in languages such as R and python, programming languages commonly used in the big data practices, actively prototype forms that did not simply conform to the implicit and pervasive injunction to 'tell stories with data'?

In this respect, the elementary character of the repository count was usefully grounding. Technically, the number is relatively easy to approximate in the GithubArchive data. A simply GoogleBigQuery produces the number in roughly 2.0 secs having processed around 40Gb of repository URLs:

```
library(bigrquery)
query1 = "SELECT count(distinct(repo.url))
FROM
[githubarchive:year.2011],
[githubarchive:year.2012],
[githubarchive:year.2013],
[githubarchive:year.2014],
[githubarchive:year.2015]"
repo_count = query_exec('metacommunities', query = query1)
## Auto-refreshing stale OAuth token.
```

The result: 31490949 repositories.

Could we re-count such capital numbers in order both to further highlight their dynamic composition through flows of association and to highlight some of the highly reactive, imaginary boundary work they might do as they materialise imaginaries of totality, globality or infrastructural control? Could configurative numbers in both their compositional and imaginary-materialising multiplicity be counted? Whilst there is much configurational work involved even in beginning to count things heterogeneously on an infrastructural scale, I found myself drawn by the transience of configurations and their imitative composition. Both concerns – transience and imitation – are not highlighted in any of the other re-counts of the GithubArchive data. They only became salient to me amidst many other failures to find any interesting story, stable signal or statistical regularity in the Github timeline data.[5]

When we count people or things (such as software projects), the working assumption is that they have some duration and substantial presence. This assumption, however, does not hold very true at the scale of large data streams, where, like subatomic particles in a collision, people and things rapidly and unpredictably flash in and out of existence. Transience and instability are artefacts of the data stream. Frustrated by our seeming inability to find anything in the GithubArchive data apart from the obvious importance of well-known software projects such as linux or android, we were forced to accept transience and ephemeral visibility as a common mode of existence

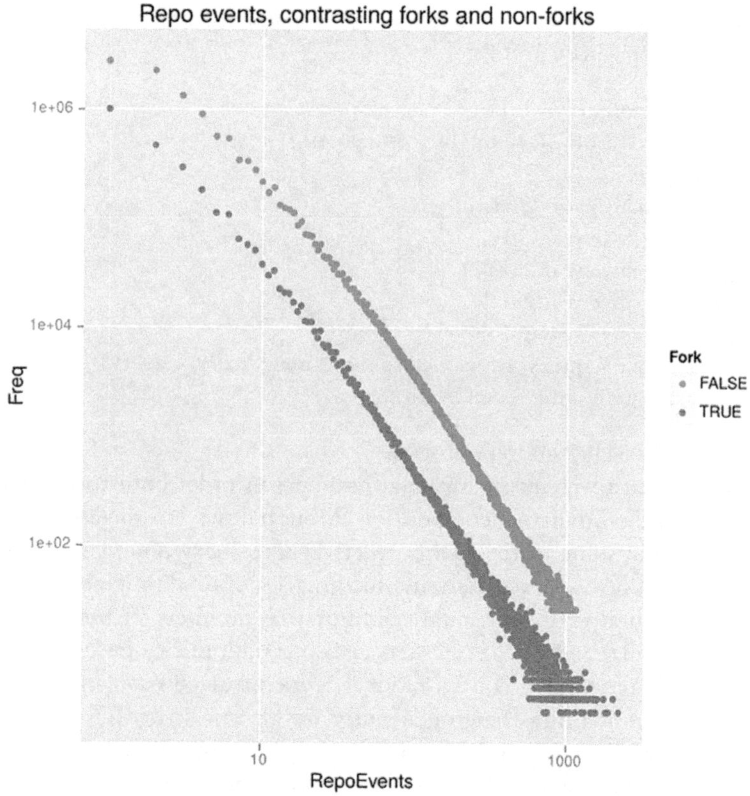

Figure 7.3   Events associated with repositories

on Github. The transient visibility of people and things in the data takes many forms. The vast majority of repositories on Github are very short-lived. They attract one or two events. A great proportion of events in the timeline data were absorbed into ephemeral repositories (if that is not too great a contradiction in terms). Millions of repositories blink into visibility on the timeline for a brief period before falling back into obscurity. Yet they survive in the capital number. Figure 7.3 encapsulates this imitative flux. On the left side, millions of repositories receive fewer than five events during the 18 months. On the right, fewer than fifty repositories receive more than a thousand events. A similar pattern appears in the other capital number: while some 'people' emit many thousands of events, others trigger only a few. Already, then, the capital number of repositories on Github takes on a different composition when viewed from the perspective of duration.

The massive asymmetry between the relatively few long-duration repositories and the vast mass of transient, abandoned repositories is definitely not another corroboration of 'the long-tail' distributions that social media exponents such as Clay Shirky and Chris Anderson began discussing more than a decade ago and that may have had a large part to play in many of the intensely individualising tendencies of big data analytics, targeted advertising, predictive feeds and recommendations. (For instance, one reason that Amazon.com stocks so many obscure products is that the long tail of sales of these items is potentially more important than the sales of a smaller number of best-sellers (Brynjolfsson et al. 2006; Anderson 2009).) Rather than the long tail of coding, a scale-free network of code-hubs on Github (itself a hub in networks of code-related infrastructure), or even simply waste, noise or something to be discarded, we might trace the working of associative processes through highly skewed distribution of events.

I can give only a brief indication of some prototyping experiments. For instance, counting just the unique names of repositories in the timeline data, counting how often and when they appear as event in the data stream begins to suggest something about the composition of the capital number of repositories. Almost two-thirds of the repositories in Github inject only one or two events into the timeline data stream ever. This means that twenty million of the thirty million repositories are just flashes in the timeline data appearing as one or two events.

What are these events? The event of creating a named repository is primary, followed by the event of pushing (putting something into a repository – a 'commit'), and then act of copying ('forking') another repository. People 'fork' other repositories frequently. If we just count the event of creating a repository by copying or forking it, more than half all repositories are copies of existing repositories ($1.665343710^{\{7\}}$). If every ForkEvent on Github creates a new repository, more than half of the repositories are direct copies. Acts of copying occur on many scales and at various levels of infrastructural and associative complexity. This copying is vital to the 'sharing' practice of Github coding. Of the several hundred million events in the timeline dataset, approximately 151891374 or 31 per cent of all events in the Github

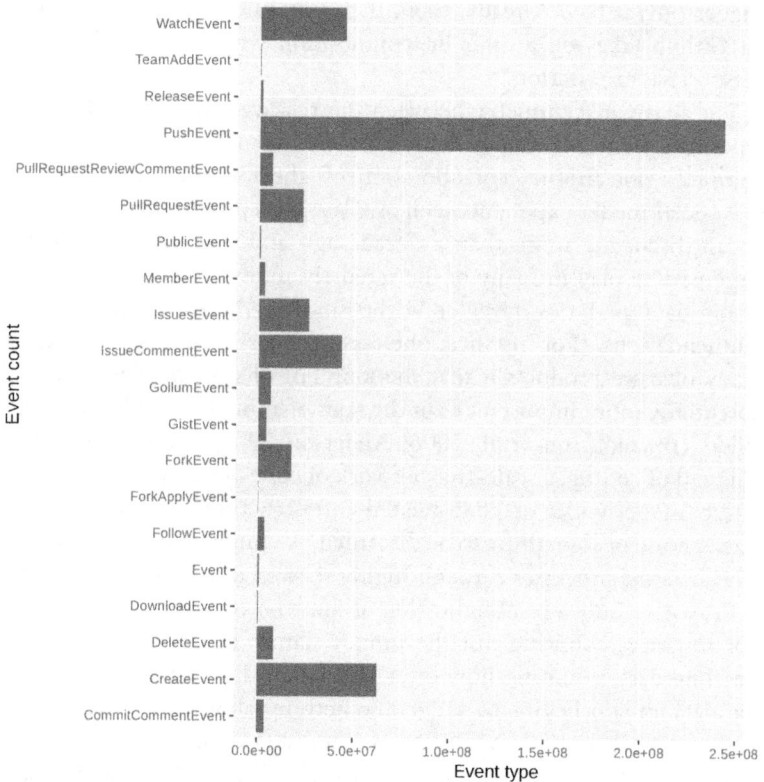

Figure 7.4 Event counts on Github 2011–2015

timeline data arise from copying, watching, commenting on or otherwise observing other repositories. (See the WatchEvent, ForkEvent,
PullRequestEvent,and IssueEvent counts in Figure 7.4.)

The growth of associative imitation

```
##
## Attaching package: 'readr'

Retrieving data: 2.1s
Retrieving data: 4.0s
Retrieving data: 5.9s
Retrieving data: 7.8s
```

```
Retrieving data: 9.7s
Retrieving data: 12.2s
Retrieving data: 14.1s
Retrieving data: 15.7s
# 160 lines removed
Retrieving data: 161.9s
Retrieving data: 165.4s
Retrieving data: 170.3s
Retrieving data: 174.2s
Retrieving data: 178.2s
```

While it is hard to grasp the texture of imitative processes in event data, they figure deeply in the composition of the capital numbers. We can observe some localised aspects of propagation of imitation by going beyond the formatted data of the API or GithubArchive data. Much social media platform data relies heavily on unique names (hence, for instance, Facebook's insistence that every user has a single unique identity). Yet the associative play of names (of people and things) attests to processes of associative imitations that continually overflow any singular naming. In the years 2012–15, both mobile devices and user interfaces were being intensively transformed in complex ways (e.g. the growth of apps, and the transformation of webpages from static HTML-formatted text to thoroughly dynamic script-driven surfaces composed for many elements). While these transformations were not directly the work of big data practices, they are intricately connected to it by virtue of the proliferation of devices, the deeper integration of networks of association they implement and, not least, the changes in the texture of contemporary experiences of interfaces. Both Figures 7.5 and 7.6 attempt to figure something of this proliferating-integrating process of change. Both figures count imitations in the form of copying code, but in ways that go beyond the formal copying mechanisms offered by Github itself (for instance in the 'Fork' button that appears on the top right of any repository on Github).

```
## Parsed with column specification:
## cols(
## repo_name = col_character(),
## created_at = col_datetime(format = ""),
## cnt = col_integer()
## )
```

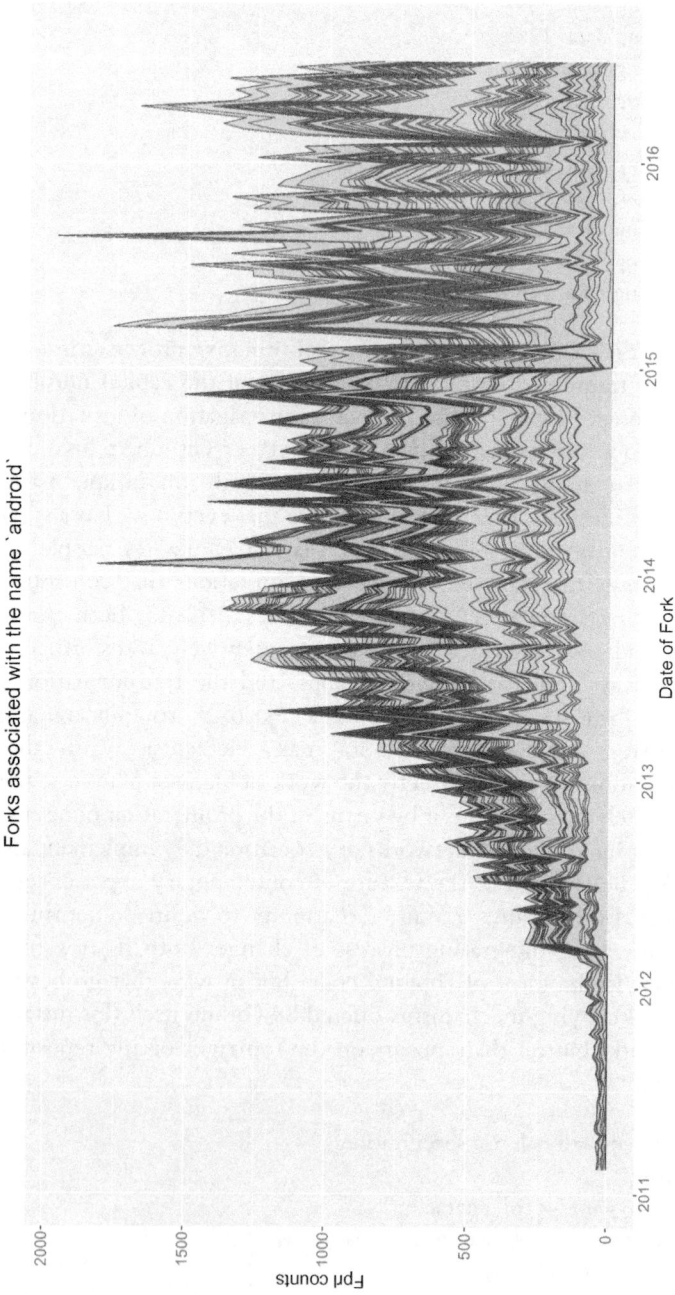

Figure 7.5 Repository forks associated with the name android

Forks associated with the name `bootstrap`

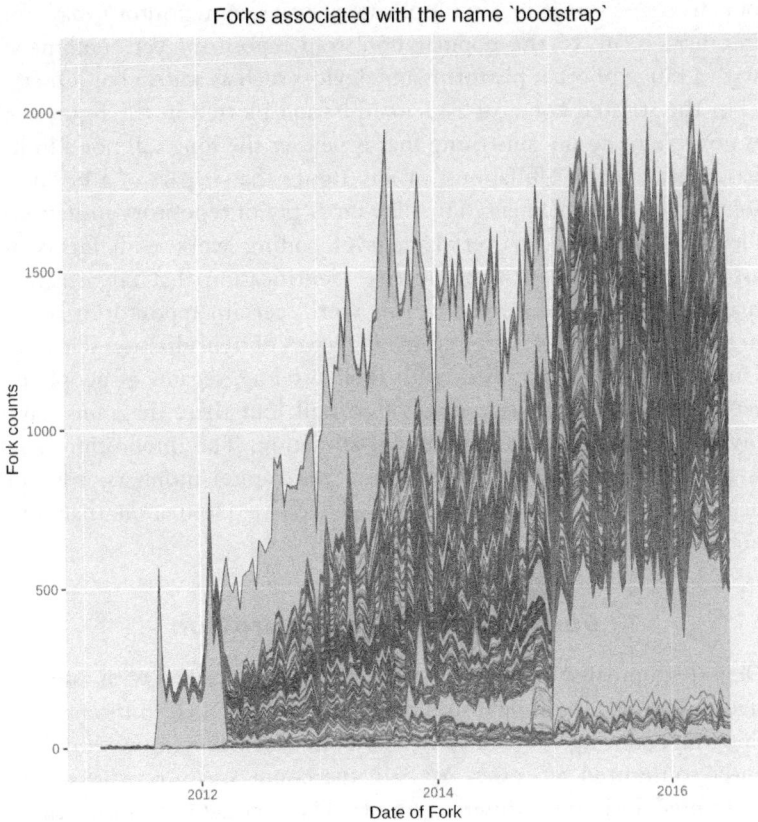

Figure 7.6 Repository forks associated with the name bootstrap

We might call this form of composition, as it configures capital numbers, *stacked associative imitation*. Associative imitation appears in two different ways in these figures. The broad bands of colour rippling horizontally across the base of the figures graph the counts of copies being made each day on Github of popular repositories such as android or bootstrap using the Fork action. (In forking, the repository name remains the same.) But the much more dense striations running above the base ribbons, seen for instance in Figure 7.5, count repositories whose names combine the base repository (e.g. android) but vary it in some way. These repositories associate with the base repository, but diverge from it in a multiplicity of ways. A repository may, for instance, relate to the popular bootstrap repository yet combine it with a range of other platforms and devices such as android or jQuery.

In the striated zones of associo-imitation plotted in the figures, it is possible to count something that is neither the long tail nor a link-based network of affiliations, or any figure that is part of a business solution or an implementation. The cross-ply of repository imitations identifies the average everydayness of coding work with forms of associative investment and affective identification that range across many different repositories. In this work, certain repositories act as high-visibility markers around which waves of hybridisation stack up. Unlike the capital numbers with their total aggregates of people or repositories, the imitative fluxes that bulk out these diagrams have diverse networks of association and affiliation. The implication here is that, by counting elements within the capital numbers, we can begin to glimpse the pathways of generative circulation that join together contemporary technologies.

Decapitalising configuration

Densely populated with ephemeral repositories, stacked with associative imitations, the capital number 29 million seemed in the light of these re-countings to be a sieve-like entity, overflowing with differently configured processes. Yet still the count was not exhaustively accounted for in these different counts. The very act of counting these imitations has a device-specificity, in its reliance on the Github platform API, the GithubArchive timeline dataset, the GoogleBigQuery cloud analytic's platform, and indeed Github itself as the repository of the code and text comprising this article (Metacommunities 2016a). Whenever we count or calculate in any form, device-specific configurations materialise in the numbers. The expansively contagious nature of imitation inevitably encounters device-specific configurations.

One sense of how numbers embody device-specific configurations can be seen by examining high event-count repositories on Github. The top 0.1 per cent of repositories attract around 26 per cent of all events during 2011–15. (The query decapitalises the repository names for the purposes of aggregation (e.g. a repository called DotFile will be counted along with dotfile).) Given the flattening of the names to lower case produced by this query, we cannot readily see how those events are distributed. But these highly eventful repositories, which comprise only a tiny percentage of the 29 million on Github, absorb many events. What happens in these high-event-count repositories?

Several major traits appear in these high-event-count repositories. Many events come from off-platform. Github, despite its own figuration as a hub where coding is done socially, functions as an element in wider configurations. For instance, the repository *eclipse.platform. common* accounts for almost two million events in the timeline data. A single repository attracting two million events (or almost 1 per cent of the total event count in the timeline data) suggests something highly significant in the geography of coding work. Perhaps the fact that *eclipse* is itself part of the Eclipse Foundation, 'an amazing open source community of Tools, Projects and Collaborative Working Groups' (Eclipse Foundation 2016) with almost a thousand of its own projects, might help explain the large number of events. More significantly, the high-frequency event traffic in eclipse.platform. common is an example of how Github itself functions as part of a configuration. The eclipse repositories are not actively developed on Github. They are mirrored – frequently copied – from the hundreds of git repositories found at git://git.eclipse.org. Mirroring practices attest to the capital importance of Github in coding cultures, but they also suggest that the value of Github is not paramount. Organisational life carries on elsewhere, outside the workflows and social coding mechanisms facilitated by Github. Like many other significant repositories (linux, android, mozilla, apache), high event counts often configure Github itself as part of a wider network of relations.

Conversely, even where repository events do originate on Github, many of them concern Github or technical configurations closely associated with Github itself. For instance, the list of names of high-event-count repositories centres on a few highly repeated names such as *test*, *dot*, *sample* and *try_git*. The many repositories that contain the term *dot* as in *dotfile* or *vimdot* suggest that Github repositories act as stores for the settings and configurations specific to coding work (e.g. *vimdot* repositories hold customised settings for the popular *vim* text editor). Terms like *test*, *hello*, and *try* or *demo* also stream through this set of repository names. These repositories often attest to non-code uses of Github and sometimes (for instance, in the case of *KenanSulayman/heartbeat* with its several million commit events) to surprising or experimental repurposings of the Github platform.

Do configuration-oriented practices around Github affect the capital numbers and the value and importance they are meant to convey? Configuration is, as science and technology studies scholars have emphasised, vital to the very existence of technologies. If many of the 29 million repositories on Github function as elements in the configuration of coding work rather than as bodies of code in their own right, then any account of what happens cannot assume that analysis of Github data primarily concerns 'how people build software' (Github 2015). Or, put more constructively, it suggests that much of what counts as software on Github – code repositories – in actuality concerns the arrangements that people make with each other and themselves in order to work with and inhabit information infrastructures. In this respect, the capital numbers are always also configurative numbers. There is no work on software without the 'how' of building software, the configuration work.

Even if we only added one repository to Github, our – the five researchers directly involved in the research – work on the Github API, GithubArchive datasets and the GoogleBigQuery platform was full of configurative events. The repository for this project contains thousands of lines of code written in Python, in R and in specialised languages such as SQL (Structured Query Language) (Metacommunities 2016a) as well as tens of thousands of lines of text distributed across thirty branches of the repository. According to the Github API, user *rian39* added around ten million lines of code and deleted eight million, leaving a net contribution of around two million lines to the metacommunities repository during the years 2012–16 (Metacommunities 2016b). In terms of ethnographic notebook writing, even if these lines are never read, this is an impressive level of inscription. While those numbers might be read as attesting to extraordinary levels of code productivity, they actually include many lines of data stored in the Github repository, alongside code, drafts of documents and configuration-related information. The deletion of eight million lines suggests that some of the main activities in the repository were changes to do with cleaning up, tidying and rearranging files and documents in the repository.

```
## opening file input connection.
## ..
Found 22499 records...
Imported 22499 records. Simplifying...
```

```
## Warning: closing unused connection 7 (https://api.github.com/
   repos/
## metacommunities/metacommunities/branches)
## Warning: closing unused connection 6 (https://api.github.com/
   repos/
## metacommunities/metacommunities/contributors)
## Warning: closing unused connection 5 (https://api.github.com/
   repos/
## metacommunities/metacommunities/languages)
## closing file input connection.
## Saving 5 x 4 in image
```

Perhaps this level of contribution activity to a repository suggests something important about the prototyping of configurative numbers in big data practice. Most of the ten million lines added and eight million lines deleted were configuration-related work as we - I in particular - sought to make sense of capital numbers such as 29 million, and tried to differentiate that sense-making from the flood of data challenges, hackathons and other usages of the GithubArchive data that were also offering geographical, sentiment, logistic and temporal narratives about 'how people build software'. In the process of trying to re-count the capital number, we 'built software' that generated four hundred or images, one hunndred or so data files, and around one thousand other files. More than 22,000 queries on GoogleBigQuery took place. Figure 7.7 shows something of the flow of data involved in this effort. By mid-2016, 80 terabytes of Github data had been searched, queried, tallied, counted, sorted and arranged according to the job logging supplied by the Google Compute Platform. This includes one day in August 2013 where 12,000 jobs were executed. It appears as a steep ascent on the left side of the graph. Traversing 40 terabytes, and generating a bill of around \$US2000, the events of that day triggered a 'reaching out' from Google Compute marketing department who were interested in our 'use case'. Why write so much code, process so much data, create so many figures and images, and indeed organise all of this work in the sometimes maddeningly precise version control system of a git repository on Github?

Conclusion

Where does this leave 29 million repositories? Halved by all the repositories with no more than a single event, halved again by all the

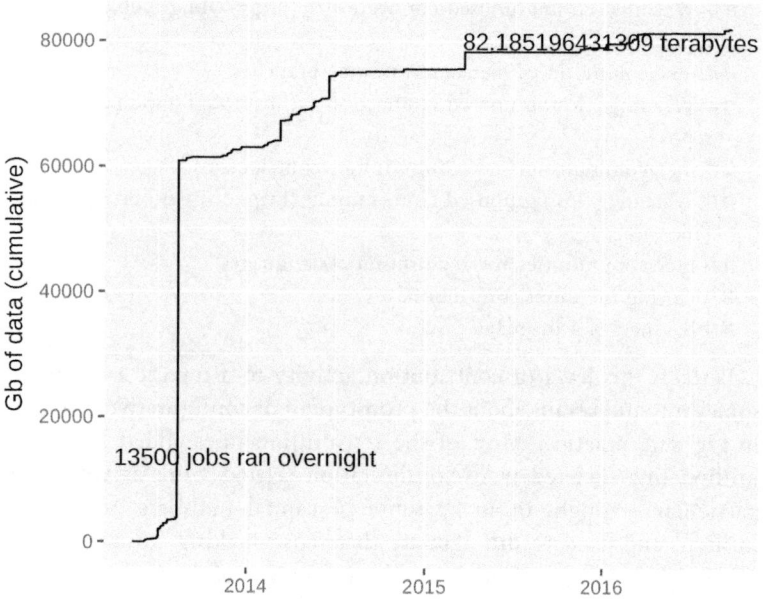

Figure 7.7 BigQuery processes terabytes in counting a
capital number

repositories that are a copy of other repositories, hollowed out by all
the repositories where people do not build software but use the repository for some other purpose (as a mirror site for instance), millions of
code repositories remain. Github placed the full source code of two
million repositories on GoogleBigQuery in mid-2016, perhaps reflecting the reality that the thirty million or so other repositories were
not going to add new stories to the platform.

Suchman suggests that configuration always entails both composition of elements and materialising imaginaries. It takes work to get
contemporary digital data and associated large numbers to do something other than augment the count of capital numbers and their
platform-centred aggregates. *Configurative numbers*, I have suggested,
is one term for prototypical enumerations and re-countings that seek
to map the composition of capital numbers, and to follow some of
the imaginaries aggregating in them. We saw how that re-counting
runs along the same lines as the many attempts to 'storify' data flows,
yet whenever we turn to associative-imitative fluxes, or to very

extensive configuration work that saturates the data stream with links to what happens elsewhere, the stories told with data start to become unstable, unfamiliar and at times a little more interesting.

Notes

1 A recent special issue of the *Journal of Scandinavian Social Theory* on numbers offers a useful variety of engagements with the status of number. See for instance Guyer (2014) on percentages or Gerlitz and Lury (2014) on 'kudos' ratings.
2 What is an imaginary? I will not address that question directly here, but all concepts of imaginary (ranging from Lacan's to the more recent proliferation of imaginaries in humanities and social science (McNeil et al. 2016)) concern a sense of wholeness or completion that allows formations of identity, inclusion, belonging and otherness to take shape. For an example of the concept of imaginary in an account of software and coding, see Kelty 2005.
3 Code for the research project can be found at https://github.com/metacommunities/metacommunities.
4 Slightly complicating matters, the single Github timeline dataset has now been retired on GoogleBigQuery and the data now takes the form of separate tables for each day, month and year since February 2011. More recently, the full contents and histories of over two millions Github repositories have been published as a GoogleBigQuery dataset (GoogleInc_2016a).
5 Nearly all of our attempts to make sense of the data can be found in the Github repository https://github.com/metacommunities/metacommunities. The scripts, plots and pieces of writing found there, however, are not highly ordered. The key results lie scattered across different branches of that repository. The somewhat tangled, messy aggregate of materials there attests to our strenuous but often incoherent efforts to find valid statistical regularities in a dataset characterised by tremendous heterogeneity and messiness. More interestingly perhaps, that repository can be understood as an ethnographic notebook.

References

Anderson, Chris. 2009. *The Longer Long Tail: How Endless Choice Is Creating Unlimited Demand*. London: Random House Business.

Brynjolfsson, Erik, Hu, 'Jeffrey' Yu and Smith, Michael D. 2006. 'From Niches to Riches: Anatomy of the Long Tail'. SSRN Scholarly Paper ID 918142. Rochester, NY: Social Science Research Network. http://papers.ssrn.com/abstract=918142 [accessed 4 March 2018].

Bucher, Taina. 2013. 'Objects of Intense Feeling: The Case of the Twitter API: Computational Culture'. *Computational Culture* 3: 1–9. http://computationalculture.net/article/objects-of-intense-feeling-the-case-of-the-twitter-api [accessed 4 March 2018].

Dabbish, Laura, Stuart, Colleen, Tsay, Jason and Herbsleb, Jim. 2012. 'Social Coding in GitHub: Transparency and Collaboration in an Open Software Repository'. In *Proceedings of the ACM 2012 Conference on Computer Supported Cooperative Wor*: 1277–86. ACM. http://dl.acm.org/citation.cfm?id=2145396 [accessed 4 March 2018].

Eclipse Foundation. 2016. 'Eclipse – The Eclipse Foundation Open Source Community Website'. www.eclipse.org [accessed 4 March 2018].

Fischer, David. 2013. 'GitHub Data Challenge II'. David Fischer (blog). 4 May 2013. www.davidfischer.name/2013/05/github-data-challenge-ii/ [accessed 4 March 2018].

Foreman-Mackay, Dan. 2014. 'The Open Source Report Card'. 14 February. https://web.archive.org/web/20140214105201/http://osrc.dfm.io [accessed 4 March 2018].

Gage, Deborah. 2015. 'GitHub Raises $250 Million at $2 Billion Valuation'. *Wall Street Journal*, 29 July. www.wsj.com/articles/github-raises-250-million-at-2-billion-valuation-1438206722 [accessed 4 March 2018].

Gerlitz, Carolin and Lury, Celia. 2014. 'Social Media and Self-Evaluating Assemblages: On Numbers, Orderings and Values'. *Distinktion: Journal of Social Theory* 15(2): 174–88.

Git. 2014. 'Git'. http://git-scm.com [accessed 4 March 2018].

Github. 2014. 'Results of the GitHub Investigation'. *GitHub*, 21 April. https://github.com/blog/1823-results-of-the-github-investigation [accessed 4 March 2018].

Github. 2015. 'About · GitHub', 16 December. https://web.archive.org/web/20151216055610/https://github.com/about [accessed 4 March 2018].

Gómez, Ramiro. 2012. 'Exploring Expressions of Emotions in GitHub Commit Messages'. *Gekksta*. http://geeksta.net/geeklog/exploring-expressions-emotions-github-commit-messages [accessed 4 March 2018].

Google. 2016. 'Github Timeline Data on Google BigQuery'. https://bigquery.cloud.google.com/table/githubarchive:github.timeline [accessed 4 March 2018].

Grigorik, Ilya. 2012. 'GitHub Archive'. http://www.githubarchive.org [accessed 4 March 2018].

Guyer, Jane I. 2014. 'Percentages and Perchance: Archaic Forms in the Twenty-First Century'. *Distinktion: Journal of Social Theory* 15(2): 155–73. doi:10.1080/1600910X.2014.920268.

Guzman, Emitza, Azócar, David and Li, Yang. 2014. 'Sentiment Analysis of Commit Comments in GitHub: An Empirical Study'. In *Proceedings of the 11th Working Conference on Mining Software Repositories*; 352–55. MSR 2014. New York, NY: ACM.

Hardy, Quentin. 2012. 'Dreams of "Open" Everything'. *Bits Blog*, 28 December. http://bits.blogs.nytimes.com/2012/12/28/github-has-big-dreams-for-open-source-software-and-more [accessed 4 March 2018].

Jenkins, Henry. 2004. 'The Cultural Logic of Media Convergence'. *International Journal of Cultural Studies* 7(1): 33–43. http://ics.sagepub.com/content/7/1/33.short [accessed 4 March 2018].

Kelty, Christopher. 2005. 'Geeks, Social Imaginaries, and Recursive Publics'. *Cultural Anthropology* 20(2): 185–214.

Kelty, Christopher. 2008. *Two Bits: The Cultural Significance of Free Software*. Durham, NC: Duke University Press.

Latour, Bruno. 1996. *Aramis, or the Love of Technology*. Translated by Catherine Porter. Cambridge, MA, and London: Harvard University Press.

Marcus, George. 2014. 'Prototyping and Contemporary Anthropological Experiments with Ethnographic Method'. *Journal of Cultural Economy* 7(4): 399–410.

Marres, Noortje. 2012. 'The Redistribution of Methods: On Intervention in Digital Social Research, Broadly Conceived'. *The Sociological Review* 60(S1): 139–65. http://onlinelibrary.wiley.com/doi/10.111 1/j.1467–954X.2012.02121.x/full [accessed 4 March 2018].

Mayer-Schönberger, Viktor and Kenneth Cukier. 2013. *Big Data: A Revolution That Will Transform How We Live, Work, and Think*. Boston, MA: Eamon Dolan/Houghton Mifflin Harcourt.

McNeil, Maureen, Haran, Joan, Mackenzie, Adrian and Tutton, Richard. 2016. 'The Concept of Imaginaries in Science and Technology Studies'. In *Handbook of Science and Technology Studies*. Edited by Ulrike Felt, 3rd ed. London & Thousand Oaks, CA: Sage Publications Ltd, 435–64.

Metacommunities. 2016. 'Metacommunities/Metacommunities'. *GitHub*. https://github.com/metacommunities/metacommunities.

Roussell, Dennis. 2015. 'Octoboard'. *Github Activity Dashboard*, 1 August. https://web.archive.org/web/20150801193208/http://octoboard.com [accessed 4 March 2018].

Russell, Matthew A. 2013. *Mining the Social Web: Data Mining Facebook, Twitter, LinkedIn, Google+, GitHub, and More*. O'Reilly Media, Inc. http://books.google.co.uk/books?hl=en&lr=&id=_VkrAQAAQBAJ&oi=fnd&pg=PR4&dq=github&ots=JqiqtzTxmK&sig=sfea4ce1ue2XYt_dERD41VpSTS4 [accessed 4 March 2018].

Straube, Theodore. 2016. 'Stacked Spaces: Mapping Digital Infrastructures'. *Big Data & Society* 3(2): 1–12.

Suchman, Lucy. 2012. 'Configuration'. In *Devices and the Happening of the Social*. Edited by Celia Lury and Nina Wakeford. London: Routledge, 48–60.

Takhteyev, Yuri and Hilts, Andrew. 2010. 'Investigating the Geography of Open Source Software Through GitHub. http://takhteyev.org/papers/Takhteyev-Hilts-2010.pdf [accessed 4 March 2018].

Thung, Ferdian, Bissyandé, Tegawendé F., Lo David and Jiang Lingxiao. 2013. 'Network Structure of Social Coding in GitHub'. In *17th European Conference on Software Maintenance and Reengineering (CSMR), 2013*, 323–26. IEEE.

Part III

Experiments in/of data
and ethnography

8

Transversal collaboration: an ethnography in/of computational social science

Mette My Madsen, Anders Blok and Morten Axel Pedersen

This chapter chronicles and reflects on the experiences of working ethnographically within, alongside and in collaboration with a large-scale interdisciplinary experiment in so-called computational social science, one of the important transnational frontiers for the mobilisation of big social data in recent years. Starting in 2013, the three authors have taken part in the Social Fabric/Sensible DTU project, a large-scale interdisciplinary research programme partly funded by the University of Copenhagen, Denmark. As part of its grand ambition to develop the technical, methodological and theoretical tools needed to transform the big data revolution into 'deep data' research, this project has sought to make continuous recordings of social interactions on all smart-phone-based communication channels (call logs, SMS, Bluetooth, GPS geolocation etc.) among an entire freshman class (N = 800) at the Danish Technical University (DTU). At the same time, a variety of other kinds of data have been produced through the deployment of more established social-science methods, ranging from surveys and structured interviews to participant observation undertaken by embedding an anthropology PhD student within the freshmen class for a year. This arrangement has served to position this anthropologist (the main author of this chapter) at right angles to both the students in the study and the other researchers studying them. As such, her experiences offer a privileged access point for addressing the pressing questions and challenges that arise when seemingly disparate data worlds and research practices, associated with computational and ethnographic approaches, come to rub closely off each other.

Based on recounting, from the ethnographer's point of view, a number of 'collaborative moments' at the awkward intersection of computational data science and ethnographic fieldwork, the chapter explores not so much the disciplinary commitments involved in this interdisciplinary encounter as the nature of that very collaborative relationship itself. Of crucial importance here is the fact that, in ways not too dissimilar from more classical contexts of participant observation, working as an anthropologist as part of the Social Fabric/ Sensible DTU research project has entailed continuous oscillation between practising ethnography *in* a (partly) computational social-science framework and doing an ethnography *of* the very scientific data practices and infrastructures involved. Rather than thinking about this oscillation either as a distanced gaze akin to that of a science and technology studies (STS) observer or as a neutral epistemic meeting point for comparison or convergence, we prefer to think of it as involving what we call 'transversal' collaborations, instantiating forms of non-coherent, intermittent, yet productively mutual co-shaping among partially connected knowledge practices and practitioners. Such rethinking of the actual and possible relationship between computational and ethnographic approaches in practice is crucial, we argue, for understanding new social data 'complementarities' (Blok and Pedersen 2014) and their epistemological, ethical and political ramifications.

Ethnography in and of big, social data worlds

Over recent decades, researchers in anthropology, sociology, human geography and STS have engaged in many collaborative and cross-disciplinary endeavours in order to experiment on new forms of complex data-generation, analysis and visualisation. This emergence of digital, computational, transactional and otherwise 'big' social data has given rise to new realignments, as well as new fissures and bifurcations, within, across and indeed beyond the social sciences. Disparate data formats – transactional, digital, ethnographic, numerical, visual etc. – have come to rub off and emerge from one another, which has resulted in the new challenges and opportunities for doing innovative, reflexive, socially and ethically grounded research in an age of 'big and broad' social data (Housley et al. 2014; see also Ford

2014; boyd and Crawford 2012; Nafus and Sherman 2014; Kockelman 2013; Wilf 2013; Knox and Walford 2016). Evidently, a rethinking of the relationship between computational and ethnographic data and methods is crucial as part of understanding these emerging social data 'complementarities' (Blok and Pedersen 2014) and their ramifications. Among other things, this poses the following questions, at once practical, political, epistemological and ethical. How should such otherwise disparate data worlds be combined or mixed? Can and should different bodies of data originating from apparently incommensurable research arenas and experimental designs be 'added up' into one another? At issue here is the question of how much is shared and how much is different across 'big' and 'small' datasets, and under what conditions such disparate datasets – or data worlds – can be brought into mutually productive interaction with each other.

These are some of the questions that the authors of this chapter have been working on over recent years as part of a team of anthropologists and sociologists from the Copenhagen Centre for Social Data Science (SODAS), a new interdisciplinary research and teaching initiative hosted by the Social Science Faculty at the University of Copenhagen. In this chapter, we follow up a previously published programmatic intervention (Blok and Pedersen 2014) to explore a specific question pertaining to this emerging collaborative space of ethnographic-cum-digital data generation and analysis.[1] The specific question we wish to focus on here revolves around the problem of what 'collaboration' between or across different disciplines might mean and entail both within and outside the academy. An extensive social scientific and STS literature pertaining to this question already exists, including work concerned with the relationship between qualitative ethnographic data and different kinds of quantitative data, whether deemed 'digital', 'computational' or not. Within the field of anthropology, for instance, a fast-growing body of predominantly very critically minded literature has discussed the supposed mutual hostility of and/or interdependence between 'small' and 'thick' qualitative ethnographic data formats and 'big' or 'deep' digital data formats in the worlds of computational social science (Stoller 2013; Erwin and Pollari 2013; Curran 2013; Taylor and Horst 2013; Boellstorff 2013; Ford 2014; Boellstorff and Maurer 2015; Abramson 2016).

It is precisely this incipient discussion in the fertile transdisciplinary landscape between anthropology, sociology and STS we wish to intervene in here. We do so on the basis of our participation in a research team (colloquially known as the 'AntSoc Group') within the Social Fabric/Sensible DTU project, a large-scale computational social-science research programme based in Copenhagen. As part of a grand ambition to develop the technical, methodological and theoretical tools needed to transform the big data revolution into 'deep data' research (Stopczynski et al. 2014; Sekara et al. 2016), Social Fabric made continuous recordings of social interactions from all smart-phone-based communication channels (call logs, SMS, Bluetooth, GPS geolocation etc.) among an entire freshman class (N = 800) at the Danish Technical University (DTU), while also gathering a variety of other kinds of data through the use of more established social-science methods ranging from surveys and structured interviews to participant observation. For three years, 25-plus computer scientists, physicists, economists, psychologists, philosophers, sociologists, public health researchers and anthropologists thus collaborated to map the 'social fabric' of DTU, incorporating also 'thick' ethnographic data obtained from 'embedding' an anthropology PhD student, Mette My Madsen, within the freshmen cohort for a year. Here, disparate data worlds and research practices associated with computational and ethnographic approaches come to rub closely off each other and therefore represent a promising laboratory for 'testing' various ideas about the meetings and/or clashes between different registers and genres of quantitative and qualitative data.

Our argument in this chapter, and our motivation for coming together to write it in the first place, departs from an initial hypothesis that My's positioning within the Social Fabric project offers a unique vantage point for gauging and assessing this large interdisciplinary experiment. As already mentioned, My was, so to speak, positioned at right angles to the students under study and the (other) scientists studying them. As such, her experiences might be seen to offer a privileged access point for addressing the many questions and challenges that arise in such meetings across disparate data worlds. Accordingly, in what follows we shall see neither an argument about the necessity of one science or data-type being greater than the other, nor a critique of any of the sciences or data-types involved. What we shall see, however, is how clashes and negotiations of differences in research praxis, scientific language and thinking, as well as understandings about the nature of data, constituted the very fabric of interdisciplinary collaboration.

The methodological point of departure of this chapter, then, is that My's role as an anthropologist within the Social Fabric experiment has taken the form of an oscillation between practising ethnography *in* a computational social-science framework and doing an ethnography *of* the different data practices and infrastructures involved, to paraphrase George Marcus's influential article, 'Ethnography in/of the World System: The Emergence of Multi-sited Ethnography' (1993). However, here we use Marcus's 'in/of' distinction to convey a somewhat different point, one that pertains to the relationship between anthropology and social data science.[2] Rather than thinking about My's role as a vantage point from which one might cultivate the sometimes rather smug and distanced gaze of a traditional 'participant-observer', or conversely an epistemic meeting point allowing the smooth convergence between several disparate perspectives in the manner of the cosmopolitan version of the traditional anthropological hero (Strathern 1996), we suggest thinking of My's role in this experiment, and our team's role in Social Fabric more generally, as involving 'transversal collaborations'. In using this term, in this chapter we are seeking to point to and explore forms of non-coherent, intermittent and yet productively mutual co-creation among partially connected knowledge practices and practitioners. Essentially, what we are trying to accomplish by talking about collaborations as 'transversals' is the cultivation of a conceptual vocabulary and an analytical language by which we, and potentially others practising ethnography in and of the world of big data, may adequately describe and critically examine their own practice.

Indeed, if the ethnography 'in' versus 'of' distinction constitutes our methodological ground, 'transversality' delineates our theoretical frame. According to Tine Gammeltoft, an anthropologist working on medical subjectivities and state power in Vietnam, 'transversality' in mathematics 'is a notion that describes how spaces can intersect; a transversal is a line that intersects other lines' (Gammeltoft 2008: 573). What makes this concept so useful for anthropologists and other social scientists, Gammeltoft suggests, is that it allows one to trace affects 'across spaces that are otherwise kept conceptually separate. Rather than structuring the analysis through oppositional categories,

this approach draws analytical attention toward shifting and symboli-
cally laden figures of cultural and political attention, focal points in
which emotional density is high and power and desire mingle' (2008:
573). In short, we envisage the concept of transversality as denoting the
process whereby disparate 'ethnographic moments' (Strathern 2004)
generated in multiple times and places (and by different researchers)
are conjoined into objects of anthropological inquiry and comparison.

What makes this and other recent anthropological invocations of
transversality[3] so useful for our present purposes is the fact that diverse
phenomena that are otherwise perceived to be 'far apart' can be
brought together in capricious assemblages, which, crucially for what
we wish to accomplish here, *retain* some of the complexity and dynamics of the original components and scales that they more or less seam-
lessly or messily 'stitch together' (Blok et al. 2017). Indeed, we further
suggest, it is precisely this non-reductive feature of transversality as a
concept which so aptly captures the peculiar *scale-shifting role* that My
has played in the Social Fabric/Sensible DTU experiment. Instead of
conceiving of My's movement between different experimental 'sites'
within Social Fabric as involving oscillation between inside and
outside vantage points, it is more productive to think of her (and the
positioning of ethnographers in big data experiments more generally)
as a *transversal data-point herself.* In that sense, she was subject to a line
of flight that criss-crosses and stitches together otherwise disparate
data worlds.

With this description of My's role as a transversal line of flight that
is orthogonal to the one defined by the 'in'/'of' binary in mind, we
are now ready to commence the more ethnographically descriptive
and reflexive part of this chapter. Accordingly, over the following
pages we recount in some detail a strategically selected sample of six
'ethnographic moments' (Strathern 1999) – or, to paraphrase Anna
Tsing, 'sites of awkward engagement' (Tsing 2005) – that My has
experienced over the last five years of working within, alongside and
in collaboration with the wider interdisciplinary experiment in computational social science, one of the important transnational frontiers
for the mobilisation of big social data in recent years. By recounting, from an ethnographer's point of view, a number of 'collaborative moments' originating from the always awkward and sometimes
conflictual intersections of computational data science and ethnographic fieldwork, in what follows we thus explore not so much the

disciplinary commitments involved in this interdisciplinary encounter as the concrete nature of that very collaborative relationship itself. In keeping with ethnographic convention, we describe the collaborative moments and encounters in the first person and present (i.e. the perspective of My as an ethnographer), only to resume, in the final section, our more collective and retrospective (and theoretically presumptuous!) voice by way of summarising and reflecting upon the analytical lessons that may be contained in the six encounters (that is, another scaling of sorts).

Enter

My PhD proposal was focused on how freshman students who did not know either each other or the institutional culture at DTU would form and negotiate friendships. I wanted to investigate this by using qualitative data from doing long-term fieldwork among freshman students, which involved me entering DTU as a freshman myself. (The students in question were all aware of the fact that they were participating in a scientific research project. They had been formally presented to the embedded anthropological researcher and partook in the research project in line with the rules of informed consent.) My proposal was thus a classic anthropological study with very little concern for the methods of other disciplines or other data types. It turned out that the panel had decided to promote my PhD proposal over other anthropological proposals because of at least one quality that was unique to me compared to the other applicants: the fact that I knew next to nothing about either interdisciplinary collaboration or big data. Of course, this was only revealed to me two years later, maybe to ensure my honest confusion and discomfort when engaging in our interdisciplinary computational social science work.

As such, I was positioned as a purely anthropological element in the larger interdisciplinary project, not unlike how other researchers were positioned as elements of their own sciences. Being an anthropologist with a classic anthropological project, I was the only one in the interdisciplinary team of Social Fabric/SensibleDTU who worked solely with unquantifiable, qualitative data. Because of my very anthropology-centred position, from the beginning I was almost destined to have very little clue about what was going on in relation to my fellow researchers at Social Fabric who were working primarily with digital or at least quantifiable data. Rather like a bull in a china shop, I delicately tried to blend into our shared office space, but kept putting my foot right in it. Soon I found myself in a position rather like the 'matter out of place' described by Mary Douglas (1966), as something that simultaneously implies both the existence and the contravention of an established order, a point through which both order and disorder are simultaneously revealed.

However, in the context of our collaborative research, it seemed as though we were not dealing with one world of order but with many, each of which constituted the potential disorder of the other. This 'out-of-place-ness' was enhanced even further when, on entering the field of DTU, I was hooked up to a data-gathering SensibleDTU smartphone, just as the freshman students were. Uniquely among the other researchers in the project, therefore, I had my very own digital data trace or digital double, if you like. Because of this arrangement, I came to be extended in a transversal 'out of place' manner myself, as a sort of continuum between the non-digital and digital data spheres or worlds. Consequently I always had the potential to belong to one or the other world, but at the same time also always dragged a tail of inappropriate otherness with me, resulting in moments of awkward confrontation and interdisciplinary negotiation over 'ordering'. In the following, we shall see a series of such moments of awkward confrontation between the ethnographer (me) and a number of researchers from other disciplines engaging in interdisciplinary collaboration.

Preliminary negotiations over 'what is interesting'

Let me start by giving a brief description of the preliminary pilot study conducted by the Social Fabric team in which the AntSoc group also came into being. This took place from 2012 to 2013, a year before the actual Social Fabric/SensibleDTU project set sail, and it turned out to have a major impact on the broader, full-scale study (in part because it was mobilised in order to obtain the larger amount of research funding). Throughout the year of the pilot study, members of the preliminary research group conducted a series of interviews with DTU students, did observational studies at DTU and had meetings where we discussed our findings and possible themes and scenarios for further research. As time passed, the discussions became more thematically shaped, shared interests were identified and small interdisciplinary sub-groups started to form.

One such sub-group consisted of Peter, a sociology Master's student, and myself, the anthropology PhD student. We had many interesting discussions of concepts and theories we found mutually interesting. I was surprised that we had so many theoretical points of interest in common across our disciplines and to a large extent could inspire and help each other with readings and ideas. Gradually our discussions started becoming more and more centred on our specific interests in the project and how we imagined our collaboration playing out. One day these discussions inevitably arrived at concrete suggestions on how to collaborate, but here something unexpected happened:

> My: 'I have this idea that I developed during my Master's project, but did not get the chance to really work with, this idea about viewing persons, I mean social beings, as some kind of amoeba, right!? [Passionately I start drawing] Like this, so that we can regard them as flexible constellations of indefinite components.'
>
> Peter: 'But why do you want to know that?'
>
> My: 'Ahem ... because it could possibly help us with new understandings of what both a person and a network is ... I thought that maybe heat-mapping could help in showing this, so ... one blur could be seen as a one-person-constellation.'
>
> Peter: 'What you are saying is not interesting. It's not interesting because that's what a network already shows.'

Peter went into an equally passionate explanation about how to understand a node in a node–and-tie network structure. While his hands gesticulated in the air, energetically forming balls, rods and explosions, I leaned back, arms crossed, highly sceptical. What had just happened? Our collaboration was going so well – why this sudden breakdown? Who was he anyway, this sociologist? My thoughts flew to a number of sociology articles and books I had read. In my mind I summarised how the introduction, theoretical parts and conclusions would always be very interesting, but the analysis or proof parts would be full of incomprehensible calculations and visual illustrations. Still watching Peter explain, my thoughts drifted away as I started wondering how something in this world could be 'not interesting' and how the argument for this claim could rest on explanations of hypothetical dots and lines. Like magic, Peter started to rematerialise in front of my eyes, now appearing as some exotic 'other', no longer as a collaborative partner but as someone who was indeed different from me, someone I would like to study.[4]

In the brief encounter sketched out above, it is not so much that my ethnographic, rather Strathern-inspired interest in distributed persons was deemed uninteresting because epistemologically it was too divergent. Rather, it was deemed uninteresting because, from the point of view of people dealing in node-and-tie networks, it seemed banal. Interdisciplinary collaboration was more or less unfamiliar to all of us, and many conversations circled around a 'supply and demand' kind of thinking in the way that everyone would think about demands concerning their own research interests and merely invite other researchers to supply confirmation, visualisation or further stabilisation of their imagined arguments (as we shall see more examples of in the following). Instead of fertilising each other's interests, we withdrew into our own disciplines, as if pushed back by the question of 'what is interesting'. Our mutual dissatisfaction about the other's claim to be 'interesting' drew us into core ways of argumentation and point-proving belonging to our different disciplines. As the interdisciplinary research went on, it became clear that figuring out how and around what to collaborate was not the easiest of tasks. Still, even this rather basic form of collaboration-as-negotiation would lead to more interesting insights, as the following section is meant to suggest.

Disparate data worlds and the possibility of an ethnographic wormhole

As time went on, the pilot study ended, and the actual project fell into shape and was funded. For the Social Fabric/SensibleDTU research project, many more smartphones were handed out to voluntary freshman students than in the pilot. However, and in spite of great efforts being made to attract the students by providing them with the newest and most state-of-the-art technology and updates, not all the phones (1000) ended up being handed out to freshman students ($\cong$ 800). This was of concern to the computational social scientists from DTU. First of all, although they wanted more phones handed out for more and better data granularity and density, it was equally important for them to provide the students with an attractive and useful product in return for their participation in the project. As already mentioned, they had chosen a state-of-the-art phone to fulfil that goal, and on top of that they had developed several self-tracking visualisations that the students could enter from their phones and hopefully find useful or at least interesting. However, when it was discovered that not all the phones had been handed out, the computational social scientists came to question whether their product was sufficient and if not, *why*.

One day the leading computational researcher at DTU asked me if I 'could somehow find out why some students did not participate in the project'. Several reasons had occurred to the researchers at DTU. It was, for example, possible that some students did not want to be part of SensibleDTU for ethical reasons, that they had simply overlooked the opportunity to participate in SensibleDTU or that some would have preferred to be given Apple phones out of habit or principle. The DTU researchers were well aware of all these issues, but it was primarily guesswork – qualified, but nevertheless guesswork, the lead researcher explained to me. Furthermore, yet other issues might have been at stake, issues that the DTU researchers 'in reality' had no way of knowing. The lead researcher was worried that the DTU researchers' guesses did not reflect the real reasons why not all the phones had been handed out. Moreover, validating them and rejecting them computationally would be time-consuming and with little guarantee of an efficient outcome. Without much thinking, I immediately replied to his request by agreeing to 'ask some of the students why'.

To my surprise, that answer triggered an impressed facial expression on the part of the computational researcher, along with a very enthusiastic comment that it would be 'valuable information!' The exclamation in his statement filled me with pride. Pride, because I realised in surprise that the act of me talking to students might actually be of help to the computational researchers. Not only that, what I could provide in the way of ethnographic qualitative data about the issue would be 'valuable information' for computational, hard-nosed quantitative research. But there was also this horror of it, because why was I suddenly being given this authority to establish the 'true' nature of the problem with the phones without any of the 'guesswork' that the computational researchers apparently operated within? Should I as an ethnographer accept the implied position of someone who was somehow closer to 'truth' and 'reality'? Would that in turn mean that the computational researchers were further away from reality, or simply in another 'reality'? Were there different worlds at stake here, worlds that would operate within their own data realities – disparate (or maybe desperate?!) data worlds? If so, was this moment in the computational researcher's office a sort of wormhole where the possibility of flow or travel by different and normally incompatible data between worlds existed?

I left his office feeling very flattered by virtue of the authority I had been given. But in a suppressed abdominal area there was a knot of worry: how would this interdisciplinary work turn out if the researchers in it had to defy space-time worlds in order to collaborate?

The grounded ethnographer and computational social science

Later on, and as a result of my dialogical relationship with the computational researchers at DTU about the student population (or my mediation of a dialogue between the researchers and the 'live' students), I became involved in an article that the DTU research team was writing. In it we wrote, among other points, that the embedded ethnographer 'helps to ground the mathematical modelling process' – that is, the computational research – by way of the ability of ethnographic knowledge to help answer questions of 'why' (Stopczynski et al. 2014: 7).

Throughout the year of my fieldwork, I had multiple experiences with both the computational researchers from DTU and other researchers involved in the Social Fabric project, especially those from philosophy, sociology and public health, where they would ask me 'why' questions about the live student population. Either they would ask me about my experiences with the students or they would want me to ask the students about their own experiences. In other words, they were asking me either to disclose or extract specific, concrete explanations from the live student population to answer questions, hypotheses or puzzles that the researchers were experiencing in working with the digital data, the digital students. Apparently, in the collaboration between computational researchers and ethnographer, 'grounding' knowledge – i.e. figuring out the 'true' nature of social reality at DTU – meant for the ethnographer working either as some kind of container of knowledge from which information could be extracted by posing the right questions, or as some kind of pathway through which it was possible to tap into real-life students to answer questions concerning the digital student population. In the greater scope of interdisciplinary collaboration, it seemed I had become a supply to a demand for a 'ground-truth' (as physicists would actually call it) either as a 'ground-truth' in myself or as some kind of tool that could help extract or establish the 'ground' for other researchers.

This reach for 'ground-truth' was indeed a major ongoing concern in the whole Social Fabric research team. Here, the ethnographer assumed an almost oracle-like position, the position of a medium, someone who could reach to the 'other side' and extract verification or rejection as to whether researchers were on the right track or not. For instance, one fellow researcher asked me: 'Do the students think about the ethics involved in retrieving their data from social media?', and, when I answered that I had not experienced any concerns, replied 'That's interesting; why do you think that is?', thus immediately accepting my first answer as if simply a truth. I had no second answer, only an odd feeling that was a mixture of simultaneous pride and shame – pride that I had been addressed as a professional witness who could answer questions like that; shame because I felt that answering questions like that was exactly what an anthropologist should *not* do.

The problem was not so much that the ethics of data retrieval was not my object of study, but that answering the question felt immoral in relation to the refrain imprinted in me throughout my student and professional life: 'there is no objective data-truth in anthropology'. Whereas the normal oracle's 'other side' would be the world of spirits, gods or death – that is, determinants outside the chaos of the relativity and situatedness of lived life – the oracle-ethnographer's 'other side' was in the middle of lived life and (all-too) profanely human students, with their partying, gossiping and what have you. And I, the ethnographer, was very much part of that chaotic, relational, situated social life, inhabiting a large number of personal biases that would inevitably shape everything I learned about the students. The 'ground' I saw myself enmeshed in was nothing like 'a truth'. Yet, when passing from me to my fellow researchers, my ethnographic data seemed to cross an invisible boundary whereby it changed character, becoming in the process of transition a sort of 'truth'. What was it about the various specific worlds of the disciplines involved, with their different legacies of theory, ethics and criteria of quality that made this transformation happen? What exactly was happening to my ethnographic data, my answers to 'why', when they crossed the boundaries from the realm of ethnography into that of computation?

Rawness and contamination: the digital ethnographer

As part of a collaborative project between anthropology and sociology within the larger framework of Social Fabric (the 'AntSoc group' mentioned earlier), we wanted to explore the wider potentialities for collaborative research. The idea was to pick a common object of study to explore new ways of interrelating the heterogeneous data of computational and ethnographic approaches. For this purpose, we singled out a specific social event – a party hosted at the DTU campus – with the aim of exploring the steps needed to work productively across heterogeneous digital and ethnographic data, in the sense of forcing forward new questions and criticism from our combination of normally incommensurable data types. In practice, this meant that we worked to match and interrelate fieldnote descriptions of the intensity and ebb and flow of party participants with Bluetooth signal strengths of proximity between party-going students' phones to indicate the shifting atmospheres throughout the party (see Blok et al. forthcoming).

As a starting point for the data-interrelating process, we wanted to 'stalk' me through both my fieldnotes and my digital data trace within the larger dataset – the digital ethnographer in the digital social, so to speak. We thus needed to locate the digital ethnographer in the dataset. However, after hours of work this proved impossible; the digital ethnographer was nowhere to be found in the dataset. A sociologist from our team decided to seek help from the computational researchers at DTU, where my sociologist colleague learned that my digital data trace had been removed from the larger dataset and put in its own folder. This had been done, he explained to me, out of a fear on the part of some of our other colleagues that my digital data would contaminate the dataset. He sat down at his computer and started to reinsert me in the dataset; the problem was solved and he could continue with his work.[5] I, however, was left bewildered.

'Contaminate'! What a strong word for one little ethnographer in a set of data with possibly the world's greatest granularity and depth.

I felt at once dirty and powerful. Was I really some kind of impure element that could corrupt the substance of the entire dataset? I suddenly remembered how the public health researchers in particular had problematised my presence in the digital data and how one researcher especially had stressed that my digital presence might endanger their research because of strict rules about data that applied to their work process. The data had to be as 'raw' – as natural and uncompromised – as possible, or their research would be rejected, the public health researcher had explained, a passionate blush spreading from her neck to her cheeks. The thought puzzled me. My contaminating digital presence would somehow corrupt the 'rawness' of the entire dataset and twist it into a falsely altered picture of the student population's natural behaviour? Why did the very same people who had so eagerly asked me 'why' questions about the live students at the same time decide that my digital persona had to be silenced?

It seemed that, whereas the real-life embodied ethnographer was treated as some kind of oracle, the digital ethnographer was at best useless and at worst a contaminant. Like the oracle of Delphi, my digital persona had to be removed from the social and kept firmly isolated in its own smoky cave. Still, I found it even more puzzling that it did not seem disturbing to the public health researchers that, in the non-digital life at DTU, there was a non-digital ethnographer engaging in the students' lives and quite possibly 'corrupting' a few of them in the process.

What can be shared and what cannot: accessibility standards and the qualitative databank

With all the different types of data that the Social Fabric project was generating, it could be difficult to remember exactly which channels it had been retrieved from. To solve this problem, the computational scientists from DTU made a Wiki-page with a list and explanation of all the data-types and the channels it had been collected through. I was very pleased with this solution, as I was definitely one of researchers who had difficulties remembering and understanding the digital data and how it had been obtained. I also felt curious: the computational researchers had not contacted me while creating the Wiki to ask about the ethnographic data and how I obtained it. Did they already know? Had we worked together for so long now that ethnographic qualitative data was no longer a problem for them to describe? Eager to find out, I scrolled down the list of data channels, only to be disappointed: I had not been included in the Wiki!

Brutally offended, I turned to the DTU researcher sitting next to me in our shared office space and asked with indignation why I had not been included in the Wiki as a channel of data and why qualitative ethnographic data did not occur at all on the data list? The DTU researcher looked surprised: how could they add me, he asked. The Wiki was meant to aid other researchers wanting to gain access to particular types of raw data to work with. I did not meet these accessibility standards because how would another researcher gain access to my data? If it could not be shared, then what was the point of putting it on Wiki?, he remarked in conclusion. 'I could put my field notes online', I replied snappily. But even as I said it, I knew that the greater part of the ethnographic databank was not my fieldnotes, it was my brain and the memories that could be triggered through reading my notes. Of course, only I had direct access to this databank of memories. We went into a discussion of how the ethnographic data could be retrieved by contacting me (the real-life person) directly and asking questions, making me describe situations or the like. In the end the DTU researcher promised to ask his superior about the matter, and we turned to face our computers again.

Even though I felt offended by the exclusion of my data contribution from the rest of the project, who was I to blame here? Hardly my colleague from DTU. Actually he was the one who had a point here: what to do with data that cannot be shared? It looked as if the ethnographic data was too problematic to list in the Wiki because of its inaccessibility to other researchers. On the other hand (and as described above), the ethnographic data *did* seem to be relevant to a number of the other researchers in the project, as they would ask me questions about the live student population, a relevance, as already noted, that the computational DTU researchers had described in a section of their initial paper when mentioning how valuable the qualitative data was in, for example, grounding the digital data. Maybe the actual data was not the central issue here but rather the receptacle for data and data-sharing, for what does the idea that 'raw data can be retrieved by any researchers in the project' say about the relationship between data and storage? Does it indicate that there are proper kinds of data and less proper kinds, and is the properness of data defined by how it can be stored? Was it not my data but simply *me* that was an unacceptable receptacle of storage for my own data, and is it things like access, databases and Wiki pages that determine such things?

Suddenly everything I had learned about embodiment, empathy and intersubjectivity, all cornerstones of anthropological research and data, seemed to be a major problem, incompatible with the idea of the research project I was part of. How are ethnographic data to be retrieved by other researchers in a large-scale interdisciplinary research project if the majority of them are stored inside the ethnographer's mind and body? To fulfil the relevant accessibility standards and become acceptable as a container for my own data, would I then have to imitate a digital database where other researchers could call me up and ask for specific information, which I would then give them? In this case, would I have to be available at any time? And for how long? Suddenly terms like 'data decay' and 'bit rot' acquired a very literal, morbid ring to them. The scope of interdisciplinary research had by now taken on scary proportions. With one last, long look at my computational colleague, I returned to the safety of my own research. Here, my embodied data were working just fine.

As far as I know, I have still not been included in the Wiki page. However, together with my AntSoc colleagues, I am in fact working on inserting my ethnographic data into the computational world. There must be ways of making my embodied and digital selves work together.

Too much information: the fragility of data

The AntSoc group engaged in yet another experiment. This time the aim was to examine whether we could somehow use ethnographic methods to deal with digital data. Again, we used data from a specific party held at the DTU campus. We grouped up in teams. I was with Thomas, a PhD student from sociology. We started by looking at my digital data trace to see where 'I' – that is, the digital ethnographer – was placed in the larger digital population we were working with. How many was 'I' within certain proximity of? Did 'I' stay within the largest sub-group in the student population? Did 'I' seem to have had contact with many different digital party participants? Thomas and I looked at the data while continuously trying to relate dots, lines and graphs to the ethnographic fieldnotes and memories of the event. It was going well. At some point, though, Thomas started looking doubtful: something was not adding up here. It seemed that, where the digital ethnographer had a lot of stable contact with only a few digital party participants, the live ethnographer had moved around a lot and met many different non-digital party participants. What had happened? I examined my fieldnotes more closely and found a small paragraph that indicated that I had left my bag on a windowsill at the party for around three hours. My phone (that is, the 'real' digital ethnographer) was in that bag. Happy to be of service in clarifying the puzzling discrepancy between the respective data traces of the digital and non-digital ethnographer, I immediately told Thomas about my discovery. But, unlike the computational scientists from DTU mentioned earlier, Thomas did not seem to find my discovery of the 'truth' to be 'valuable information' that could help the 'grounding' of our work with the digital data – quite the contrary. For a moment, he looked at me with a blank gaze, then he looked down, shaking his head in despair.

At first, and maybe owing to my previous success as a truth-witness and oracle of the non-digital, I did not understand his reaction. 'Amazing, isn't it? There is no theft at DTU even at parties ...' my voice faded. Then it dawned on me with irreducible embarrassment what had just happened. How casual I had been about the fact that my phone was collecting digital data that might later be of significance to research! In a horrible moment, I realised that the discrepancy between the data traces of the digital and non-digital researcher was directly proportional to my unintentional, even unconscious lack of interest in the digital realm at the time of the party. It was equally bad (of course) that this piece of information that I had so happily blurted out indicated something terrible about our digital dataset and the work we had spent all day doing; people leave their phones in windowsills! This extra, belated piece of (ethnographic) data seemed to be capable of jeopardising the creditability of all the data in the set we had been working on until then, and thus also our own findings.

Indeed, how fragile data is if it can be overturned by either the lack or the superabundance of information caused by similar interest and lack of interest of the non-digital people we study in caring about their digital selves. Ironically, it seemed that to provide credible digital data about the actions of real-life people, the latter would have had to be instructed carefully on how to act as digital data providers – as digital people. Or was it rather the other way around? Was it we the researchers who insisted that the digital and non-digital had to fit together? Was it we insisting that I and 'I' had to be the same when in fact they were not? Why was the correlation fine but the discrepancy not? I could not grasp the implications for computational social science and interdisciplinary collaboration. Rather abruptly, I got up, mumbling 'tea', and left for the kitchen, hoping that when I came back Thomas would be doing something completely different.

Exit

We have provided a series of ethnographic moments focused on the difficulties of interdisciplinary research seen from the perspective of the ethnographer and concerned with a common object: data. Let us exit the ethnographic section by highlighting a main point from the six moments, namely the general characteristic that, just when collaboration seemed to be at its best, smoothly merging heterogeneous data and methods, something was always also jarring. Either the interest points of the researchers diverged as soon as the data were to be engaged with; or data-merge was ripped apart by specific yet unshared standards of data-sharing and pollution; or the understanding of the data of one discipline would seriously disrupt the understanding of the data of another, as when ethnographic data corrupted the digital data (leaving the digital data scientist frustrated), or when ethnographic data were used as 'ground-truth' (leaving the ethnographer frustrated).

In the descriptions presented here, data is not just an object of study or mutual engagement but also a conceptual point from which a variety of different research worlds crystallised. Disciplines, after all, enact and inhabit speific data worlds with their different histories, methods and logics to inform and legitimize their interests. Simply pushing research technologies (data, methods, theories etc.) from one world to make others run more smoothly will most likely not work (after all, anthropologists have made this point many times concerning the difficulties of travelling technologies). Does this sound discouraging for interdisciplinarity? Borrowing from Mary Douglas, we have on the contrary wanted to show how data that are 'matter out of place' and often overlooked can come to serve as hinges between the disconnected worlds of research and data. In a transversal movement, the ethnographer emerges here as a data point herself, allowing new insights into the many data worlds at stake in contemporary big social data collaborations.

The social fabric of Social Fabric: remarks on transversal collaboration

Over the preceding pages, My has outlined some of her auto-ethnographic experiences of working with social big data in an interdisciplinary and computational setting. As such, what we have shown can be understood as peepholes into the very fabric that such collaboration is made of – the social fabric of Social Fabric, so to speak. Not coincidentally, the experiences highlighted here focus especially on the process of negotiating what should count as 'social data' in the first place – with data acting as both the meeting-point between otherwise disparate knowledge histories, paradigms, practices and projects (what we call data worlds), and the presumed arbiter of the relative interest, veracity and value of these respective practices. As such, a concern for the qualities of social data acts as the 'lowest' (or indeed highest!) common denominator, we might say, not only of the Social Fabric project and its various ambitions as a whole but also, and importantly, of the way we understand the oscillations contained within the transversal forms of collaboration into which My's ethnographic work in this computational social science context brought her.

Rather than showing how interdisciplinary negotiations worked *on* or *around* data, the ethnographic accounts above show how negotiations are inherently *parts of* the resultant social data themselves. The social fabric of Social Fabric – that is, the way the collaborative research went on in practice, of which we have documented ethnographic moments here – seems to show us exactly how the very data that we worked on came into being through collaborative negotiations between multiple agencies (including not just the different researchers but also the phones, the databases and of course the DTU students). In a sense, this observation would come as no surprise to an STS researcher of computational social science. What we have tried to add, however, is the sense – indeed, we think, the 'deep' and constitutive sense – in which *our very own* ethnographic observations and data are themselves mutually implicated in this setting in terms of its scalar and other qualities going from 'local' insignificance to 'global' all-knowingness. After all, the core question of what ethnography can and cannot do in a big social data setting, and how it intermittently 'grounds' or 'troubles' new computational approaches while itself being grounded and troubled in equal measure, is exactly what our account here is meant to open up. Indeed, this is also the point we attempted to convey in the introduction with reference to George Marcus's zoom-like oscillation between inside ('in') and outside ('of') vantage points.

Having set out the ethnographic moments, however, we are now in a better position to see why we insisted on adding to Marcus's observation the notion of the transversal in order to describe the form of the encounter between ethnographic and computational data worlds in the Social Fabric project as one of transversal collaboration. As we have seen, the ongoing negotiation of what was interesting; the scaling up and down from the particular to the aggregate (which we see in the qualitative grounding of vast digital datasets); the switching between different understandings of data from 'raw' to 'grounded' to 'contaminated' to 'corruptive'; and the fine balance of contextualising data with other data without adding too much or too little information – without these on-going negotiations, there simply would be no social data to work with. However, it is not simply that all social data are born through such relational and negotiated encounters, as an STS account would highlight, although this is certainly true. Nor is it the case in our heterogeneous data experiment that scaling and zooming across data formats takes on a frictionless state, as Latour et al. 2012 might be read as arguing.[6] Indeed, far from it. Rather, what seems to us interesting about our own collaborative experiences is the way social data emerge in the very partiality, non-coherence and indeed awkwardness of the encounters – that is, in their transversality.

This is certainly not meant on our part to downplay the initial sense of exasperation, perhaps disappointment and even disillusion, with which our ethnographic account in this chapter might be greeted (and to which we ourselves have also intermittently been subject). Our account is, we hope, very far indeed from being a rosy, glossed-over celebration of the epistemic wonders of interdisciplinary collaboration in general, or of computational social science collaborative endeavours (of the Lazer et al. 2009 type) in particular. Set in the average context of a motley crew of well-intentioned but only-so-human researchers from diverse intellectual backgrounds (ourselves included), My's experiences certainly contain their fair share of old-fashioned mutual stereotypes, of both the 'ethnographer-as-truth-sayer' and the 'digital-data-as-honest-signal' varieties. They also display, we believe, a whole range of the very real tensions and difficulties, as well as some of the methodological and ontological productiveness, of how interdisciplinarity works in contemporary scientific knowledge-making (see Barry and Born 2013). If anything, then, we hope to have conveyed the sense in which striving to move across ethnographic and computational data worlds is hard and challenging work, if also occasionally quite fun.

However, we intend a bit more than this for our notion of transversal collaboration – and this is where we return to the notion of the intersection of transversal lines as a focal point of heightened affective (and, we should add, related epistemic) density and desire. Under the right conditions, we argue, the intersection of otherwise disparate ethnographic and computational data practices and knowledge projects might come to attain just such qualities, and thus to suggest new and exciting avenues for overlapping but distinct (i.e. 'complementary') insights. In the present chapter, the main figure of such intersection is indeed My herself, or perhaps better, the intersection of the embodied ethnographer and her digital double in the computational dataset. As itself a transversal data point, we suggest, this intersection allows novel insights to accumulate in both 'directions', that is, in the directions of both computational social science and ethnography itself as a knowledge project. Hence, in the direction of computational social science, this positionality points towards the always already 'cooked', fragile and radically ungrounded nature of computational and other 'big' social data, thereby also opening up a conversation on other ways of relating to and manipulating (rather than simply 'critiquing') their emerging realities (see Blok et al. 2017 for one such experiment). At the right angle of intersection, then, ethnography might actually come to co-constitute the densities and relationalities conjured up by new digital data formats.

In the other direction, meanwhile, it points back to ethnography itself as an equally situated and malleable practice of data production and manipulation, one whose contours and commitments are as much up for grabs as are those of computational social science. Indeed, we need to acknowledge and affirm that it is not only computational social scientists who legitimately worry about what is happening to 'ground-truth' in a social world that is increasingly played out both within and across the blurred lines between the digital and the non-digital. Nor should ethnographers be inclined to leave exciting new images of distributed persons, dynamic and relational socialities, and scale-shifting movements from the 'micro' to the 'macro' to an emerging generation of quantitative network analysts equipped with digital trace data (see Latour et al. 2012; Ruppert et al. 2013). If we have said little about these issues in the present chapter, even as we share the sense of intellectual promise to which they gesture, this should be seen partly as a self-sobering realisation on our part that ethnography as presently practised may have as much to learn on these accounts from the innovative parts of big social data worlds as the other way around. Indeed, we would like to end this chapter by briefly reflecting on what such new 'complementarities' (Blok and Pedersen 2014) between ethnographic and computational data worlds might look like.

By way of conclusion: towards new complementarities?

In closing, let us reflect briefly on one (transversal) asymmetry that runs through this entire text and is indeed signalled in its very title. We obviously write here *as* ethnographers who use ethnographic methods, rather than as computational social scientists deploying new digital data to understand interdisciplinary collaboration (although we would certainly affirm the potential for just such studies). More tellingly, however, and throughout the text, we have also conformed to 'official' designations and expectations in speaking about Social Fabric *as* indeed a computational social science experiment, rather than (say) a way of reinventing ethnographic interest in studying campus life, young people's social networks and, more generally, well-bounded (and rather 'total') communities and institutions (as per Goffman). In a specific sense – namely, as My's PhD project – it is of course all these latter things as well, and it will eventually make its way into established anthropological conversations. Yet, it does indeed seem as if, for all our stress on the mutual transversality (so to speak) of this collaborative research setting, we are not quite ready to describe it *as* (simply) ethnographic. Why this asymmetry?

Beyond rehearsing well-worn points about academic hierarchies and the contemporary 'hype' for 'big', digital and computational social research methods (which is not to say that such observations are not important or do not pertain to our setting), there is also, we believe, a more principled and eventually more far-reaching point at stake. Indeed, simply to redescribe our interdisciplinary research setting as 'ethnographic' through and through – in the sense of dealing in what are taken to be inherently local, embodied, interpretative (and so on) forms of knowledge, even where this is (presumably) 'obscured' by the lure of the digital gaze – would be to miss what seems most radical and most promising about this setting. In words that we have used before (Blok and Pedersen 2014), we take this to be exactly the complementarity, in a strictly epistemic sense – i.e. the simultaneity of mutual incompatibility *and* mutual dependency in observational apparatus – of ethnographic and digital-computational forms of knowledge. In this light, our present chapter should be read as searching for the right vocabulary – a transversal one, we argue – in which to recognise and render operational such complementarity of ethnography in the actual practice of computational social science. Given the exact same, well-known power asymmetries and exclusions that shape this domain, we think of this as an inherently ethical and political move of ('transversal') critique.

Yet, this still leaves open the further and implied question, one to which we intend to return in future research, as to what it might mean for the project of ethnography itself to make it mutually dependant on digital-computational forms of knowledge. As we suggest elsewhere on the basis of our own experiments (Blok et al. 2017), one thing it must mean is a willingness to transpose *both* ethnography *and* computational social science on to a *third* plane of social investigation, one that is transversal to but not co-terminus with either. While we ourselves are still searching for this plane, notions such as the ephemeral, the affective, the effervescent, the absent, the distributed and the non-relational come to mind (see also Ruppert et al. 2013). Around all of these notions, ethnographic and computational approaches arguably find themselves equally challenged, yet also sufficiently (non-) aligned, for there to be a mutually overlapping angle and productive interest. It is our hope that the transversal line of flight across the otherwise disparate data worlds set forth in this chapter may come to inspire more experimental endeavours at the mutually intersecting, yet still too often mutually hostile, endeavours of ethnography and 'big' social data.

Notes

1 For a different take on these issues, in the form of an in-depth case study of quali-quantitative experiments carried out by our team, see Blok et al. (2017).

2 As is well known, Marcus's original agenda was to capture the (then) new anthropological interest in large-scale transnational or 'global' cultural, social, economic and political processes. The 'in' versus 'of' distinction played a central role in this project, for it was only by acknowledging that anthropologists were not imprisoned 'in' the seemingly small, local and bounded scale defined by the single fieldsite but also could and should conduct their fieldwork by 'following the people' (as Marcus famously put it) across multiple and unbounded sites that anthropology was going to be rescued from its obsolete 'small' subject matter and become able to conduct studies 'of' global phenomena and flows. Our use of the 'in'/'of' binary is different from Marcus's not just by virtue of the subject matter (globalization versus social data science) but also with respect to the assumptions about scale (Strathern 1996; Holbraad and Pedersen 2009, 2017; Wastell 2001) that undergird any discussion of ethnographic data and methods, whether 'digital', 'global' or what have you. Accordingly, instead of conceiving of My's perpetual oscillation between a positioning 'inside' the Social Fabric and her other, more detached vantage point on the 'outside' of this experiment as a movement between two scales of 'smallness' (the local) and 'bigness' (the global) respectively, we are more interested in exploring the messy scale-making practices whereby these two 'sizes' of data and methods first came into being and have since been reproduced.

3 In a recent article, for example, Pedersen and Nielsen (2013) have used the concept of transversality to compare the different temporalities of a multi-sited ethnographic dataset from a large collaborative research project on Chinese infrastructural projects in Inner Asia and Africa (2013). To capture how what they call the 'time of the field' stitches together a simultaneity of disparate temporalities, whose mutual relationship is neither linear nor cyclical but transversal, Pedersen and Nielsen introduce the concept of a 'trans-temporal hinge', which they define as a 'middle

point that connects the multiple temporalities' of a given anthropological research project and its different fieldsites.

4 In a previous version of this section, the question was asked whether this conversation between Peter and I revealed not only disciplinary differences but also gender differences, i.e. 'mansplaining'. The comment has been much appreciated by both the authors and the larger AntSoc research team. However, and as the reader has probably noticed, 'mansplaining' has not been brought up in this section. This is primarily because of two points I will elaborate on here. First, 'mansplaining' indicates a situation where the male who is doing the explaining in reality knows less about the topic then the woman he is explaining it to. However, this is not the case here, as Peter is explaining how a note-tie network is understood and theorised *in sociology*. Since he is a sociologist and I am an anthropologist, it is unlikely that he would in fact know less about understandings in his own discipline than I would. The significant fact, I would still argue, is in the way we persistently keep to our own science's understandings of 'what is interesting', as if this was the only correct way to perceive the matter. Second, in judging Peter's explanation as 'mansplaining', I am simultaneously being judged as subject to it and therefore someone who has been rendered inferior within our relationship. This sort of judgementalism towards me I would very much like to resist. To this I can just say that I did not feel inferior in the situation but rather felt a sudden alienation from Peter as an exotic 'other'. To make these two points more clear the section has been elaborated to give more context of Peter and my relation-history and to show more of my agency or reaction in the exhibited situation.

5 Or, more correctly, he inserted me in the copy of the dataset that we came to work with. Of course, 'I' could not be allowed into the 'real' dataset.

6 We do not claim much originality on this point, as similar observations about frictions have been made by, for example, Housley et al. 2014. Nevertheless, it is still worth emphasising in this context, as there is arguably something distinct and specific about the particular frictions involved when working across computational and ethnographic data worlds. For an elaboration of this point, see Blok et al. 2017.

References

Abramson, A. 2016. 'What in/is the World is/of Big Data? Fieldsights – Cultural Anthropology'. https://culanth.org/fieldsights/833-what-in-is-the-world-is-of-big-data [accessed 16 March 2017].

Barry, Andrew and Born, Georgina. 2013. *Interdisciplinarity: Reconfigurations of the Social and Natural Sciences.* New York: Routledge.

Blok, Anders, Carlsen, Hjalmar Bang, Jørgensen, Tobias, Madsen, Mette My, Ralund, Snorre and Pedersen, Morten Axel. 2017. 'Stitching Together the Heterogeneous Party: A Complementary Social Data Science Experiment'. *Big Data & Society* 4(2): 1–17.

Blok, Anders and Pedersen, Morten Axel. 2014. 'Complementary Social Science? Quali-Quantitative Experiments in a Big Data World'. *Big Data & Society* 1(2): 1–6.

Boellstorff, T. 2013. 'Making Big Data, in Theory'. *Firstmonday* 18(10). http://firstmonday.org/article/view/4869/3750 [last accessed 21 February 2018].

Boellstorff, T. and Maurer, B. 2015. *Data, Now Bigger and Better!* Chicago: Prickly Paradigm Press.

Boyd, D. and Crawford, K. 2012. 'Critical Questions for Big Data: Provocations for a Cultural, Technological, and Scholarly Phenomenon'. *Information, Communication and Society* 15(5): 662–79.

Curran, J. 2013. 'Big Data or "Big Ethnografic Data"? Positioning Big Data within the Ethnographic Space'. *EPIC 20013*, 1. www.epicpeople.org/big-data-or-big-ethnographic-data-positioning-big-data-within-the-ethnographic-space/ [last accessed 21 February 2018].

Douglas, M. 1966. *Purity and Danger: An Analysis of Concepts of Pollution and Taboo.* London: Routledge.

Erwin, K. and Pollari, T. 2013. 'Small Packages for Big (Qualitative) Data'. *EPIC 2013*, 1. www.epicpeople.org/small-packages-for-big-qualitative-data/ [last accessed 21 February 2018].

Ford, H. 2014. 'Big Data and Small: Collaborations between Ethnographers and Data Scientists'. *Big Data & Society* 1(2): 1–3.

Gammeltoft, Tine. 2008. 'Figures of Transversality: State Power and Prenatal Screening in Contemporary Vietnam'. *American Ethnologist* 35(4): 570–87.

Holbraad, M. and Pedersen, M.A. 2009. 'Planet M. The Intense Abstraction of Marilyn Strathern'. *Anthropological Theory* 9(4): 371–94.

Holbraad, M. and Pedersen, M.A. 2017. *The Ontological Turn. An Anthropological Exposition.* Cambridge: Cambridge University Press.

Housley, W., Procter, R., Edwards A. et al. 2014. 'Big and Broad Social Data and the Sociological Imagination: A Collaborative Response'. *Big Data & Society* 1(2): 1–15.

Knox, H. and Walford, A. 2016. 'Digital Ontology'. *Fieldsights – Cultural Anthropology.* https://culanth.org/fieldsights/820-digital-ontology [accessed 16 March 2017].

Kockelman, P. 2013. 'The Anthropology of an Equation: Sieves, Spam Filters, Agentive Algorithms, and Ontologies Of Transformation'. *Hau: Journal of Ethnographic Theory* 3(3): 33–61.

Latour, B., Jensen, P., Venturini, T., Grauwin, S. and Boullier, D. 2012. '"The whole is always smaller than its parts". A Digital Test of Gabriel Tardes' Monades'. *The British Journal of Sociology* 63(4): 590–615.

Lazer, D., Pentland, A. (Sandy), Adamic, L. et al. 2009. 'Life in the Network: The Coming Age of Computational Social Science'. *Science* (New York, NY) 323(5915): 721–3.

Marcus, George. 1993. 'Ethnography in/of the World System: The Emergence of Multi-sited Ethnography'. *Annual Review of Anthropology* 24: 95–117.

Nafus, D. and Sherman, J. 2014. 'Big Data, Big Questions: This One Does Not Go up to 11: The Quantified Self Movement as an Alternative Big Data Practice'. *International Journal of Communication* 8: 1784–94.

Pedersen, Morten Axel and Nielsen, Morten. 2013. 'Transtemporal Hinges: Reflections on a Comparative Ethnographic Study of Chinese Infrastructural Projects in Mozambique and Mongolia'. *Social Analysis* 57(1): 122–42.

Ruppert, E, Law. J. and Savage, M. 2013. 'Reassembling Social Science Methods: The Challenge of Digital Devices'. *Theory Culture & Society* 30(4): 22–46.

Sekara, V., Stopczynski A. and Lehmann S. 2016. 'Fundamental Structures of Dynamic Social Networks'. *Proceedings of the National Academy of Sciences* 113(36): 9977–82.

Stoller, P. 2013. 'Big Data, Thick Description and Political Expediency'. *Huffington Post*, 16 June. www.huffingtonpost.com/paul-stoller/big-data-thick-description_b_3450623.html [accessed 4 March 2018].

Stopczynski, A., Sekara V., Sapiezynski P., Cuttone A., Madsen M. M. et al. 2014. 'Measuring Large-Scale Social Networks with High Resolution'. *PLoS ONE* 9(4): e95978.

Strathern, Marilyn. 1996. 'Cutting the Network'. *Journal of the Royal Anthropological Institute* 2(3): 517–35.

Strathern, Marilyn. 1999. *Property, Substance and Effect. Anthropological Essays on Persons and Things.* London: Athlone Press.

Strathern, Marilyn. 2004. *Partial Connections.* Walnut Creek, CA: Altamira Press.

Taylor, E.B. and Horst, H.A. 2013. 'From Street to Satellite: Mixing Methods to Understand Mobile Money Users'. *EPIC 2013*, 1. www.epicpeople.org/from-street-to-satellite-mixing-methods-to-understand-mobile-money-users/ [accessed 21 February 2018].

Tsing, A.L. 2005. *Friction: An Ethnography of Global Connections.* Princeton: Princeton University Press.

Wastell, Sari. 2001. 'Presuming Scale, Making Diversity'. *Critique of Anthropology* 21(2): 185–210.

Wilf, E., Cheney-Lippold, J., Duranti, A. et al. 2013. 'Toward an Anthropology of Computer-Mediated, Algorithmic Forms of Sociality'. *Current Anthropology* 54(6): 716–39.

9

The data walkshop and radical bottom-up data knowledge

Alison Powell

How, and under what circumstances, would it be useful to produce big data from the bottom up? The assemblages that we consider to be part of the production and positioning of big data are themselves large-scale: the computing power required to deal with multiple forms of digital data, the analytics processes required to derive sensible or logical predictions, the institutional meaning-making apparatus required to create frameworks and application spaces for this data are all easier to mobilise top down. In an article on big data from the bottom up (Couldry and Powell 2014), Nick Couldry and I foreground individual agency and reflexivity as well as the variable ways in which power and participation are constructed and enacted. But the kinds of civic assemblages that we identified as examples of bottom–up big data don't operate in the same way as those from the top down. This chapter examines some strategies for examining public matters of concern in relation to data production, following from and developing from previous efforts at surfacing and valorising situated knowledge in particular urban contexts, and identifying how 'bottom–up' data subjectivity could become collaborative and collective through the use of participatory meaning-making processes. This approach allows us to attend to who is asking the questions about big data, and, further, lets us think about how data gets to be 'big' in the first place, who asks the questions that make it big (in size as well as importance) and how one might ask different kinds of questions. This chapter focuses on the genesis and development of the Data Walking project (see http://www.datawalking.org) as a means of asking differ-ent questions about 'big' data, space and local knowledge.

The data walk

The 'data walk' or 'data walkshop' is a radically bottom-up process of exploring and defining data, big data and data politics from the perspectives of groups of citizens, who walk, observe, discuss and record connections between data, processes of datafication, and the places that they live in. This produces an opportunity for collabora-tive and collective reflection on and production of ideas about data. Briefly, it works like this: after a large group discussion that opens out avenues for defining or understanding data, participants are assigned specific observational roles based on their interests, and take a walk in a local area in a small group. Each member of a walking group has a particular role in observing and documenting encounters with data, and each group is tasked with observing places and spaces that they interpret to be 'data calm' and 'data rich' and where they may observe 'data activations' where data (as defined by the walkers) intersects with other modes of being in the world. This could be the intersection of data and citizenship, the relationship between data and bodies or the construction of value in relation to data. They are also asked to identify places of data resistance. At the end of a walk, where the groups have been asked to document their movement with a map, observations, collection of physical objects, they need to tell others a story of their journey. Data walking can be used as a tool for civic engagement (Balastrini 2017), or within a broader set of reflections on specific social or economic processes (Crutchlow et al. 2016). These applications work through data walking's potential to create a phenomenology of data, and link this process to previ-ous ethnographic explorations that focus on space, movement and context in the production of knowledge (Lee and Ingold 2006). Through the framework provided by the observational roles and the kinds of data relationships they are asked to observe, participants construct a narrative for how they define and critique data in place. The whole experience, based on an encounter between participa-tory ethnography and devised performance, opens out a process and possibilities not only for 'doing big data' from the bottom up but for creating new ways of being with and ways of knowing about data in everyday life. Examples of the intersections are given later in the chapter.

This chapter outlines the genesis of the data walk as I've practised it, focusing in particular on the contribution of artistic practice to social science research and the necessity for creating new modes of interdisciplinarity to address the phenomena of data. The chapter also describes how the data walk process operates to articulate data to other concerns, employing many of these interdisciplinary elements. It charts my unfolding engagement with art practice and the insights that this provided to social scientific and public engagement work and identifies how these processes help to move beyond a focus on 'data subjectivity' as the primary way that datafication is experienced. It reflects on the data walk process as a means of surfacing the everyday experiences and reflections that many people have in relation to data by involving people with interests and concerns about data in ethnographic practices of observation and reflection. The chapter suggests that 'top-down' data assemblages need not necessarily be contested with parallel 'bottom-up' ones but perhaps instead with alternative modes of making sense. In conclusion, it reflects on the outcomes of this process not only as a form of community or civic engagement and as a conceptual tool for generating alternative epistemologies and ontologies for big data as well as datafication, highlighting that challenging narrow, instrumental or coercive use of data may also involve creative and expressive knowledge production.

Genesis of the data walkshop

As this chapter discusses, walking reflections have been used by philosophers, psychogeographers, urban planners and community organisations to explore relationships between people, ideas, knowledge and space, and sometimes to locate local assets (my version of the data walk began as a teaching tool, specifically intended to provide students with a physical, spatial and sensorial experience of the ethnographic experience of data proliferation, while helping them to understand the concept of situated knowledge (Haraway 1988). One of the expectations of the original student workshops was that students would come to understand not only how one's particular position of observer renders the experienced world of the city into data, but also how multitudinous this data might be.

The exercise was devised as a conceptual counterpoint to the celebratory rhetoric of big data, and undertaken at the same time as students read polemical celebrations of big data (Mayer-Shönberger and Cukier 2013) and their critiques (boyd and Crawford 2012). Over the course of several years I used the model in many contexts, including with the artist Paula Crutchlow and the Furtherfield Gallery in Finsbury Park, north London, and Exeter in the south-west of the UK as part of the Museum of Contemporary Commodities project, with urban planners at a seminar hosted by the Centre for Big Data Ethics and Microsoft Research in Cambridge UK, with data ethics PhD students in Copenhagen, social activists at the World Social Forum, and interested researchers, students and locally based workers at two sessions sponsored by the Learning Technology Innovation centre at the London School of Economics. From the beginning I was interested in using the loose form of the 'walkshop' to create a space for the exchange of different ideas, and to learn about how people with different expertise understood or defined data. As time passed I also began to see how the 'data walk' as an event, staged the possibility for new forms of collaborative knowledge production.

Originally based on a proposal for 'flashmob ethnography' framework intended to create more participatory forms of ethnographic practice (Forlano 2010), the data walk also integrates Adam Greenfield's network walkshops where attention is directed to digital networks as they appear perceptively in city space. Forlano's version of the walking experiment called for small groups to explore areas that they were unfamiliar with, with each member of the group responsible for a particular feature of the ethnographic encounter: photography, map-making, thick description and interviewing. In Forlano's original experiment, the goal was to observe 'the role of values in urban infrastructure and the built environment (including public spaces, retail shopping environments, restaurants and cafes). Specifically, the workshop encourages participants to look for and document tensions, surprises and counter-intuitive findings' (Forlano 2010). This practical approach seemed especially appropriate to introduce to my students, who were simultaneously debating the significance of big data for social research. I also directed the students to examine places that Greenfield found suggestive of the connection between network, space and civic action:

Places where information is being collected by the network.

- Places where networked information is being displayed.
- Places where networked information is being acted upon, either by people directly, or by physical systems that affect the choices people have available to them.

Combining Greenfield's focus on spaces of mediation with Forlano's structured roles for non-expert ethnographers provided a framework to direct the walk and also a means for students to narrate their findings, but it also set up a way for the students to distribute expertise between themselves, and to transform their insights into potential action. In the first walkshops, the walking and observing were followed by a workshop using 'critical making' to interrogate the relationships that the students observed and to imagine potential reinterpretations or critical futures. Critical making has been lauded as a means to inspire active citizenship (Ratto and Boler 2014) and celebrate everyday practice and experience of life. Critical making focuses on how do-it-yourself creative production can act as a form of everyday political and social critique. In applying critical making as a pedagogical tool (Powell 2012b) I introduced students to ideas of thinking together through material and bodily practice (Crawford 2009) and continuing Hertz's (2012) activist design project of using critical design and critical making to advance alternative futures.

The walking, observing, reflecting and remaking originally appeared within a frame inspired by de Certeau's attention to everyday life (1984), Benjamin's celebration of walking and reflection in the Arcades project (trans. 1999), the psychogeographic tradition and other radical reinterpretations of life in designed spaces such as the Situationists. Walking and watching are practices that create the cultural life of cities, and I wanted to articulate these practices to the technological mediations that I had been investigating in other research, particularly on the concept of the 'smart city' as it evolved over time (Powell 2008, 2011, 2016). If attentive walking could bring new spaces, new phenomena and new knowledge into being, perhaps it could also serve as a way to bring new understandings of data.

Conceptual antecedents: rethinking the smart city and the objective god-eye

The observational approach was also inspired by Haraway's (1988) concept of situated knowledge. Following Haraway's acknowledgement that the 'god-eye' of science must be made to see in a particular way, the workshops also intended to highlight the inevitable consequences of deciding that one thing, rather than another, might become data. From the beginning, the walks had a constructive orientation: students were asked to use the multiple types of ethnographic data that they had collected to produce future interventions in the city spaces they observed. This was not only 'data analysis' but a play or commentary on the possibility (or not) of intervening in how cities are mediated and experienced.

I had been interested for some time in the mediation of city experience through technology, and in particular in the structure and experience of 'smart cities' as locations where particular types of technological mediations (like the idea of data being generated, gathered and processed to generate insights about the world) might become part of the repertoire of understanding. I'd already written about how activists who installed wireless internet networks might be thought of as 'rewriting' their own city by layering their own vision of it technologically (Powell 2016). I followed scholars who reflected on 'the insertion of procedure into human knowledge and social experience' (Gillespie 2014). This notion of procedure in turn reframes how data is understood and positioned in relation to prediction or potential: 'what makes something algorithmic is that it is produced by or related to an information system that is committed (functionally and ideologically) to the computational generation of knowledge or decisions' (Gillespie 2014: n.p.). I was thinking a lot about the design of smart cities, the ways that particular discourses of data seemed to frame a 'calculative' exercise of citizenship. I had been considering how citizen science, open data and other civic movements built new politics from producing, curating or calculating data (Powell 2016). But I found it difficult to step outside the technological framework and see data in a broader context.

Current critical scholarship on the 'smart city' – the framework that motivated my initial development of student walks – assumes that specific kinds of data are produced within large-scale civic projects (mostly public–private partnerships) and that this particular form of datafication produces a kind of ideal data city. This is the totalising vision of the smart city pilloried by Greenfield as 'any-space-whatever … generic technologies on generic landscapes in a generic future' (Greenfield 2011: 149). The assumption is often framed in the way that Flyverbom and Madsen express it: 'the city that becomes visible is a city that fits in with existing projects and strategies' (Flyverbom and Madsen 2016: 149). The datafied 'smart city' might, as Gabrys (2016) conceives of it, be a Foucauldian project where citizenship ceases to be connected with the exercise of rights and responsibilities and begins to be related to the capacity for citizens to act as sensors, absorbing and presenting computational information. Gabrys writes, 'participation involves computational responsiveness and is coextensive with actions of monitoring and managing one's relations to environments, rather than advancing democratic engagement through dialogue and debate' (2016: 9). This view of citizenship and participation in the data city is active and responsive, but unfolds what Gabrys calls a 'biopolitics 2.0', a biopolitics of construction in and through the calculative. This is similar to what Cheney-Lippold (2011) understands as the 'soft biopolitics' established in relation to the identities constructed by and through the correlations that emerge when one processes online data.

Within the critical literature on 'smart citizenships' some scholars (Tironi and Criado 2015) ask whether citizen production of data like 'collaborative mapping' might establish another opportunity to slow down the intensification of calculation, or display different forms of sensitivity. They wonder if this might be part of a bigger project of cosmopoliticisation, as Isabelle Stengers (2010) calls it, where new potentials are made public without concern for praise or criticism, and where new modes of engagement with urban data might be possible. Many other scholars, like Ratto and Boler (2014) and DiSalvo (DDIB2014) take this perspective as a means of supporting the experimental approaches of DIY technical and cultural subcultures. Aligned with other DIY movements (Powell 2012a, 2015) and interventions in urban spaces (Corsín Jiménez 2014), experimental and cosmopolitical data citizenships experiment with the potential for a computational world. But as much as these ways of thinking open out new contours for smart city life, to me they also raised questions about whether, how, and under what circumstances different kinds of people living in cities might be able to question and intervene in the idea that city life has become datafied or computational. The data walk began to appear as a way to open out discussion and DIY practice beyond people already engaged in it.

Interdisciplinary encounters

My ideas about walking, data and ways to devise an open engagement with data and cities expanded through an interdisciplinary encounter and subsequent work with artists. In early 2015 I was invited to Furtherfield Gallery in Finsbury Park, north London, to meet the artist/ geographer Paula Crutchlow, who was starting a project called the Museum of Contemporary Commodities. Paula was working with the geographer Ian Cook on MoCC (Crutchlow et al. 2016), which was a research-creation-engagement project aimed at examining trade (in)justices as collective future heritage. Paula and Ian wanted to lead a walk as part of their programming. I thought I could modify my teaching tool as a public engagement strategy, and connect my interest in data to Paula and Ian's interest in trade. As part of this project I led two data walks with groups of artists and local residents around Finsbury Park. Later, I travelled to Exeter to host another data walk at the Museum of Contemporary Commodities pop-up.

This encounter and the resulting conversations transformed and enhanced the perspective and the process of the data walk. Paula had been using walking as a research creation tool for many years as part of her wider practice in performance making. She was integrating this with ethnographic process through MoCC, conceiving of this as critical art practice. She explains:

Devised theatre often consists of democratic and non-hierarchical experiments where the framework for what is being made is set up by the collaborating group who write, assemble, edit and perform the materials together ... Cross disciplinary processes are shaped by participants' views, beliefs and life experiences and, when situated outside theatres as site-specific or mobile, the sense of place in all its 'thrown togetherness' (Massey 2005) becomes central to event dramaturgy. MoCC was co-designed to combine these approaches with Ian Cook's followthethings pedagogical focus on trade (in)justices and cultural activism (Crutchlow et al. 2016). The research aim was to collaborate with other academics, technologists and publics across disciplines to produce what George Marcus calls 'para-sites' 'intermediate forms, platforms and digital compositions, contemporary contraptions ...', critical art objects and events that 'push' ethnographic texts back into the production of field work by posing pedagogical challenges and experiments. (Cantarella et al. n.d.)

Where I had been considering the idea of observing data as a corrective to an objectivist 'smart city' frame and as part of a strategy of civic conversation, Paula and Ian had a more specific focus on the experiences of people trading and valuing in and near Finsbury Park, and on the phenomenal experiences of datafication of space and commodity relationship, which often produced feelings of guilt in relation to a 'perceived lack of personal agency and empowerment within globally networked systems of governance' (Crutchlow et al. 2016). Grounded in her training and experience as a performance artist, Paula's perspective on walking included a focus on movement and the transformative experience of participating in an intentionally 'disruptive' creative act. Her view of the walk revealed to me its potential as a new phenomenological experience and a way of producing alternative knowledge about the city, using performance to destabilise social hierarchy and reform the potential for collective experience. Paula writes:

The data mediations of increasingly privatised and hyper-surveilled urban space render the poetic tactics of walking in the city as imagined by de Certeau more likely to contribute to administrative strategies of consumption and security than to acts of creative resistance. Pervasive datafication and its concrete shapings of places, practices and flows might also raise questions as to whether it's desirable or even possible to develop subjectivities that are outside of or resistant to these processes (Smith 2016). Data walkshops are not the kind of exceptional cultural practice that we might understand theatre to be, but their deeply social and convivial performativities help us to unpack, negotiate and story data mediations in ways that acknowledge and use these contexts to generate potential for new performances that are consciously, purposefully and artfully constructed. (Crutchlow et al. 2016)

In the course of working with Paula and Ian I came to see the power and value of using structured small groups to create shared definitions of 'data', 'information' and 'knowledge' in a non-hierarchical way, which aligned with my interest in using data walks to investigate partial perspectives and different ways of constructing knowledge. I also learned that one of the features of this kind of work was a decentring of research expertise through involving people in a structured experience akin to a performance. In the walkshops that we held together, playfulness dominated and subjectivities shifted among artists, researchers and residents. Participants, with their specific roles to perform, observed the world but also experimented with playing at observing the world. Rather than assuming that ethnographic observation collects truthful observations, this perspective points out how much our situated knowledge is constructed through our experience, and invites us to shift that experience, and to be reflective about what the shift produces. Paula characterises the narrative reporting of the walks this way:

> On returning, embodied and imaginary practices are used in a performative re-journeying of the route, where participants are both experts in their own experience and collectively responsible for representing the group findings. Constructed as provisional, discursive and held in common, these re-visionings de-centralise the researcher's authority, creating fragile inter-subjectivities and layered imagery that are perhaps suggestive of how temporary and contingent the structures of data mediation are themselves. Through both close reading of structures and the imaginative play of group narrative they generate tactics for resistance, the means for subversion, and propositions for pedagogical artworks that question and re-value. (Crutchlow et al. 2016)

This encounter provoked me to think very carefully about how much of the meaning or significance of data was dependent on its mediation and interpretation, and how for any of the different kinds of people attending the walkshops, from urban planners in Cambridge to students in London and artists in Exeter, data might mean different things, things that could be surfaced through the shared experience of the walk. Fundamental questions about what constitutes data, how any data might be contested, or how experiences of datafication might be challenged or reimagined, emerge from this process.

Data walk process: data walkers make trouble

Building on Paula's identifications of the radical potential to reposition subjectivity and disrupt the process through which we encounter data in everyday citizenship, I began to focus more on the phenomenal experience of the data walk (in line with the long history in social science and art practice, including Lee and Ingold (2006) and Cantarella et al. n.d.) but in particular on how this performative, phenomenal experience introduces new ideas about expertise and data politics. I opened up data walks as a process of experience and inquiry to many different groups, targeting meetings and contexts where I thought the approach might be complementary. The organisers of these events advertised the data walks, and interested participants appeared. This meant that over time I held walks with many different kinds of people, from urban planners to community advocates, PhD students to residents of many different sorts of neighbourhoods in many different kinds of cities.

I began to see how the experience of destablilising expertise and learning on the move in a small group created new pathways for learning and for sharing knowledge, as well as generating processes of individual reflection on the nature of expertise. One of the artists at Finsbury Park specified that their favourite feature of the walk was the chance to meet different local people and understand how they were thinking about some of the same issues. Other participants in other walks also highlighted this exchange of expertise as a key feature of the experience. In a small group, with no leader, with defined responsibilities to document as well as to respond, all knowledge is revealed as situated. When organisers asked for responses from participants about what they particularly appreciated about the walks, people responded that they enjoyed 'the chance to observe data in the street with others' (Montreal) and 'everyone's enthusiasm – and everyone's suspicion of the environment' (Exeter). A 'suspicion of the environment' brings to mind Gabrys's notion of 'environmental subjectivity' or an orientation of the self to the environment. But this subjectivity is not necessarily constructed only through observation of data but rather through the critical manoeuvres that participants used to interpret data. Even so, subjectivisation through data is not the only way that people experience data, and a performative method can help to introduce others and to move encounters with data from the individual to the collective. As the project matured, I built the DataWalking.org website to explain the process and open up exchanges with others experimenting with it.

Situating and reflecting on surveillance

Some work in geography as well as communication studies assumes that urban mediation consists of what Flyverbom and Madsen call 'data produced by objects' (2016: 1) – the strata of data produced by sensors and cameras. As the emerging literature on data, space and value indicates, this data becomes integrated into organisational, calculative and decision-making processes that structure the experience of urban space. A narrow view of 'environmentality' might suggest that the data produced by objects helps to construct that subjectivity. But our walks suggest that it is the performance of observation and narrative reconstruction that produces this subjectivity, and that this can be transformative, especially as it produces new forms of collective or collaborative knowledge. One common element of critique was the experience of observing traces of data-based surveillance. In every walk, some participants photographed the banal architecture of surveillance: blank-surfaced round surveillance cameras hanging from above in university campuses and privatised shopping areas, passcode-protected gates and doors that close spaces off to those without the data, and railway station turnstiles with RFID readers that collect data on who passes.

But many of these installations are inscrutable on their own. It is impossible to know whether the camera is functioning, or how the RFID transport data is packaged up and sold – much less to whom. The frustration at the unknowable and inscrutable enrolment of individuals into the 'calculative frame' caused many data walking groups to look elsewhere and to create, through their attention, different kinds of data assemblages. Sometimes this happened through a violation of the social expectations that permit us all to tolerate such inscrutable installations. In Copenhagen, a group walking near a newly constructed public library building in an official 'campus' area encountered a large brushed metal pole, similar to a telephone standard, about a metre and a half at the base. They circled it and stood taking photographs until a security guard appeared from inside the building. The object, it emerged, was part of a perimeter security project – which the walkers learned in a long interview with the security guard. In this interview (which some non-Danish participants found surprisingly open and revealing), the guard described how the perimeter system was installed to prevent graffiti being painted on the wall of the building. The group found this particularly striking as a building about 100 metres away was covered in graffiti – but they were informed that this was a 'graffiti zone' and the public library needed to be protected from it. Here, attention to data and its ambiguities produces new relation and new understandings of geographies and politics.

Investigating data assemblages

In several other walks, participants focused on what they saw as evidence of 'the digital' in the city – observing web addresses, telephone numbers and indications of networked information systems laid over physical spaces. They photographed and described occasions when web addresses were posted (or, in one case, carefully hand-painted) on exterior buildings and speculated on what might have been implied by these links between the physical world and the online world. In Copenhagen, a non-functional web address was written on to the wall of a community gardening and social support project housed in a weathered wooden hut. Walkers juxtaposed the invitation to access information on the Web with the many different kinds of concrete data and information (including tools, plants, soil, labels and instruction) present around the gardening shed. This experience echoes other work on the layers, and splinters, of data geographies (Kitchin 2014; Graham and Marvin 2001; Crang and Graham 2007).

Such apparatus of data subjectivation are therefore not the only, or far from the most important, elements of datafication experienced in everyday life. Our data walks revealed another set of constructive processes. Critical data scholars focus on how the operations undertaken on and in relation to data structure its value and power. Classification, organisation, processing and visualisation of data are defining features. As Gitelman (2013) has identified, the imagination of data is in some measure always an act of classification, of lumping and splitting, nesting and ranking, though the underlying principles at work can be hard to recover. 'Once in place, classification schemes are notoriously difficult to discern and analyze' (2013: 8f). I initially imagined that data walks might intervene in these classification processes by providing the opportunity for walkers – as citizens – to observe, audit, or resist surveillance or data classification, but instead they exploded it.

The huge range of ways that data walkers interpreted the question of 'what is data?' blew up my expectations that technologically mediated data would be the primary focus for reflections about knowledge or citizenship.

Participants developed nuanced ways to get beyond the performance of tactics against strategies, and instead plunged into the conceptual challenge of looking for and observing different kinds of data, or, as one participant put it, the potential to 'see the invisible'. In Montreal, participants reflected on the collapse between data and information, the consequences of permanent tracking of shared cars and bikes versus the temporary appearances on city streets of the 'non-datafied' versions, and the significance of different kinds of data for knowledge of place and its potential inequalities. They photographed 'non-datafied' bus stops in counterpoint to the data-linked, sensor-enabled systems for parking and car sharing, and tried to see community gardens as 'data' that illuminated potential processes of communal transformation to self-organised commons. Rather than seeing data as quantity as Maurer and Boellstorff discussed, walkers understood data as the quantitative and qualitative elements that are important to a particular community – one of the Montreal walkshops derived this definition.

Data for someone else – decentred perspectives on data

Another persistent fascination, likely linked to the non-hierarchical repositioning of expertise within data walks, was an interest in the data or information that walkers knew was important to a system, but which they couldn't interpret. In Finsbury Park, the markings under train tracks fascinated one group of walkers, who read the combinations of letters and numbers as important data destined for another audience. In Montreal, walkers read graffiti along with barcodes and identification markings as 'information that we can't know about'. 'Data produced by objects' is only one way urban life has become datafied, although it is often the focus of attention and critique. For example, Thrift's most recent (2014) work on 'sentient cities' concentrates on the ways that new data produced by sensing technologies.

Instead, other processes might be equally relevant, for example the classification and knowledge production based on this. The walkshops suggested ways to reflect and reimagine which things are worth attending to: in three walkshops participants used technological tools to expand their observation of 'the invisible'. In Finsbury Park one of the artist-participants reappropriated a domestic scanner to produce data–glitchy photographs, distorting the usual visual perception of the city by (incorrectly) rendering it as data. If data are 'produced by objects' in this assemblage, the production is faulty – so what does that make the result? In Copenhagen a group programmed a random walk generator as an algorithmic intervention into the choices that they might make in directing their walk – a significant portion of their walking time thus included negotiating with and eventually reprogramming the algorithm. In Montreal, one group used their mobile phones to display the number of WiFi signals at different points along a busy street, including markers on the maps that they made as to where most WiFi spots could be found. Later in London, a reporting narrative from one group of walkers melancholically mused on the inability of the members to really understand what they were passing by in the city. Without being forced to pay attention, they had inadvertently walked past dozens of locations of historical significance. When we attend to the city as a site of data it changes what it is: historical monuments become only one set of elements that might surface from a space of invisibilities and power relations.

Data walk outcomes

Processes of counter-subjectivication

Data walking potentially produces a way to create different experiences of data subjectivity that engage with new definitions, contentions and resistant positions. In particular, these are constructed from relationships *between* participants as they collectively seek to define and make meaning from data. These collective subjectivities exist beyond the helpless passivity that so many theorists claim must result from producing data that is then used by corporations (van Dijck 2014), beyond the open data auditing that requires entrepreneurial subject positions (Irani 2015). They move data subjects into a space that might respond to, as Birchall puts it, 'the demand not to be reduced to, and interact with, data in ways delimited by the state; to resist the terms of engagement set by the two faces of shareveillance (i.e. sharing data with the state and monitoring that shared data)' (2016: 9). In some data walkshops I asked participants if what they had learned changed how they acted in relation to data. None of the participants mentioned limiting the data that they produced, necessarily, or even changing their behaviour to avoid producing data that might fit into the assemblages we discussed. Instead they considered how the practice of walking and thinking and paying attention changed their city and provided 'heightened awareness of potential places to intervene' (Montreal).

If participants are attending to data as evidence of surveillance, they may find it. But by performing expertise within a data walk, people can make other things filter into view, 'become data' and connect to other people and other matters of concern (Latour 2004). Data walking might be considered a strategy for becoming a data citizen. Across the different groups I met, a few shared themes emerged. One was an interest in attending to the liminal – to the edges and curiosities of urban life, and where these were inflected by, resistant to or integrated into data systems. In London a group I walked with received a wonderful lecture on the development of post boxes and the way that this disintermediated communication – creating a binary system of 'stamped/not stamped' mail. In Cambridge one group fixated on the traces left by fallen leaves, which they wished to be able to interpret with as much factual meaning as the affective power the arrangement created for them.

People also navigated in interesting ways the barrier and balance of datafication by forcing visibility of the invisible in some cases, and by trying to document the everyday excesses of datafication: composing maps of their walks by noting the positions of maps placed in the street, documenting competing and contradictory numbering systems inside university buildings and at bus stops, or proposing new data interventions to highlight assemblages that are less visible – like proposing to collect data on the use of the Exeter Pound local currency. For some people, there seemed to be a politics to this – a push against full datafication where this might bring optimisation: 'what would be the point of a totally organized city? Where nothing happens?' (Montreal).

In the last data walk before the time of writing, I heard back from one of the participants, who had been particularly taken with the form of the walk, which he saw as linking the objectivist and phenomeno-logical views of data. He noted that by providing distinct roles the walks not only distributed or destabilised expertise, they also nar-rowed the 'data' that would be collected. Similarly, requiring a map forced a performance of a narrative that also created a particular specification for the knowledge. I agree; this play of structure and movement is one way to break down the distinction between data as 'what is given' (perhaps even fact) and data as something that must always be made, through observation, expertise, filtering, contestation and narrative, in conversation with others. Data walks, through their collaborative and performative structure and invitation to phenom-enal experience, create a method for creating different kinds of data, but also for challenging some of the ways in which top-down big data paradigms are narrowing the ways that data might be experienced or researched.

Paying attention and staying with the trouble

The data walk process, with its focus on paying attention and attend-ing to the liminal, also suggests ways and means to undertake what Isabelle Stengers calls 'paying attention' (2010) and Haraway 'staying with the trouble' (2015). Both of these feminist philosophers suggest that current ways of thinking about science – that is, thinking about 'data' objectively – block us into thinking reductively about our rela-tionships to the worlds that we build as well as those into which we come. This is at the root of Haraway's (2015) critique of the concept of the anthropocene – the notion that it has been human activity itself that has so transformed the living world and our relation to it. She acknowledges that the Capitalocene might be more descriptive, given that the scale and intensity of changes to world-systems have emerged with changes to scale, rate/speed, synchronicity and complexity. Fun-damentally, Haraway suggests that the way forward is to push into a Cthulucene, a world-thinking mode that 'entangles myriad tempo-ralities and spatialities and myriad intra-active entities in assemblages – including the more-than-human, other-than-human, inhuman, and human-as-humus'. Taking these new positions makes spaces of theory that are large enough to help 'reconstitute refuges, to make possible partial and robust biological–cultural–political–technological recu-peration and recomposition' (2015: 160). This species-being position seems far from the interest in observing human-made mediations involving abstract data within human-made cities. Philosophically, however, the data walk's intense focus and attention to the construction of mediations and their meanings start to make the assumption of a 'god-eye' seem untenable – along with the idea that only certain kinds of actions get to be rendered as data.

The stories of liminality, of inscrutability of the data and information produced in cities, speak to the troublesome nature of mediation, which is one way that 'the being of humankind is to be outside itself' as Bernard Stiegler (1998) argues. Kember and Zylinska (2012) push this further, calling for an ethics that acknowledges this 'productive engagement with alterity'. As media begin to settle into becoming data, then radical media studies might perhaps be encouraged to see, reckon and manufacture data differently. I encourage other researchers to pull out these threads and develop them as datafication sinks into the communicational everyday.

Conclusion

My data walks resulted from a wish to intervene in a space where data is often viewed as objective, and where its 'bottom-up' subjectivity is often oriented to the individual, not the collective. When it is viewed as constructed or phenomenological, scholars have struggled to create room for people's situated, everyday, emotional or non-expert knowledge in relation to this construction. Over its evolution and encounters with other walking traditions and their political and philosophical positions, my version of the data walk has specified a framework for radical, collective, bottom-up knowledge creation and sharing, with an element of performative practice. It has proved capable of being articulated with the interests and concerns of a range of different people who have listened, walked, observed, defined and laughed about data, information, knowledge and place. It has produced collaborations, friendships, misunderstandings and the capacity to listen to many retold stories about 'what we started to see emerging' as groups of strangers walked in cities and tried to perceive relationships that were not always visible – and then tried to tell stories about them. To counter the emerging ontological frames that fix data as something larger than the individual, forever controlling and inscrutable, and the epistemological frameworks that claim data as truth, the walks may provide a radical relief. These activities, in their sheer humanity, reposition knowledge and feeling, opening up the possibility that data might be created through these performative acts. Can they act as full counters to the datafied experience of everyday life? That is not the question. Can they provoke joy, curiosity and engagement? New ways to tell stories and new ways of thinking about why data matters? Perhaps yes, and that is what matters.

References

Balestrini, M.E. 2017. 'A City in Common: Explorations on Sustained Community Engagement with Bottom-up Civic Technologies' (Doctoral dissertation, University College London).

Benjamin, W. and Tiedemann, R. 1999. *The Arcades Project*. Cambridge, MA: Harvard University Press.

Birchall, C. 2016. 'Shareveillance: Subjectivity Between Open and Closed Data'. *Big Data & Society* 3(2): 1–12.

Boyd, D. and Crawford, K. 2012. 'Critical Questions for Big Data: Provocations for a Cultural, Technological, and Scholarly Phenomenon'. Information, Communication & Society 15(5): 662–79.

Cantarella, L., Hegel, C. and Marcus, G. n.d. 'A Week in Pasadena: Collaborations Toward the Productive Encounter'. *Field* 1 (spring): 53–94.

Cheney-Lippold, J. 2011. 'A New Algorithmic Identity: Soft Biopolitics and the Modulation of Control'. *Theory, Culture & Society* 28(6): 164–81.

Corsín Jiménez, A.C. 2014. 'The Right to Infrastructure: A Prototype for Open Source Urbanism'. *Environment and Planning D: Society and Space* 32(2): 342–62.

Couldry, N. and Powell, A. 2014. 'Big Data from the Bottom Up'. *Big Data & Society* 1(2): 1–5.

Crang, M. and Graham, S. 2007. 'Sentient Cities Ambient Intelligence and the Politics of Urban Space'. *Information, Communication & Society* 10(6): 789–817.

Crawford, M.B. 2009. *Shop Class as Soulcraft: An Inquiry into the Value of Work*. New York: Penguin.

Crutchlow, P., Cook, I. et al. 2016. 'Museum of Contemporary Commodities, Artwork Research Assemblage'. www.moccguide.net [accessed 24 February 2018].

De Certeau, M. 1984. 'Walking in the City'. In *The Production of Everyday Life*. Berkeley, CA: University of California Press, 91–110.

DiSalvo, C. 2014. 'The Growbot Garden Project as DIY Speculation through Design'. In *DIY Citizenship: Critical Making and Social Media*. Edited by M. Ratto and M. Boler. Cambridge, MA: MIT Press, 237–65.

Flyverbom, M. and Madsen, A.. 2016. 'Sorting Data Out: Unpacking Big Data Value Chains and Algorithmic Knowledge Production'. In Die Gesellschaft der Daten: Über die digitale Transformation der sozialen Ordnung. Edited by F. Süssenguth. Bielefeld: Transcript Verlag, 140–61.

Forlano, L., 2010. 'Flash Mob Ethnography Workshop'. *Ethnographic Praxis in Industry Conference Proceedings*, 2001(1): 307.

Gabrys, J. 2016. *Program Earth: Environmental Sensing Technology and the Making of a Computational Planet*. Minneapolis: University of Minnesota Press.

Gillespie, T. 2014. 'The Relevance of Algorithms'. In *Media Technologies: Essays on Communication, Materiality, and Society*. Edited by T. Gillespie, P. Boczkowski and K. Foot. Cambridge, MA: MIT Press, 167–84.

Gitelman, L. 2013. *Raw Data Is an Oxymoron*. Cambridge, MA: MIT Press.

Graham, S. and Marvin, S. 2001. *Splintering Urbanism: Networked Infrastructures, Technological Mobilities and the Urban Condition*. London: Psychology Press.

Greenfield, A. 2011. 'Systems/Layers Walkshop'. www.dcrc.org.uk/events/systemslayers-walkshop-adam-greenfield [accessed 24 February 2018].

Haraway, D. 1988. 'Situated Knowledges: The Science Question in Feminism and the Privilege of Partial Perspective'. *Feminist Studies* 14(3): 575–99.

Haraway, D. 2015. 'Anthropocene, Capitalocene, Plantationocene, Chthulucene: Making Kin'. *Environmental Humanities* 6: 159–65.

Hertz, G. (ed.). 2012. *Critical Making*. www.conceptlab.com/criticalmaking [accessed 4 December 2017].

Irani, L. 2015. 'Hackathons and the Making of Entrepreneurial Citizenship'. *Science, Technology & Human Values* 40(5): 799–824.

Kember, S. and Zylinska, J. 2012. *Life after New Media: Mediation as a Vital Process*. Cambridge, MA: MIT Press.

Kitchin, R. 2014. 'The Real-Time City? Big Data and Smart Urbanism'. *GeoJournal* 79(1): 1–14.

Latour, B. 2004. 'Why Has Critique Run out of Steam? From Matters of Fact to Matters of Concern'. *Critical inquiry* 30(2): 225–48.

Lee, J. and Ingold, T. 2006. 'Fieldwork on Foot: Perceiving, Routing, Socializing'. In *Locating the Field: Space, Place and Context in Anthropology*. Edited by P. Collins and S. Coleman. Oxford: Berg, 67–86.

Massey, D. 2005. *For Space*. London: Sage.

Mayer-Schönberger, V. and Cukier, K. 2013. *Big Data: A Revolution that Will Transform How We Live, Work, and Think*. New York: Houghton Mifflin Harcourt.

Powell, A. 2008. 'WiFi Publics: Producing Community and Technology'. *Information, Communication & Society* 11(8): 1068–88.

Powell, A. 2011. 'Metaphors, Models and Communicative Spaces: Designing Local Wireless Infrastructure'. *Canadian Journal of Communication* 36(1): 1–39.

Powell, A. 2012a. 'Democratizing Production through Open Source Knowledge: From Open Software to Open Hardware'. *Media, Culture & Society* 34(6): 691–708.

Powell, A. 2012b. 'Critical Making, Teaching & Politics'. In G. Hertz (ed.), *Critical Making*. www.conceptlab.com/criticalmaking/ [accessed 20 February 2018].

Powell, A. 2015. 'Open Culture and Innovation: Integrating Knowledge across Boundaries'. *Media, Culture & Society* 37(3): 376–93.

Powell, A. 2016. 'Coding Alternative Modes of Governance'. In *Code and the City*. Edited by R. Kitchin and S.Y. Perng. London: Routledge, 178–95.

Ratto, M. and Boler, M. (eds). 2014. *DIY Citizenship: Critical Making and Social Media*. Cambridge, MA: MIT Press.

Smith, P. 2016. 'Walking and Subjectivities'. Accompanying presentation, Asylum Topographies, Bethlem Gallery, Kent.

Stengers, I. 2010. *Cosmopolitics*. Minneapolis: University of Minnesota Press.

Stiegler, B. 1998. *Technics and Time, 1. The Fault of Epimetheus*. Stanford: Stanford University Press.

Thrift, Nigel. 2014. 'The "Sentient" City and What It May Portend'. *Big Data & Society* 1(1): 1–21.

Tironi, M. and Criado, T.S. 2015. 'Of Sensors and Sensitivities. Towards a Cosmopolitics of "Smart Cities"?' *TECNOSCIENZA: Italian Journal of Science & Technology Studies* 6(1): 89–108.

Van Dijck, J. 2014. 'Datafication, Dataism and Dataveillance: Big Data between Scientific Paradigm and Ideology'. *Surveillance & Society*: 12(2): 197.

10

Working ethnographically with sensor data

Dawn Nafus

This chapter is primarily about methods. I work in Intel Labs, the research and development organisation at Intel. Since 2007, I have been asking research participants to collect digital data about themselves, and giving it back to them in forms designed to stimulate conversation. I invite participants to reflect on data as matters of concern, not matters of fact (Latour 2004), and they largely respond in this spirit. Much like the chapter from Powell (Chapter 9 above), and in the spirit of the broader turn towards critical geographic information systems (GIS) (Wilmott 2016) and community-based participatory research (Corburn 2005), this approach evolved as a way to reclaim the situatedness of data, and create space for more participatory, humanistic ways of engaging with data. This space necessarily sits alongside positivist modalities of using datasets, and occasionally creates room for dialogue between positivists and those who value situated knowledge. Even those who value generalisability as a goal, and treat situatedness a bias to be avoided, often can agree that best person to explore what a dataset means is often the very person to whom it refers. Perhaps more significantly for anthropology, this approach offers ethnographic opportunities that are hard to come by in other ways. Data evokes the past without fully predefining it, and that opens up conversations between researcher and the participants who understand the context behind it.

My first goal for this chapter, then, is to describe in a relatively straightforward way what this research practice involves for those who might be curious about adapting it for their own research situation. The considerations for setting up the research and working with these forms of data are non-trivial, but the approach can be done by those of us who do not possess engineering or data science skills. This was not always the case. Five or ten years ago, working with sensors used to be much more difficult. Even today, sensing systems can be tricky to set up, and data visualisations can fall flat. Working with data as a qualitatively trained person always produces a certain amount of hesitance about where one's capacities reach their limits, and when it is necessary to seek help from others. Therefore, I hope to share some of the pitfalls and possibilities I have found.

These research practices have evolved in a context where the material infrastructures available have been transforming. In a sensor-rich world, the same tools that create massive data stockpiles at technology companies and scientific laboratories also create smaller, but still richly analysable data streams that have a different sort of value. Sensor data creates circumstances where analysis can grow numerically complex even when that data refers to a single person, let alone a whole community (Nafus 2016). The technical systems that people access as consumers show data in ways that are quite different from what data scientists can see, who have fuller access to those systems. Indeed, this unequal access has been a chief complaint about contemporary big data cultures (Andrejevic 2014). Not only can large institutions black box the algorithms they use to parse data, they can also take advantage of the cross-population insights that cohere only when data points are collected across many people (Pasquale 2015).

While this is clearly a problematic aspect of institutional power, there is also a significant technical challenge that has largely been overlooked by social-scientific commentary. Even if companies or publicly funded research projects did become more transparent about what they do with data, either by choice or through legal mandate, what tools are realistically available for data subjects – the people to whom data refers – to create alternative views, or appropriate the data in ways that suit their agendas better? What tools would facilitate meaningful participation in big data? The systems that professional data scientists use offer the broadest possible flexibility to make a wide range of calculations, but their use presupposes advanced mathematical and computer science skills. Yet my research had been showing that 'ordinary' people do in fact have something to say about which patterns matter and which patterns do not. Big data is not just about esoteric calculations that require machine learning algorithms. A simple recurrence in time can still show something conceptually simple and useful beyond expert circles, yet still be hard to achieve in a spreadsheet.

Threaded through the methodological work described below, I have also been participating in technical work to address this problem. The software project I co-lead, Data Sense, attempts to facilitate 'lay' data exploration by people who do not possess coding or statistical skills. The project is a technical response to what I had been seeing as research participants encountered data with me. This software is but one of many developments in the technological infrastructure that makes it conceivable for non-experts to use sensor data for their own purposes.

A secondary goal for this chapter, then, is to contribute to the discussion about the entanglements between materials, sociality and methods. The introduction to this volume argued that, in a data-saturated world, it should not be surprising that data might be found in ethnographic accounts as artefacts that participants already have, and as artefacts that ethnographers set out to collect. When I began using this approach in 2007, I did not encounter research participants who already had data I was looking to collect. Now when I do field-work participants regularly offer their Fitbit data, or ask the research team to look more deeply at data they have, like air quality data. The tools and the distribution labour in research have changed, too. When I started this work, it was in collaboration with a computer scientist, who departed our lab leaving a sizeable hole in the lab's research practice. I did not know at the time that the software I would later help develop, in conjunction with other technological developments on the market, would also fill some of that hole. Although I cannot do everything a computer scientist can do, changes in the available technology mean that as a non-engineer I can now get some mean-ingful data out of a sensor system, parse it in some limited ways and know what to ask for when the situation requires someone writing a script to do the job. The interdependencies between materials and methods, and the distribution of labour, become clearer as they evolve in the long term. That trajectory is what I wish to show.

This transformation in research practice underscores the argument made by the social life of methods approach (Law et al. 2011; Ruppert et al. 2013; Savage 2013), which suggests that methods cannot be disentangled from the ongoing social lives they are designed to comprehend. What starts as one person's method becomes another person's everyday practice. The changes in my research practice also echo the inventive method (Lury and Wakeford 2012), in that they show that 'it is not possible to apply a method as if it were indifferent or external to the problem it seeks to address … if methods are to be inventive, they should not leave that problem untouched' (Lury and Wakeford 2012: 3). Indeed, I hope to suggest that taking the social life of methods seriously also means intervening in the tools that sustain cultures of big data. It is not enough to comment on the emergence of new technical systems as if we ethnographers were untouched by them. Nor is it enough to merely appropriate the techniques and technologies of other research practices to conduct ethnography. While not every anthropologist needs to become invested in actively shaping big data systems, I hope to demonstrate that an ongoing anthropological and sociological voice in their making is worthwhile both for our discipline and for our research participants, who are as entangled in a data-saturated world as we are. The materials matter to what others can do with big data, and what we can do with it, too.

In the methodological account that follows, I rely on a loose, somewhat shifting figure of the reflexive data subject. Like Couldry and Powell (2014), Kitchin (2014), Wilmott (2016) and others in this volume, I take the view that big data methods should make space for reflexivity and participation by data subjects. While my approach bears some resemblance to 'trace ethnography' (Geiger and Ribes 2011) in studies of computer-supported collaborative work (CSCW), where researchers immerse themselves in online documentation to understand the social relations that generated them (see also Dumit on 'data archaeology' in Chapter 11 below), like Dumit I place much more emphasis on speaking to live human beings about data. Here, participants' reflections can extend into a research practice in its own right. In some projects, participants have simply commented on data as presented to them, while in others they have posed their own research questions, used their own methods and formulated notions of appropriate data collection, parsing and visualisation. In some others still, participants wished to exercise some control over the research agenda while leaving it to researchers to specify how their agendas translated into numerical form. Where reflection ends and research begins, or where an ethnographer's methods end and another's begin is not something that can be assumed *a priori*. Nevertheless, in a data-saturated world, it is safe to assume that reflexive data subjects have their own agendas with data in some way.

In what follows, I focus on three particularly illustrative projects, one on computer use, one on stress among family caregivers and one on environmental health. I show the methodological considerations that emerged in attempting to give participants data to reflect upon, and how the methods shifted in response to changing the technological circumstances and the positionalities of the people with whom I was working.

Ethnomining

In 2007, our team received a request from a strategic planner hoping to collect some market intelligence about how people were using laptops. He wanted a research project where software would detect computer use, as opposed to ethnographers asking people about how they used their computers, or observing them. He wanted those measurements to fit into the demographic categories that form the currency of market research. Do women use laptops more frequently than men? Do young people's laptops use more power than older people's, because perhaps they use video more heavily? At Intel, anthropology had traditionally been used for identifying underlying social changes that created risks or opportunities for the business, and my colleagues and I were not keen to abandon this remit in order to answer a basic market research question. However, this was 2007, and device telemetry (i.e., using software to create data about how a device is used) had not yet become standard practice. This made it a technical research problem alongside a social one, and so we took on the project despite some reluctance.

We formed a small team consisting of a computer scientist and two anthropologists, including myself. Aware that this method would never adequately capture what computers meant to people, we designed the project to mix ethnographic interviewing with what would later be called big data. Our team developed and placed software on 169 people's laptops that recorded everything that happened on those laptops on a second-by-second basis over the course of a month and a half (keystrokes, power state location, etc. – everything that was detectable, excluding the contents of documents or online materials). The computer scientist we worked with, Tye Rattenbury, shared our scepticism about reducing matters to demographic categories, but he also showed us that there were alternative ways of parsing data. His epistemological flexibility meant we did not encounter the transversals described by Madsen et al. (Chapter 8 above). Tye did not just meet us half-way, but got curious about anthropological approaches to research, which in turn stoked our own curiosity about how he was thinking about data. This situation created the mutual trust necessary to experiment with new methods together.

Tye found that there simply *were* no patterns that meaningfully mapped on to demographic categories. No way of breaking down the data produced anything statistically significant in those terms. In an attempt to see if there were other patterns to see, he printed out a full wall's worth of data visualisations. Each chart showed when a participant's computer was used lightly or intensely for the study period. The only pattern that seemed to hold was that these 169 people tended to not use their computers during normal sleeping hours – not exactly a huge finding. When it became clear that the original request was utterly unworkable, the project began to rely more heavily on the ethnography. For a sub-set of research participants we printed out large, poster-sized plots of the data, and asked them what they thought the data showed. That work demonstrated that, across the board, people were using computers in times they thought of as interstitial – in times between the times structured by kinship, waged labour and so forth. We called this approach 'ethnomining', because at the time working with big data was not 'analytics' but 'data mining'. The favoured terms are inevitably fleeting.

With this approach we were able to show both qualitatively and quantitatively what we initially could not see by playing data scientists. Contrary to the mythical 'power user' we had been asked to find, all of the computer users interacted with their computers in short stints most of the time. My colleague ken anderson knew this to be a long-standing phenomenon (he had coined the term 'Internet snacking' some years before), but we did not expect that it suffused computer use so completely. Once the ethnography showed us what was worth looking for, Tye made the relevant calculation that Intel used to redesign a chipset to accommodate interstitial use – not the sort of

Figure 10.1 Interviewing with big posters of data about computer use

change that our strategic planner expected, but a result none the less (Anderson et al. 2009).

The research payoffs for our odd, early experiment surprised us. We were surprised by the ease with which people were able to make sense of, and reflect on, a large complex dataset when it pertained to themselves. We worried that the complex plots would be illegible, but in the end what mattered was their ability to see the dates and times, and flurries of activity. The temporal patterns facilitated discussions about daily habits, what it means to keep a schedule, what constitutes productivity and relaxation etc. Some participants would use the data to show their lack of a regular schedule, and to insist on how busy they were. Others would use a tightly orchestrated regular schedule to insist on the same thing. This got us into a discussion about the relation between discourses of busy-ness and practice that we could not have had otherwise. We were also surprised that people we interviewed requested to keep the data posters we had made for them.

They enjoyed having their lives reframed in a way that was open to their own interpretations. The data was 'real', in the sense that it faithfully recorded bursts of keystrokes, but it was an open, partial record that said nothing about what those keystrokes were about. These were partial indications whose full meaning only the data subject could supply.

At a practical level, there were many aspects of our workflow that proved difficult. There was the temptation to underestimate the amount of technology support that research participants need to ensure that data is collected at all. In this first project, we had written our own software that was not easy to install, and checking that data was indeed being collected was non-trivial. We ended up having to send the software on USB sticks through the mail, and asking participants to return them full of data, but we could not rely on the exact specifications of each person's software and hardware set-up. Each computer behaved just that little bit differently. In fact, this proved so unwieldy that, when we did an extension of this study in Portugal and Bulgaria, we structured the research so that there was an initial interview where we got to know the person or family, and did the installation of the technology ourselves.

Another difficulty was the sheer amount of work involved in designing, testing and compiling the plots. Just as the first round of interview questions never really 'works' in traditional fieldwork, so too we needed to test whether the printed-out plots were evocative at all, using our own data. We could not adjust the plots on a person-by person basis because of the time pressure involved. If too much time had elapsed between the data collection period and the time when we sat down with participants to talk about that period of time, their memories would fade. Even just running the scripts to generate the plots, and print them, was itself significant labour.

In a predecessor for this study (Aipperspach et al. 2006), my collaborators learned that visualisations that paint a 'complete' picture make for poor interview materials. In that work, researchers had created a visualisation of patterns of people's movement inside a home, and interviewed the data subjects about what it might mean. The responses there had been quite flat. Participants were more likely to say 'yup, I must have been on the couch a lot' than to tell stories about what being on the couch meant to them. In the ethno-mining study, there was a 'flaw' in the data that proved advantageous. The location data in our study was not human-readable, and often reported a change in location when there was none. This vagueness proved to be exactly the invitation we needed to get people beyond 'yup, I was there' to thinking through where they could have been, or if it was a computer glitch. The thinking out loud in turn brought out discourses of busy-ness and routine that proved significant to the work. As we proceeded in these interviews, we had to work out a delicate balance between giving participants enough of an explanation of how the graphs worked so that they stood a chance of interpreting them at all, and giving not so much that we ended up with flat responses, or telling them what to think. Finding this balance has remained an ongoing issue.

Caregiving

While the ethnomining process was used more or less in a similar way in subsequent projects (see, for example, Nafus and Beckwith 2016), by 2015 the material circumstances had shifted in some important ways. One was that consumer-grade sensing technologies like Fitbits had proliferated, which meant that the possibility for using sensor data in research expanded beyond click data or document version data to include what could be sensed about a body, or an environment. Culturally, new expectations had developed about what that data indicated. Participants in the Quantified Self community, for example, had begun to use data from these devices to turn medical research methods 'inside out' (Greenfield 2016), and discover something medically and personally meaningful about their own bodies that sometimes drew on medical expertise, and at other times challenged it. Indeed Data Sense started in part as an effort to help them do this. More broadly, data analysis tools and infrastructures had become more stable and easier to use. New tools like Tableau meant that with good familiarity with data structures it was possible, without coding, to do many data visualisation tasks inappropriate for spreadsheet programs. Application Programming Interfaces (APIs) – an important way of getting data out of a sensor device – had also become fairly common and more reliable. Many companies had come to understand the importance of offering 'raw' data export, often with vociferous pressure from the many Quantified Self participants who needed that capability to do research on themselves.

These changes set the stage for the Atlas of Caregiving project, a Robert Wood Johnson-sponsored pilot project led by the Family Caregiver Alliance to examine stress among family caregiving (Mehta and Nafus 2016). In this work, we asked caregivers to use a set of sensing gadgets that detected stress-related phenomena for a 24-hour period. We also asked them to keep a log of their activities, so that we could interview them about it afterwards and together identify what specific aspects of stress were causing the most trouble. As my collaborator Rajiv Mehta put it, the primary purpose was to 'see what we could see'. The sensors were being evaluated for their research value at the same time as we were trying to understand the substantive issue of stress among caregivers.

This was also an action research project, meaning that the goal was not merely to respond to the scholarship on family caregiving but to test whether collecting and examining data were directly useful to the caregivers involved, as is the case in the Quantified Self community. The people who participate in Quantified Self are different reflexive data subjects from family caregivers. Quantified Self participants tend to have elaborate ideas about what kinds of data collection, parsing methods and experimental design are going to yield the most insight, while family caregivers are usually preoccupied with other things. Still, their homes were not free of data, but contained elaborate spreadsheets, filing systems, medical data and the occasional Fitbit that kept things afloat. Both Mehta and I had been deeply involved in the Quantified Self community, and so we had a loose sense that, if caregivers were shown a new way of collecting data, they might stand to benefit in practical ways from reflecting on it.

In this study we spent a good deal of time evaluating newly available technologies for their suitability in research. The criteria we used for evaluation were the following (for further details, see Mehta and Nafus 2016).

Signal: What is the data claiming to indicate, and is that claim credible? In our case, we were looking for indicators of stress, but there are no direct indicators of stress to be had. Instead, there are proxies, like heart rate, electrodermal activity (EDA) and sleep disturbances. These only partially indicate some types of stress, some of the time, and also indicate a whole lot else like exercise or a humid room. We also examined whether the device is prone to returning missing data, or implausible data such as spikes in heart rate reaching 170.

Sampling rate: How often the device takes a reading (known as sampling rate) can affect what a researcher can do with the data afterwards. A device that takes a reading every second can tell a researcher about some types of physiological responses that one taking a reading every minute cannot. However, a file that takes a reading once every second is also 60 times larger than a file that takes a reading once a minute, and that impacts in the requirements for storing the data, the ease of moving it between collaborators and ease of working with it. Fine-grained data might or might not be necessary, depending on the researchers' conceptualisation of how long the phenomenon in question plays out, and the participants' ability to recall the details of what was happening (which in our case was not at the second-by-second level).

Parsers: Sometimes data can be parsed in different ways to extract different kinds of indicators. Activity trackers regularly parse movement data into steps or sleep, for example. Parsing algorithms like these are rarely available off the shelf and not easily deployed. In our case, we contacted stress-sensing researchers who allowed us to use a parser that would convert EDA data into more sophisticated signals that they believed are more likely to be tied to stress.

Battery and data storage: As with the initial 2007 study, devices do not always behave in the way that one would hope. Batteries might need frequent recharging, or the device might fill up with data and need to move it off the device and into long-term storage more quickly than a research participant can get to a connection. Some devices successfully sync better than others, which impacts the level of intervention necessary from participants or researchers.

Burden on participants: A device that was particularly unsightly, physically hindering or inappropriately gendered might be difficult for participants to use for any sustained length of time. Technology babysitting, like syncing data from device to online storage, might require unavoidable work from the participant. As our study also involved participants keeping a log of their activities, which was a significant burden, we also limited electronic data collection to a 24-hour period specifically so that no one would have to recharge a battery or deal with syncing issues on top of keeping a log, and that on top of caregiving.

Compatibility with participants' systems: Our device-vetting process revealed that many devices and mobile phone apps are specific to a particular operating system, or otherwise depend on what participants have access to. Setting up an in-home sensor might require high-quality broadband access that participants don't always have. In the caregiving study, we did not load software on to people's devices largely to avoid this problem, but that choice meant we could record only for a short amount of time, and record one participant at a time. In subsequent projects where the research questions demanded a longer sensing period, we had to make sure to use devices that could work with both Apple and Android systems, and do more technical support to ensure they were successfully loaded on to the participants' phones.

Data export and data format: Not all devices provide the ability to export data. Some popular devices offer export of daily summaries, but require customers to pay more or have a developer account to get the full dataset available (software like Data Sense and Zenobase provides a way to work around this problem). Many potentially viable devices were rejected for this reason. Also, not all data types are interoperable. We did not fuse together numerical data, handwritten logs and images taken once every minute into an interactive visualisation because this would have required building bespoke software. Similarly, timestamps can be inconsistently formulated across different devices, making it tricky to compare across different data. Some data analysis tools will help with the timestamp alignment, and someone more technically minded can overcome the time-formatting issues in a spreadsheet program. In the end, we showed participants each data type (noise level, heart rate etc.) separately in part to avoid these issues.

Data giveback: Data giveback can be as simple as sending participants spreadsheets, but this is not likely to be particularly useful. Many consumer-oriented sensors provide interfaces that research participants can use to peer into their data, but sensors designed for research use might not provide this. It can also be a source of frustration if the interfaces are poorly designed or inappropriate to the context (for example, if the device 'nudges' the user into exercising more when the data is being collected to indicate stress). It might be sufficient to provide participants visualisations produced by the project.

Because we were sensing a 24-hour period, and people quickly forget the details of a single day, our turnaround process was much tighter than in the computer-use study. We held an initial interview where we also set up the gadgets, revisited the participants the next day to collect the gadgets, and then Rajiv immediately produced plots in Tableau which we used the following day for interviewing. Because we had selected a research-grade sensor, we did have to write a script to be able to plot the data, but this would not have been necessary with a consumer-oriented device. Still, it also required learning to use new software (Tableau) and developing an overall strategy for the types of plots that would be necessary. Here, we focused on simple area graphs for each of the numerical datasets, one that contained data for the full duration of study and another that zoomed in to times that appeared notably stressful.

As with previous studies, what the data evoked proved much more ethnographically productive than the stories it told directly. Because our set-up involved multiple modes of sensing, the discrepancies between the different accounts often proved interesting. In the inter-views, images from body-worn cameras and handwritten logs helped participants recall the events of the previous day. The logs helped us understand how participants framed those events, and indicated their subjectively experienced stress. One particularly telling interview shows how these modalities came together. Nadine's son, a Type 1 diabetic, had a continuous glucose monitor, which sent her alarms on her phone when his glucose was out of range. Sometimes it indicates a real problem, and sometimes the alarms were spurious.

On our second interview Nadine explained how the alarm woke her up multiple times in the night, and early in the morning her son had an infection she had to take care of. Later that morning the glucose monitor was going off again, and she was desperately trying to get hold of her son and her husband, both of whom could resolve the problem. So far, there are three stressors in the account: a medical situation, the difficulty reaching the people who can resolve it and the need to respond to the situation on very little sleep. This incident was playing out while she was in a meeting with one of her volunteer organisations. She said, 'So in the school meeting it was really the worst, and I felt so bad because I'm constantly texting and there's this counsellor sitting with a direct view of me ...' So now we have a fourth stressor, which is the social stigma of appearing to not be properly paying attention at a meeting.

We then looked at the pictures together. She had written down the incident as happening at 8:15 am, which was the start time of the meeting, and had marked it as having very high subjectively felt stress levels. Her heart rate data appeared to show a fairly large surge just after 8:15, and so at first we thought we had a small discrepancy in time (8:15, as she had remembered it, versus just after 8:15 when the heart rate spiked). When we looked at the camera data for 8:15, though, we saw her not in the meeting but still bicycling to the meeting. The surge lasted for the duration of the incident as she describes it, which means that the sensors were picking up on some biological manifestation of what she was experiencing. But the minor discrepancies in the starting time suggested one additional important layer to the stress. When we showed her the camera data from that time period, she noted 'I think it was probably really that I thought, "Oh, we have this meeting afterwards. But now I need to concentrate on this."' She told us about how she was worried about letting down someone she would encounter in the next meeting, which to us spoke to the tremendous cascade of responsibilities she was carrying, and how they were interwoven temporally.

A positivist would be inclined to use the story to underscore the poor recall capabilities of human beings. We used it instead to think about how stress might be a layered phenomenon, where the first version of the story is not a lie or a mistake but the part of the story remembered as worth telling. Subsequent versions of the story, mediated through different resources, showed that a cascade of responsibilities were working together. The 'full story' is not what made it interesting; the fact that it came in layers, with different parts remembered in different ways, is what gave it meaning. We came to suspect that this might be saying something about how stress builds up, and becomes culturally and socially inflected. These nuances became visible only by making room for, and valuing, human 'error'.

Real Time Health Monitoring

In this final section, I wanted to add some thoughts about this approach for community-based participatory research (CBPR). In the caregiving pilot, there was an aspiration that the research should be useful for at least some of the participants involved. In this last project, Real Time Health Monitoring, a coalition of environmental justice groups had been looking for research that could identify the health effects of air pollution from a point source polluter in their area. Being familiar with how members of the Quantified Self community answer questions like this, and, by this time, having a prototype of software that could ease some of the data-wrangling challenges the problem posed, I became interested in exploring what it would take to help these groups answer their question. I collaborated with Gwen Ottinger, an STS scholar who had a longer history with these groups as they advocated for high-grade air quality sensors to be put in place, and Randy Sargent, a computer scientist at Carnegie Mellon University's CREATE Lab, which had created an important infrastructure for making air quality data accessible (esdr.cmucreatelab.org). The installation of air quality sensors was itself an important victory, but the question quickly became how to make good use of them. Gwen and I worked with the coalition to enable them to set up a small, participatory pilot study that equipped nine volunteers to with various health-related devices to report symptoms. If these tended to occur at times when there was a spike in pollution, it could indicate something significant to them.

Here we followed the same device-vetting procedures as in the previous study, provided the high levels of technology support for participants that we had learned would be necessary and continued the process of meeting with people individually to explore what the data meant to them. In those individual meetings, I did not prepare visualisations ahead of time, as Data Sense enabled me to try out various visualisations interactively in the interview itself, and annotate them. This reduced substantially the amount of data preparation necessary beforehand, but limits the study to the patterns that Data Sense handles well. (There are also now other similar tools available, such as databasic.io, Fluxtream and Zenobase, which offer analogous improvements and tradeoffs.) This was a new evolution in my research practice, as for the first time it was up to me to handle the data movement from the device to the place where it would be analysed. While there were some hiccups, including one of the data collecting apps going out of business entirely during data collection, in general I found this now feasible to do without specialist skills.

However, the environmental justice groups were acting as a community, not as individuals *per se*. That added additional layers of complication. In the caregiving study, we could analyse data on an individual-by-individual basis, but here the participants themselves were asking questions about what was shared between them. Specifically, they were looking for correlations with the pollution levels that they shared physically. Data Sense was designed for individual use by Quantified Self (QS) community members, and so it creates grids of pairwise correlations for a small handful of data referring to a single individual. QS participants were largely wary of correlations across a population, and so Data Sense did not contain a notion of a population, even though here it was central.[1] What it did have was a notion of data sharing and exchange, and so, to hack this feature for community use, we created a series of grids by sharing data into one account. Each grid showed one pollutant and as many participants as we could fit in. These showed whether the group was correlating with the pollutant while exposing the individual variation. Some participants were more strongly affected than others. This attempt at numerical commensuration without a population-wide measurement would likely make epidemiologists unhappy, but it suited the purpose of discussing with the group whether there was a possible relationship worth further research. It invited conversation about whether pollution was affecting those with chronic health problems more severely, or people living closer to or further from the main polluter. Seeing the range of individual responses invited people to imagine how they were a part of the whole in a new way.

While this project did convince me that it was feasible to do this kind of data work without the aid of a data scientist, and, in the future, by citizen groups themselves with a bit of training, 'empowerment' also comes with its costs. I anticipated the heightened scrutiny, and pre-emptive discounting, any further calculations would receive because they were made by newcomers to these forms of mathematics, primarily by women, and by people who were seeking the evidence base they needed to advocate for change. The increased level of mathematical complexity also created more room to get it wrong for the wrong reasons. For example, in the course of working with the data, we discovered that some of our data had numerical qualities (non-normal distribution) that Data Sense was not optimised to handle. It took the intervention of someone more fluent in statistics to spot it, and figure out a workaround. While we put ourselves in a position to be able to defy genres of big data calculation and expose the limitations of epidemiology – to get it 'wrong' for the right reasons – we also risked stumbling into problems that others have indeed thought more deeply about, like non-normal distribution, that, if not caught, could be used by others to undermine the whole thing.

Unfriendly scrutiny is always just around the corner for these groups. At some point my inventive method – the use of consumer devices to make non-standard data compositions that suited a human lifeworld if not expert-driven health research – becomes not just an interesting, novel research approach but a matter of responsibility to others who would also have to live with this. These groups will have to decide whether to use calculations like these to make claims through idioms of science or idioms of storytelling, and my method sat precisely in the middle. The middle might be ethnographically rich, but, in some circumstances, dangerous waters. These are real pollutants, and real fights about bodily harms that are not helped by uncertainty. We swam in these waters nevertheless on the faith that doing so meant that far-away experts would no longer monopolise the tools of knowledge production. In that sense, perhaps we were not just 'seeing what we can see' but learning *how* to see, rooted in this particular social world that included data, software, hardware, people and landscape.

Conclusion

When I began working on Data Sense, I did not expect to end up hacking on it as a matter of methodological necessity. The trajectory, however, shows how the social life of this ethnographic method is caught up in the evolution of the materials at hand, and does not leave untouched the worlds it is designed to comprehend. My story has been one of decreasing reliance on collaborators to do the data wrangling, which is not a claim that collaboration is problematic, but a claim about the capacities that open up when anthropologists take the social life of methods seriously, not just as the outcome of research practice but as part of the research itself. This methodological evolution shows, from a particular point of view, the changing material circumstances as they have unfolded across the last ten years. Indeed, the changing materials available are not some exogenous force but something anthropologists can and should actively participate in. When we approach data systems as something that is a part of the social worlds in which we work, and not merely the latest flight of fancy of funding bodies dazzled by the magical power of computation, we tap in to longer-standing anthropological traditions of deep engagement with the social worlds we write about. If data is a contemporary form of storytelling, then anthropologists are only just beginning to take the leap in telling those stories with the people we work with. It might be easier to do this with tools that we also have a hand in creating.

It is not difficult to imagine how it is that our research participants tell their stories with data, yet somehow we struggle to imagine doing so for our own. Stories with numbers are not stories we usually tell. Self-trackers and environmental justice advocates regularly receive criticism from those who they challenge about how they are not scientific enough, use poor experiment design, etc. These accusations are cut from the same cloth as the ones that anthropologists have endured for a very long time. They are born from a preoccupation with generality that both anthropologists and these groups find untenable. We can be clear-headed about the epistemological politics of large data systems and nevertheless see how supposedly dubious numbers, coming from such suspect sources as non-professionals and Othered researchers, might yet become powerful in unexpected ways.

Note

1 The Data Sense team, at time of writing, has since explored the design requirements that would be necessary to create appropriate cross-population aggregates.

References

Aipperspach, R., Rattenbury, T., Woodruff, A. and Canny, J. 2006. 'A Quantitative Method for Revealing and Comparing Places in the Home'. In *International Conference on Ubiquitous Computing Proceedings*. Berlin and Heidelberg: Springer, 1–18.

Anderson, K., Nafus, D., Rattenbury, T. and Aipperspach, R. 2009. 'Numbers Have Qualities Too: Experiences with Ethno-Mining'. In *Ethnographic Praxis in Industry Conference Proceedings* 1. New York: Blackwell Publishing Ltd, 123–40.

Andrejevic, M. 2014. 'The Big Data Divide'. *International Journal of Communication* 8: 17–36.

Corburn, J. 2005. *Street Science: Community Knowledge and Environmental Health Justice*. Cambridge, MA: MIT Press.

Couldry, N. and Powell, A. 2014. 'Big Data from the Bottom Up'. *Big Data & Society* 1(2): 1–5.

Geiger, R.S. and Ribes, D. 2011. 'Trace Ethnography: Following Coordination through Documentary Practices'. In *System Sciences (HICSS), 2011 44th Hawaii International Conference on Systems Science*. Piscataway, NJ: Institute of Electrics and Electronics Engineers (IEEE), 1–10.

Greenfield, D. 2016. 'Deep Data: Notes on the N of 1'. In *Quantified: Biosensing Technology in Everyday Life*. Edited by D. Nafus. Cambridge, MA: MIT Press, 123–67.

Kitchin, R. 2014. 'Big Data, New Epistemologies and Paradigm Shifts'. *Big Data & Society* 1(1): 1–12.

Latour, B. 2004. 'Why Has Critique Run Out of Steam? From Matters of Fact to Matters of Concern'. *Critical Inquiry* 30(2): 225–48.

Law, J., Ruppert, E. and Savage, M. 2011. 'The Double Social Life f Methods'. CRESC Working Paper Series, 95. http://research.gold.ac.uk/7987/1/The%20Double%20Social%20Life%20of%20Methods%20CRESC%20Working%20Paper%2095.pdf [accessed 4 March 2018].

Lury, C. and Wakeford, N. (eds). 2012. *Inventive Methods: The Happening of the Social*. London: Routledge.

Mehta, R. and Nafus, D. 2016. 'Atlas of Caregiving Pilot Study Report'. https://atlasofcaregiving.com/core-research/pilot-study [accessed 16 June 2017].

Nafus, D. 2016. 'Introduction'. In D. Nafus (ed.), *Quantified: Biosensing in Everyday Life*. Cambridge, MA: MIT Press.

Nafus, D. and Beckwith, R. 2016. 'Number in Craft Situated Numbering Practices in Do-It-Yourself Sensor Systems'. In *Critical Craft: Technology, Globalization, and Capitalism*. Edited by C. Wilkinson-Weber and A. DeNicola. London: Bloomsbury Press, 115–34.

Pasquale, F. 2015. *The Black Box Society: The Secret Algorithms that Control Money and Information*. Cambridge, MA: Harvard University Press.

Ruppert, E., Law, J.and Savage, M. 2013. 'Reassembling Social Science Methods: The Challenge of Digital Devices'. *Theory, Culture & Society, Special Issue on 'The Social Life of Methods'* 30(4): 22–46.

Savage, M. 2013. 'The "social life of methods": A Critical Introduction'. *Theory, Culture & Society* 30(4): 3–21.

Wilmott, C. 2016. 'Small Moments in Spatial Big Data: Calculability, Authority and Interoperability in Everyday Mobile Mapping'. *Big Data & Society* 3(2): 1–16.

11

The other ninety per cent: thinking with data science, creating data studies – an interview with Joseph Dumit

Joseph Dumit and Dawn Nafus

Editor's note: This is a jointly edited transcript of an interview with Joseph Dumit (professor of Science & Technology Studies and Anthropology) about the Data Studies undergraduate minor being designed at University of California at Davis. This programme began in late 2015, and is led jointly by Dumit and Duncan Temple Lang, director of the Data Science Initiative at UCD, professor of Statistics, and formerly of Bell Labs.

DN: How did Data Studies become an interest of yours?

JD: The immediate genesis was meeting with an alumnus, Tim McCarthy, who had been a social science major and went on to work in senior positions at a series of international banks and financial institutions. He was concerned that Liberal arts majors were declining, even though it was the critical thinking skills of the liberal arts that were incredibly valuable in his career. He was concerned that, when he was starting out, companies hired liberal arts majors and then trained them for one to two years. But today, companies can't afford to train anyone for more than a couple of weeks, even though they do want critical thinking skills. This was juxtaposed with my observations that many students in the social sciences and humanities are interested in how technology is changing the world, and have critiques of it, but for various reasons are never getting their hands on data. Partly that's because they think it's math, or they think the bar to entry is learning how to program.

When we met, we discovered a shared interest in teaching data skills, and critical thinking around data as a means to, at minimum, get them jobs. We wanted to make sure this was doable, however, so a team of us visited senior people at over twenty large and small Silicon Valley companies, banks, a grocery chain company, consulting agencies etc., asking them what they would like to see out of liberal arts majors. They all said that students do need to know Excel – it's a legacy standard that companies can't really get out of – but they also wanted people who, if you asked them a question, could tell you that you were asking the wrong question. They were hiring recent computer science and statistics graduates as data analysts, but one complaint was that, if you gave many young data analysts a problem, they could too easily give you an answer. They would not necessarily take the time to reflect and say, 'Maybe this is not the right question'. The companies were very interested in being able to also get critical thinkers who talk the language of data science, and who know what a data science question is, but who don't necessarily have to know the algorithms in order to engage with them.

Then Duncan Temple Lang and I discussed what it would take to design a set of classes geared toward liberal arts majors (social sciences and humanities students) to learn enough about data handling and data science to be able to apply their critical thinking skills to work in government, industry or NGOs *alongside* data scientists. This would be a minor that would complement, not replace, their major: Data Studies.

DN: DID ANY OF THESE COMPANIES GIVE YOU AN EXAMPLE OF WHY REFRAMING THE QUESTION HAD BUSINESS VALUE?

JD: One company had engineers and data scientists designing front-end interfaces for managing hundreds of databases at a time, and what they ended up with was an interface full of all the information *available*, but not the information that was *needed*. Another example was a bank trying to optimise credit scores, and they needed to take into account the regulatory context (see also O'Neil 2016). Given a particular set of data, there might be an algorithm that would optimise the selection of good credit versus bad credit given that dataset. The regulatory context is constantly changing, so what you can and can't do is something you have to take into account as you optimise the answer, otherwise you might optimise the answer in an illegal or unfair way. That means you have to ask: why do we have this dataset versus another, and are there biases in that dataset so we can tweak it a little, or seek more data?

DN: YOU PROPOSED TO ME THAT WE SHOULD TALK ABOUT 'THE OTHER NINETY PER CENT". WHAT DO YOU MEAN BY THAT?

JD: In order to design classes for Data Studies, I'd been reviewing textbooks for data science, looking at online courses etc., and at the beginning of each, there was a nice acknowledgement that 'figuring out the question' and 'data cleaning' were the most important things that a data scientist does, and it often takes eighty to ninety per cent of their time. But then the book will only spend ten per cent of the contents on cleaning, ninety per cent about algorithms and programming, and almost nothing on clarifying the question. (There are, however, a couple books (O'Neil and Schutt 2013; Peng and Matsui 2015) that do devote a whole chapter to clarifying and cleaning). 'The other ninety per cent' challenges the irony where textbooks are saying that ninety per cent of your time is going to be spent on one thing, but then focus all of their effort on something else.

Data science is in this funny space. Duncan had started his career in the Statistics and Data Mining group at Bell Labs, where exploratory data analysis (EDA) and figuring out what the real problem was and what data matters was how data scientists spent their time. That was a place where these skills were as important as algorithm-tuning. Duncan was one of core developers of the statistical computing language R, designed precisely to focus attention on thoughtfully exploring data visually as well as numerically (see Mackenzie 2007). He had been writing articles and books for over 17 years about refocusing classroom time on giving students a feel for the data (Nolan and Temple Lang 2015). He had been flipping curriculum using case studies and online tools like Piazza to put students into a collective learning environment. In fact one of the hardest skills to teach was one that all good programmers use: being willing to ask questions online and make use of collective wisdom when wrestling with data and tools.

Occasionally experts do talk about experience – that if you do this long enough you start to get better at asking questions. But the idea that there are actual fields where people are trained to think critically and expansively about interpretation, and to be rigorous about ambiguous situations rather than avoiding them, is absent. These books and courses don't mention, for example, how you should understand the range of your stakeholders – not just those who are invested in your results but those who are potentially affected by the way you analyse and present your data.[1] They might give one example of how a particular stakeholder is important, but the idea that there's a whole discipline devoted to mapping stakeholders and understanding social implications and feedback effects is avoided. Anthropologists and sociologists are trained in how to interview, and how to ask questions that might not just lead stakeholders to the answer they think you want but allow them to reveal to you what they actually care about. Of course, in some amazing world, people would actually just tell you what they want, but sometimes they don't know, or sometimes the right answer is at the intersection of multiple stakeholders. In these situations you do not necessarily need long interviews, but you do need careful interviews with them.

Cleaning has its own sets of mysteries to deal with. We started the introductory class by making students answer a survey of 30 questions by filling in text boxes. We asked them their name, their year in school, how many friends they had on Facebook, sibling rank, favourite movies, shoe size etc. And then we give them their own collective data back, and said: clean this so we can ask questions about possible trends in the class and whether we can use the survey to potentially predict things. They immediately saw that the way most of them answered the questions did not make cleaning the data easy. They learned that they should regularise how people input shoe sizes, for example. Sometimes with sibling rank, students from Asian countries will put their rank among male children if they are male, or among female if female. It didn't occur to them to rank all the children together, just like it didn't occur to other students that rank might be separated by gender. As they tried to clean up the data to be able to quantify it, they came to see that every decision they make about cleaning the data is going to affect them or their friends directly. There's no right answer in most cases, so we have a discussion about that, and about how each form of cleaning is 'political', meaning that each decision affects the future of how the data will be understood because it will delete some data that others might consider important, collapse some differences and emphasise others.

DN: HOW DO YOUR STUDENTS ENCOUNTER THIS BROADER NOTION OF 'BIAS', WHEN SOCIETALLY THERE ARE MUCH NARROWER NOTIONS OF WHAT BIAS IS?

JD: In one approach, we used Latanya Sweeney's (2013) work on bias in algorithms that pull up Google Adwords that can be racially biased even though the algorithm probably did not have a human behind it except someone who decided that first name was a variable to throw into a giant machine-learning algorithm. Sweeney's discussion of the ethics of algorithms was incredibly helpful for students (Brennan 2015). We also used Cathy O'Neill's presentation to TalksAtGoogle (TalksAtGoogle 2016) and her work on *Weapons of Math Destruction* (O'Neil 2016) describing the work that ProPublica and others had conducted on policing and sentencing to get them to understand that something could be *both objective and unfair*. For instance, if arrests are racially biased, then predictions based on crimes will be racially biased. 'Objective' was always indexed to the dataset as it was gathered. It was indexed to drawing a box around a problem and saying 'Given this data or this criteria, this is an objective answer.' The question was not whether it was biased, because all samples and all collection mechanisms are biased in the sense that they have made choices, but she emphasises that what matters is whether it is unfair in terms of the outcome. If the outcome is unfair, you would reconsider the algorithm and the particular form of objectivity being built in.

We could then extend this to seemingly different workflows. If a company is comparing sales and bonus from different regions, the way in which sales are counted ends up being political and potentially unfair. The people who get urban regions versus rural regions can get penalised in different ways, and there is always fighting over what is going to be the metric. These metrics are also data-formulating and cleaning problems, because there will always be outliers and someone who says 'You can't count that one the same way as this one.' It's important for students to understand that here is where decisions are made, and, once you start putting algorithms on it, you are going to carry forward any choice you made. If you haven't explored the data and just run with it, you are really building in a type of bias that no one will necessarily notice. To not have people spending serious time exploring data is, from an employer point of view, dangerous. Maybe that person has to gather together the stakeholders to say, what do we do about these differences in how things are counted or with our outliers? It's in our training data, or base set, so it's going to bias our future.

So the first step was getting them to see that there is more than one 'logical' way to do something, and more than one 'objective' answer. Some students end up still thinking that bias is only race, but they do get to the point where they can see that racial bias is made up of a bunch of choices to do with initial data choices, question formulation and cleaning, and doesn't necessarily have to do with how the algorithm was designed. Rather bias often has to do with how data are not independent of the algorithms that they are put into. The next stage is showing that all data is biased and that is an important starting point, which they all got when we worked with the airline data. But you are right that on the test there were students who defaulted to the idea that bias equals race or other key social catego-ries. My hope is that is that, with more classes that emphasise how to think critically, with and about data and unfairness, they can learn to extend these arguments.

When we take it to actual datasets, like an airline flight delay dataset, they start to see how even something that looks very neutral, when you dig into it, you see layers and layers of politics. I was trying to teach them the concept that politics here is just making decisions where it affects others, to the extent that that algorithm gets employed in some way. Politics isn't always 'bias', but it is a change. Or rather, it is bias but it's not evil – it's inevitable. It's a choice. It's more impor-tant to be able to explain the results to the public, or to an employer, and say why you made the decisions you did. This means leaving a trail of why I cleaned it this way, and that I did indeed clean it. Otherwise it's just magic; it's just, 'I have an answer' and no one can go back and say 'Why not clean it this way?'

DN: Tell us more about that airline dataset. Why was it good to work with?

JD: This dataset is a favourite of data scientists because it is large – over five million domestic flights per year for starters. It's a database maintained by the US Bureau of Transportation. Every flight is one entry in a giant spreadsheet with over a hundred measurements (Excel columns). It includes data about when the flight took off, how long it was on the runway, when they closed the doors, when it was supposed to land, when it actually landed, how much it was delayed or early, and if delayed why. Our whole course was designed around cases with actual data in all of their messiness, and having students imagine having stakeholders, and work through how different stakeholders might want different types of information. It could be someone who is trying to fly back and forth between San Francisco and New York every week, and wants to know which airline or flight has the least chance of being delayed. Or, it could be American Airlines wanting to know which categories it is beating United in, so they can make a campaign around it. It could be someone taking a vacation next year, and that person might be interested in lost luggage, but the data doesn't have that. So if they say they really don't want to lose their luggage, the answer is to find another dataset.

DN: Is that what you mean by teaching them how data is already political – it's designed for the needs of certain people, but not other people?

JD: Yes. Furthermore, we, and anyone analysing or presenting data, is making decisions about who our audience is and what they care about. So we 'censor' data, or, specifically, results in order to address what is important to our 'audience'. We hope our choices reflect the audience's goals, as well as social fairness, because there are always multiple audiences. Except in the case of a classroom test!

We started by teaching the students pivot tables in Excel. Most students' computers can handle up to a million rows in Excel, so we did a sub-set of the flights for one year from six California cities and New York cities (approximately three hundred thousand flights). We gave them enough data that they could ask questions about it. We had them first try to sit and examine the data and ask, why are there so many columns? Why is there a column for how many minutes it is delayed or early, but another column identical to that one that had zeroed out all the negative numbers so there is no 'early'? Then there was another column that showed a one or a zero depending on whether it was delayed 15 minutes or more.

As they started posing questions, they realised that each of these columns was differently useful. For example, if you averaged 'arrival time' one airline might appear much better than another one, but then you notice that it includes negative numbers for flights that arrive early. If what you meant to study was which airline had the fewest delays, especially the least long delays, then the column with delays longer than 15 minutes was far more immediately useful. We could see how the bureau started adding columns to this data so others didn't have to create them. If you were creating them on a million or a billion rows, it would take a long time. Here they just give it to you, and so the columns themselves reveal a history about who uses this data and what kinds of questions they pose to it.

Then there is the question of why is one of the columns '15 minutes or more delayed'. We could think about who thresholded it at 15 minutes and why. We wanted to ask whether '30 minutes or more' might be meaningful to someone, but we'd have to make a new column for that. We noticed that there were a lot of early flights, too. Analysts at OAG Aviation Worldwide explored the data and figured out that either the Earth is getting bigger or the projected flight time from San Francisco to New York gets longer, which means that the airlines are listing their arrival time later and later so that more flights are less than 15 minutes late (Morris 2015). Once you put a number like 15 minutes into a data threshold, and turn it into tables that are used to publicise who is on time the most, you see Goodhardt's Law at work, which says that any time an index becomes a target, it no longer functions as an index (see Strathern 1997; Dumit 2016; Griese-mer 2016). From a customer point of view, it's nice because I would rather the airline say it takes longer, and know that I have an hour to make my connection. It's good for me, and good for the airline, but it means comparing data across years becomes an interesting challenge, because the airlines are changing the flight times.

Then we get to the real cleaning question. The data is presented apparently quite clean, meaning that every box that is supposed to have data has something in it, unlike when you are at a company or in an environmental group where you get lots of missing data (see Ribes and Jackson 2013). We were trying to ask, if you have data from 2012, could you predict something about 2013? Which airline has the fewest delays for certain routes? We have them do exploratory data analysis (EDA), which is something Duncan Temple Lang often talks about (Tukey 1977). This starts with actually sitting in front of your data, looking at and thinking about it, and visualising it in many different ways. I think of this as a non-Tufte-style visualisation. Edward Tufte has a powerful approach to visualisations which show how good a map or a chart is as a measure of the distance between what someone who hasn't seen it before gets from it and what the intended meaning was. That's important. If I am the engineer or the social scientist and I know what my data means, and now I want to find the best way to graph it so that somebody else gets my meaning, I measure how much they get out of it by comparing what they understood with what I am trying to convey. Did they get enough, or too much or not the right thing? Exploratory data analysis is totally different. The analyst is the recipient of their own data visualisation and they don't know what the data means except through visualising it multiple times in lots of different ways. They try a bunch of different things to see if there's something that could be a hypothesis, and then they dig in and ask why.

DN: One thing I struggle with as someone who is still learning this is that there are some patterns that are clear in my mind because I see them so often, like recurrences by hour, or by location. They become my go-to patterns, and I'm always surprised when somebody comes up with one that is conceptually simple but not yet in my repertoire. I wouldn't explore it in those new ways because I didn't know that was even a way to explore. How do you seed the possibilities with your students?

JD: Partly we do this through having them sketch on paper what they thought relations would be [editor's note: see also Lupi and Posavec 2016]. This is so they don't get habitual. One of the dangers of most tools like Excel and Tableau is that they come with pull-down menus of charts that make a lot of choices for you, and worse, 'Recommended Charts'. The problems are (1) most of the time these charts *look good* so that, even if they don't make sense of the data, it is easy to stop and hit *print*; (2) when they choose your axes and colour schemes for you, you don't necessarily notice that they made all of these choices; and (3) therefore they don't encourage thinking about what a useful chart might be for yourself. Thus one of our exercises is always to sketch by hand charts you might find helpful as a way to think out loud about what your data means. Another practice is for our students to post their exploratory charts to one another, so they can be inspired by each other. We try to have them work in teams, so they can bounce ideas off one another. Each person tends to have partial ideas, based on their ongoing hypotheses, and they may think it's obvious and therefore don't think it is worth sharing. But when they do say or show it, someone is often inspired.

This approach is also enhanced by thinking through the lenses of different stakeholders. For example, if you care about a particular person who's flying regularly, certain things are more likely to come to mind as being important. When you think about United versus American Airlines trying to do a marketing campaign, or the ground crew and what they might be worried about, you start thinking about different kinds of relations that you then put together in a graph, and different temporal signatures might come to matter.

For example, as we were exploring and looking at the data for 2012 and delays by month, November looked like this amazing month because it had very few delays relatively speaking. But then we did a graph that showed there were six days in November when there were no delays at all for New York airports. So we looked at it and asked 'What's that? That never happens!' We looked at cancellations, and sure enough every flight was cancelled. So then, what do you do? What's going on? Because it is real data, you can Google '2012 flight delays November New York' and what you find is Hurricane Sandy. And so now you have a cleaning issue: does the question that I am trying to answer with the data in front of me need to be cleaned of Hurricane Sandy? If I include cancellations, then November turns out to be this horrific month and I might end up telling everyone not to fly in November, but if I use delays then November turns out to be a great month. Should I just forget November, and average December and October as a more plausible stand-in for November? Should I look for which month is most like November and put that in instead? So now we are into politics. I have to make a choice here, and each choice will have different consequences for different questions. Not making a choice by just using the actual data I have is going to throw off some recommendations.

There was another occasion where we were exploring the data for airlines day by day, and found there was one period where American

Airlines was super-delayed, and United had almost no delays. This outlier only showed up with one type of graph, it was weird, but you are looking for outliers like this. So then you Google for more about what's going on: 'American Airlines flight delays September 2012'. And you find a labour dispute was going on then, and there were intentional delays. For this period of about 15 days there are tons of delays, and then American and the pilots settled their next ten-year contract. So now we have a dilemma: if I am trying to recommend to my stakeholder which airline to fly next year, do I just use the data as I have it, in which case American is not going to get recommended because it has higher delays, or do I get rid of those two weeks, averaging out that month because the dispute is settled, and it's a ten-year contract, so the odds of something similar happening next year would be almost nil? But United's contract is coming up next year … so do I take this into account by making the recommendation that says we should take into account labour contract negotiation as putting airlines at higher risk for delays? In that case, I should apply the risk of delays to the other airlines, and not to American.

This is cleaning. It's when you recognise some trend in your data that may or may not be relevant to the question, or hurt the correctness of the recommendation, and you have to make a decision as to whether to leave it in or not. Even this simple flight data turns out to have politics in it – labour disputes, hurricanes etc. Do I take Hurricane Sandy to mean that we are having worse weather and you should stop flying to the East Coast?

DN: I IMAGINE THAT ONE PROBLEM YOUR STUDENTS MIGHT BE FACING IS WHEN TO CALL SOMETHING DONE. HOW DO THEY FIGURE OUT WHEN THE EXPLORATION IS ENOUGH?

JD: Right in the beginning I give them slides that are almost like marketing slides, about the 'Deep Skills' they will be learning: being comfortable with vagueness, willingness to fail, ability to explore, being able and willing to ask for help, understanding and embracing randomness. There are students who are really good *students*, and, because of that, sometimes they run into trouble. I had one student drop the class because she was spending too much time on the assignment. She couldn't figure out how to stop because she wanted to be *right*. I had another student say that 'the word "explore" paralyses me'. Still other students have the opposite problem and just stop at the first thing that comes to mind (often the first 'recommended chart' by Excel). When I was teaching critical reading and writing at MIT, I had to develop the incompressible assignment, because all the physics students would have these problem sets that took a certain number of hours. They were incompressible. If I gave them a writing assignment next to that, they would squeeze the writing assignment into as few minutes as possible. So I ended up writing these elaborate protocols that tricked them into thinking this could not be compressed.

In Data Studies, I have to make exploratory data analysis as detailed incompressible assignments, because a lot of students have this sense that, if they were going down a route that turned out not to be interesting, they've wasted their time. How do I, as a teacher, communicate that, if you think that way, you are never going to do really good work? You need to try a bunch of things, so one of the things you really need to learn is to try things fast. So the assignment then becomes, 'show me two tries', and then 'show me two more tries'. We can then talk about the value of each try. It's about giving them a sense of progress, but the risk is always that they develop a sense that there is a set of twenty things that they could do to most any dataset, and they can apply it, and then think that they've explored all twenty relations and be done. We all want shortcuts and heuristics, but we first need to really understand that this data in front of us is specific to a time and place, it is situated in historical and cultural and regulatory settings, and therefore may not be 'the same' as previous data we have looked at. We want them to actually find a way to pause and stare at the data, to think about the question they are trying to answer, and see if the data actually answers it, or if they might need to revise the question. That's how data scientists describe it – as you stare at the data, you graph it in a few different ways, you are getting a feel for what this data is telling me. But it is *vague*; it's not anything where if your boss came by, and asked, 'What do you have?' you might not have anything better to say than, well, I've stared at it for two hours. In this sense it is akin to philosophy. That's the interesting dilemma about the pressure for speed, or pressure for results.

In teaching, I've tried various ways to discuss the assignments collectively and in groups. With any group of thirty students, I can have them all say something that is interesting to them about the data. Collectively they cover an amazing number of things, even if at first individually they all are feeling like, 'Oh, I don't really know anything, I only had one idea.' I'll say, 'But look, together you have set up a lot of interesting questions about the limits of this data for answering this question.' Patience with exploring, comfort with vagueness, willingness to fail.

DN: YOUR USE OF THE TERM 'DATA CLEANING' IS INTEREST-INGLY INCLUSIVE. IT'S A LOT MORE THAN WHAT IS SUGGESTED BY 'DATA JANITOR', FOR EXAMPLE. IS THIS FRAMING OF DATA CLEANING PARTICULAR TO DATA STUDIES AS OPPOSED TO 'ORDINARY' DATA SCIENCE, OR DOES IT REFLECT A CONSENSUS ABOUT WHAT DATA CLEANING INVOLVES?

JD: I don't know if there's any consensus at all in data science right now. I don't even know who you would go to, to adjudicate that question. Sure, many people say they know what 'core data science' is, but could you get any sample of data scientists in a room together to agree on it? It's one of those issues where this stuff might not look like 'cleaning', but it is within the area of doing exploratory analysis, looking for outliers and deciding whether to filter them. Is hurricane Sandy an outlier or not? Is a labour dispute an outlier or not? These are things where you can't avoid the fact that they should at least be part of a cleaning conversation, iterating back and forth with analysis.

The cleaning here is very much the iterative process of EDA and modelling that goes beyond data janitor and that is essential. As discussed, every operation on the data is 'political' or a decision that potentially affects different stakeholders. Therefore, the 'data scientist/ analyst' has to make them rather than have this done at an earlier stage by somebody else. Often, the cleaning is done by somebody else and we have lost a lot of information about what decisions were made. This is why we always want the raw data. In one case that the students chose, analysing the results of a large-scale US mental health survey, for convenience, the study authors provided the data in different formats.[2] However, they had collapsed several categories into one for at least one variable. This was far from apparent and changed the conclusions drawn by the students. At first they didn't realise this, and were making erroneous conclusions. So we had to go back to the raw data.

There is a fun book called *Guerrilla Analytics* (Ridge 2014). It is full of war stories about how people don't label their files correctly, or record the process by which they cleaned data, and it creates big problems down the line when someone assumes something different happened. I teach these things to students to say: You might think labelling files is something you do for yourself, but you are really doing it for other people. Whatever you do, odds are that six months from now someone is going to face your files and have to make sense of it. That person might even be you six months from now. If you don't clarify what goes where, what you actually did, and keep all your metadata close to it: that future you is going to be very pissed at the current you.

DN: SO WHY ISN'T THIS DATA SCIENCE?

JD: When I talk with data scientists, they usually say, 'Well, this *is* data science.' I then say, could we have in your curriculum a whole course, or maybe even two, devoted to just this: how to think critically about question formulation, data cleaning and bias, stakeholders mapping, multiple objectives, unfairness and politics? They will say, 'Well, I don't know if we have time for that, and every course is going to have this in it anyway.' Yes, but that means that every course is going to have the same problem you enacted for me just now, which is that it will get shrunk each time and become secondary to the algorithm types and optimisation – it will be assumed but not taught. That's why I'm calling this Data Studies: a whole minor – it's not a major – but it has its own name precisely so that there will be whole courses devoted to teaching people how to do *the critical social science and humanities work that is an integral part of data science thinking*. Data scientists will always say this is data science, and I say yes, it is, so have your students take the courses!

   This is a well-known issue in science, statistics and engineering pedagogy, where the pressure to cover the other core material means squeezing out exploratory data analysis, ethics or other things that are acknowledged as important but, in any particular battle, end up being less important than the material that the faculty in that discipline are primarily trained in. 'Data Studies' remembers that there is an additional set of skills that are required training and are equally necessary for every data scientist, as I am told by data scientists. I try not to tell them, 'You need to be doing this', I just say 'I'm doing this' and then they say 'Oh, that's data science.' I now call these things 'deep versus shallow skills', as opposed to 'soft skills'. I sometimes provocatively try calling algorithms shallow skills because they do not require long ambiguous conversations and bringing in stakeholders.

Of course, the Data Science programme and major we envision creating at UC Davis will involve a solid mix of EDA, framing questions, interpreting insights, social science and also the usual statistics, machine learning and computing. Already in our pilot classes we have had graduate students take them, and stats students take them. There is a void that needs to be filled. This is why we are experimenting with deep skills pedagogy through cases.

DN: It seems important to make the deep skills explicit – to name what these skills are, so they don't get muddled as somehow 'soft' or imponderable. In anthropology and sociology, they are made explicit.

JD: Yes! In fact, I call this work: 'data archaeology'. Archaeology is a parallel to exploratory data analysis. It involves looking at where the data came from – the provenance or chain of custody, as well as stopping and carefully thinking about what those measurements mean quantitatively. In the airline example, the airlines are sending in their own data to the agency, and it might be necessary to know that airlines are competing with each other in this common data format. An analyst at FiveThirtyEight studied another effect of the '15 minute delay' threshold, and found that for the long flights, e.g. from San Francisco to LA, you could make up the time by going faster (Montet 2014). So if the flight took off within 30 minutes of its departure time, they could make up the time by flying faster while costing the airline a little bit more fuel money, and land within the 15-minute delay window. But if they took off any later, they didn't fly faster at all since they would still be 'late'. So they were behaving in relation to the data collection rule, not in relation to the passengers who would miss a connection if they are 40 minutes late. Data archaeology is figuring out how the data got to you – what each group did, why those columns were added, and that gets you to all the possible places where you can start to ask questions.

There are ways of looking at datasets to make a guess about the culture or historical period in which those questions make sense. In a Foucauldian way, you can start to ask about the genealogy about the dataset itself, and these categories. You can then do a reverse stakeholder map and ask, why do all these columns exist here? Which people cared that they ended up here? Do I think that there are things that should have been in here but aren't? There's probably a story in that too. These questions provide a more critical sense of why you have this data and not other data in front of you, and they are relevant to what you do to that data. You recognise that the data is one piece of a bunch of possible data, and you might say we should go get other data to answer the question. Even though I could answer the question with the data I have, that might be a defective answer for the people I am trying to help. The data scientist is the last person to see that data before there is an answer floating around, and that answer gets shorn from the data. By the time you get a chart, you are no longer in a position to ask, what choices were combined to produce that?

We hope that the audience to whom the 'answer' is reported would be asking all of these sceptical questions. And a good data scientist should be mentioning any important decisions which may change the conclusion and build them into presentations as well as 'metadata' that travels with the analysis and charts. But STS scholars have long shown that, even with the best intentions, charts and graphics fly free of their qualifications. In our courses, we try to insist that titles, axes, captions and colours have to convey the real, sometimes messy, always limited, story about the data and one's conclusions.

DN: TRADITIONALLY AFTER EXPLORATION AND CLEANING, THERE'S A NOTION OF BUILDING A MODEL. FOR YOUR STUDENTS, WHAT'S NEXT AFTER THESE STAGES?

JD: I'm emphasising the front end because, in the class I taught, students were using Excel for exploratory data analysis, and the plan of the minor is that they learn to work with data scientists and their models. Other classes currently include 'Data Sense and Exploration: Critical Storytelling with Analysis', which introduces the data language R and more visualisation approaches; 'Survey of Data Analytic Concepts & Methods via Case Studies' that introduces machine-learning techniques from a historical and use point of view; electives in areas such as ethics, policy, regulation; and a capstone course that focuses on team approaches to an entire data science pipeline.

But in the introductory course we do work on simple models. For data on the *Titanic* survivors, we built up 'one by one models', where you could ask, does gender matter? or does gender *and* class matter? and then try gender and class and family size. In this way, you could build up a model that was the equivalent of one type of algorithm that would help you come up with a model of survival. The notion of a 'model', however, gets used in various ways. In statistics, problems are often tied to a sampling question – how do I tell if my sample is good enough (P-values and T-tests and so on). In data science, usually you have something much closer to the population, or found data, rather than an intentional sample. You have all the company's customers, for example, or all the flights for that year, or all the students in the class. So there is no sampling test now, but a need to recognise the data you have and its relation to the inference you want to make. There is a question of what can be predicted, for which I can look at strength of regression, or strength of association of a particular set of features. For that, I can create my own partial universe by taking eighty per cent of my data and seeing what it implies, or predicts, and figure out if there are certain features that can indicate something like survival. Once I have something that works on the eighty per cent of the data, I try to see if it works on the remaining twenty per cent. If it does, it suggests that I may be on to something. There are more sophisticated versions where I try to automate the whole process and repeat ten thousand times: select a random eighty per cent of the data, and figure out what works on that and then test it on the remaining twenty per cent. Our other classes would introduce students to types of modelling, various kinds of regressions, clusterings, machine learnings and so on. The model building, then, is trying to figure out different ways of crunching vast sets of data into better prediction than another one.

In much of data science training, as I mentioned, the model building is part of the ninety per cent of the time spent teaching. There are many different approaches, and each depends on what type of question you are asking: e.g., if you are classifying customers versus trying to predict something. There are a lot of technical choices here, which is the reason why this is ninety per cent of the textbook. But making sure you are asking the right question, clarifying the problem, figuring out what matters in the data so that models can be applied to it, these also matter and are skills that we can deepen in data studies. These hopefully have the effect of helping the students learn what data science can actually do (seeing past the hype) and being able to work with data scientists. And data scientists, at the same time, training in these data studies skills.

DN: IS IT POSSIBLE THAT SOME OF THE MISRECOGNITION IS HAPPENING HERE, IN THE SENSE THAT PERHAPS SOME FOLKS MIGHT THINK PICKING AN APPROPRIATE MODEL IS THE 'PROBLEM DEFINITION'?

JD: This is a lively debate, in that there are many blogs out there posing questions about this. There is also a debate about Kaggle and other similar data science competitions. The Kaggle approach is to provide eighty per cent of a dataset, and reserve twenty per cent to be predicted by the competing data scientists. Everyone gets the eighty per cent along with a definition of what it is – Netflix user reviews, perhaps, or pictures of fruit. Everyone optimises on that eighty per cent, usually by taking an eighty per cent sub-set of that, and trying to find an optimal model that works on it. You then submit it, and Kaggle runs it on the secret data, and gives you an answer back saying how well you did in the form of a score.

But this is the kind of problem definition where the question of whether the right problem is being asked is off the table. This is the data and you know the question, answer it, full stop. It reinforces the idea that modelling alone can get *the right answer*. However, the people that often win, or some of them, have won partly by what they call 'leakage', which is when the real world leaks into the dataset. This is defined in competition terms as a trace that's not 'supposed' to be in the data. For example, in a hospital data competition, the number system for patient IDs allowed the competitors to figure out groups of patients from different hospitals. By the rules, they 'shouldn't' have been able to do that, but they were able to use it to make a better algorithm. The very term 'leakage' proves that Kaggle poses toy problems, because it defines using the real world as breaking into the 'pureness' of the problem.

There is a side of data science that is trying to become a pure science, the way that statistics went from being applied math to a discipline, and now applied statistics then became data science. Data science is now trying to become a science that defines itself against 'applied data science'. This requires acting as if there is a world where the algorithms can be separated from leakage. But when you are in the real world, leakage is what you want. Any way to figure out a better answer is supposed to be used. In Kaggle, some people think it is a form of cheating. My son, who enters these competitions, at one point said it should be more 'real data science-y', where you try to think about the world that the data comes from and use that. He used that term in a way that I would like to see everyone use it, where leakage was the whole point, even though at the time he was really obsessed with just tuning his deep learning algorithms to better do prediction.

It might be changing, but so far the emphasis has been on the math, and pushing the limit of computational power. A good Kaggle competition is trying to find the limit of brute force, which is interesting because data science in many ways is the computational brute force approach to the problems that statistics was invented to solve without computational power. The science part of 'pure' data science is about going to the limits of the machine. When we talked to companies about this, some managers would talk about hiring a data science/ computer science graduate from an elite programme who only wants to tune cool algorithms. They are almost intentionally ignoring all the leakage. But real data is all leaks, or better put: real data is all context.

DN: Do you have a sense for why there might be that disconnect between businesses and the way data science is usually taught?

JD: I don't want to be misunderstood here. Coming up with a problem that requires all of your programming ingenuity is fascinating, and that joy and fascination is one element that's sustaining the disconnect. Companies and governments and the rest of us eventually have data that currently exceeds our computational power, so coming up with computational tricks to get new insights is amazing. As with applied statistics, there are a lot of people doing the hard work of problem formulation and poring over the data, but that is not what is taught or makes it into the news articles. At the same time, faculty at universities work on the math, that's what they publish on, so the nitty gritty of *teaching how to apply it in context* can take them away from their comfort zones. The default is therefore to teach the 'math' and 'algorithms', which also are easier to test.

But this is also a place where Duncan would remind me that statistical thinking – being able to understand and incorporate randomness and uncertainty in decisions – is at the heart of data analysis. I'm intrigued by the ability to circumscribe the world, like in a Kaggle competition, and challenge people. Given this or that 'simplified' or 'toy' problem, it's still hard. That toy problem is indexed to a real-world problem, but it turns out you can spend all your time on the toy problem. Maybe a useful analogy is to the way in which chess became a marker of artificial intelligence because it was really hard.[3]

DN: SELF-DRIVING CARS PROVIDE EXCITING ENGINEERING PROBLEMS.

JD: When engineers are imagining self-driving cars, what toy universe are they making in which they can throw all their resources at it and not solve it quickly? They are making incremental progress, but still ignoring the non-toyness of the eventual car; the car that will be making decisions about whether to kill a pedestrian or the driver, whether to get you somewhere on time by taking some risks, or play it safe.

The data disconnect is a historical one, too, where the amount of data being collected and processed has become so large that companies are realising they can still get value out of algorithm-tuning data scientists, even if they could get more value if they added better data scientists. Critical thinking is its own discipline. It's the other half of campus. Doing social science on what's the real problem among this core group of people is a field that includes management consultants. Consultants spend a lot of time learning from people in all parts of companies because companies get so siloed into different departments, and they stop talking. So they hire someone whose job it is to interview everyone. Anthropologists are in companies for the same reason: they don't stay in their box. Of course, Duncan points out: neither do good data scientists. They add value precisely through talking with different groups and putting data in context. Teaching data studies as part of data science is our goal.

DN: IN SOME PREVIOUS CONVERSATIONS, YOU MENTIONED THIS NOTION OF DATA AS A THIRD KIND OF THING. WHAT DO YOU MEAN BY THAT?

JD: I've been thinking about the sense among students and much of the rest of the world that there's a difference between qualitative and quantitative, and that they involve different skills. There is a way in which that is true, but when you are looking at data like flight delays or surveys, it is amazing how you can apply quantitative skills and interpretive skills to it. At every moment, I find that you can apply both approaches – and you do need to spend time learning to think and reason with uncertainty quantitatively, statistically and socially. I think that there is a third approach. There is a way to talk about data itself as a kind of third skill, where we recognise that there are not two approaches being applied, but you are actually applying a new approach.

My practical definition of data is: anything you can put in an Excel spreadsheet cell. I like the fact that it's in Excel, because Excel itself demonstrates why companies run on Excel. For example, the Excel date format breaks if you give it dates from the nineteenth century (we discovered this when trying to explore early cholera data). It seems like it should be easy enough to fix the date format so that all dates work, but Excel is so full of technocultural legacies that programmers cannot fix this problem without breaking everything. I tell my students that for every headache they experience trying to use Excel, it's just further proof of why companies can't get off of Excel. Excel can't get off of itself. It's proof of the inseparability of history, culture and technology.

Data is Excel with all its broken date conventions. It's not just programming, it's interpretive, cultural, historical world programming. Every piece of data has to be seen as all of those things at the same time, and if we can get to the point where we just say data and mean that, then we'll be in a much better place. Right now we just oscillate. Right now, politically speaking, I'm creating Data Studies as part of this oscillation, but good data scientists are blogging all the time about this stuff – that data can't be treated the way math wants to treat numbers. When you subtract one in Excel, it can break a date if it's from the nineteenth century. That's not just math – the data runs out at a certain point. That's why the Kaggle competitions are effectively 'toy' problems, because they are supposed to be solvable without ever having to ask where are its edges and how do leakages, politics and stakeholders reframe the questions and data. People who win by leakage are good proof that data is this other thing, this third thing, where you have to always use all of these skills, recognising that every time you write an algorithm you are also deciding the cultural and political boundaries of your data. Every time you are making choices about who to interview to make the analysis, or decide to eliminate data from November, you are making a quantitative and qualitative decision. You are influencing what that algorithm is going to make. You are never separable from these things that appear separate.

I think of data studies as training people right at that intersection. It's training them in Excel and interpretation, in a manner that they can't escape the fact that they are oscillating between the two. It's what I heard the companies saying: we need people who know how to ask the right question about sales data, or engineering data, or public access data. What they were really saying was that we need people who don't think quantitative and qualitative are separate worlds, we need people who can think data critically.

Notes

1 I use the term 'stakeholder' because it is understood across business and government, but I expand it to think through social and environmental justice concerns, drawing on STS and anthropology scholarship. (See for example Callon in Callon and Lacoste 2011; and Fortun 2009.)
2 They were working with the Substance Abuse and Mental Health Services Administration (SAMHSA) population data www.samhsa.gov/data/ [accessed 4 March 2018].
3 See Dumit 2016 for this early history of AI.

References

Brennan, Michael. 2015. 'Can Computers Be Racist? Big Data, Inequality, and Discrimination'. Ford Foundation blog, 18 November. www.fordfoundation.org/ideas/equals-change-blog/posts/can-computers-be-racist-big-data-inequality-and-discrimination [accessed 6 April 2017]. Video available at: https://vimeo.com/146814921.

Callon, M. and Lacoste, A. 2011. 'Defending Responsible Innovation'. *Debating Innovation* 1(1): 19–27.

Dumit, Joseph. 2016. 'Plastic Diagrams: Circuits in the Brain and How They Got There'. In *Plasticity and Pathology: On the Formation of the Neural Subject.* Edited by D.W. Bates and N. Bassiri. Oxford: Oxford University Press, 219–43.

Fortun, K. 2009. *Advocacy after Bhopal: Environmentalism, Disaster, New Global Orders.* Chicago: University of Chicago Press.

Griesemer, James. 2016. 'Taking Goodhart's Law Meta: Gaming, Meta-Gaming, and Hacking Academic Performance Metrics'. Paper given at Gaming Metrics: Innovation & Surveillance in Academic Misconduct, University of California at Davis, 4 February.

Lupi, Giorgia and Posavec, Stephanie. 2016. *Dear Data*. New York: Chronicle Books.

Mackenzie, Adrian. 2007. 'Plying R: A Statistical Programming Language and the Credibility of Data'. Unpublished manuscript.

Montet, Benjamin. 2014. 'Flight Delayed? Your Pilot Really Can Make Up the Time in the Air'. *FiveThirtyEight*, 24 April. https://fivethirtyeight.com/features/flight-delayed-your-pilot-really-can-make-up-the-time-in-the-air [accessed 6 April 2017].

Morris, Hugh. 2015. 'Are Airlines Exaggerating Flight Times so They're Never Late?' *The Telegraph*, 3 December. www.telegraph.co.uk/travel/travel-truths/Are-airlines-exaggerating-flight-times-so-theyre-never-late [accessed 6 May 2017].

Nolan, Deborah and Lang, Duncan Temple. 2015. *Data Science in R: A Case Studies Approach to Computational Reasoning and Problem Solving*. Boca Raton: CRC Press.

O'Neil, Cathy. 2016. *Weapons of Math Destruction: How Big Data Increases Inequality and Threatens Democracy*. New York: Crown Publishing Group.

O'Neil, Cathy and Schutt, Rachel. 2013. *Doing Data Science: Straight Talk from the Frontline*. Sebastapol, CA: O'Reilly Media, Inc.

Peng, Roger D. and Matsui, Elizabeth. 2015. *The Art of Data Science: A Guide for Anyone Who Works with Data*. Baltimore, MD: Skybrude Consulting.

Ribes, David and Jackson, Steven J. 2013. 'Data Bite Man: The Work of Sustaining a Long-Term Study'. In *'Raw Data' Is an Oxymoron*. Edited by Lisa Gitelman. Cambridge, MA: MIT Press, 147–66.

Ridge, Enda. 2014. *Guerrilla Analytics: A Practical Approach to Working with Data*. San Francisco: Morgan Kaufmann.

Strathern, Marilyn. 1997. '"Improving ratings": Audit in the British University System'. *European Review* 5: 305–21.

Sweeney, Latanya. 2013. 'Discrimination in Online ad Delivery'. *Communications of the Association of Computing Machinery (CACM)* 56(5): 44–54.

TalksAtGoogle. 2016. 'Cathy O'Neil. Weapons of Math Destruction', 2 November. www.youtube.com/watch?v=TQHs8SA1qpk [accessed 24 February 2018].

Tukey, John. 1977. *Exploratory Data Analysis*. Boston, MA: Addison-Wesley.

Index